International Perspectives on Citizenship, Education and Religious Diversity

Citizenship is high on the agenda of education systems in many of the world's democracies. As yet, however, discussions of citizenship education have neglected issues of religious diversity and how the study of religions can contribute to our understanding of citizenship. *International Perspectives on Citizenship, Education and Religious Diversity* brings together an international range of contributions from religious scholars and educators specializing in the study of religions. Together, these illustrate and explore the key questions for educational theory and pedagogy raised by drawing issues of religious diversity into citizenship education.

The chapters address and extend debates over the nature of citizenship in late modernity, highlighting local and global dimensions of citizenship in relation to issues of national, religious, ethnic and cultural identity. As well as emphasizing the role religious education has to play in citizenship education, the book also covers wider issues such as state-supported faith schools and cultural diversity in relation to common citizenship. The authors argue that critical, yet reflective, approaches to religious education have a distinct and valuable contribution to make to citizenship education. Issues addressed within the study of religions are related to new forms of global and cultural citizenship, as well as citizenship within the nation–state. Ultimately, this stimulating and original collection highlights the challenges and possibilities of teaching and learning about religion, religions and religious diversity within an inclusive educational practice.

Robert Jackson is Professor of Education and Director of the Warwick Religions and Education Research Unit at the University of Warwick. He has published extensively on religions and education and is Editor-in-Chief of the *British Journal of Religious Education*.

International Perspectives on Citizenship, Education and Religious Diversity

Edited by Robert Jackson

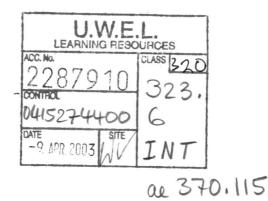
 RoutledgeFalmer
Taylor & Francis Group

LONDON AND NEW YORK

First published 2003 by RoutledgeFalmer
11 New Fetter Lane, London EC4P 4EE

Simultaneously published in the USA and Canada
by RoutledgeFalmer
29 West 35th Street, New York, NY 10001

RoutledgeFalmer is an imprint of the Taylor & Francis Group

© 2003 Edited by Robert Jackson

Typeset in Palatino and Gill by BC Typesetting, Bristol
Printed and bound in Great Britain by
Biddles Ltd, Guildford and King's Lynn

British Library Cataloguing in Publication Data
A catalogue record for this book is available from the British Library

Library of Congress Cataloging in Publication Data
A catalogue record has been requested

ISBN 0–415–27440–0

Contents

Contributors

Lat Blaylock is Executive Officer of the Professional Council for Religious Education (PCFRE), the subject teachers' professional association in England, and is an Adviser in the RE Today team. He is interested in religious education's contribution to transformations through education, and in pupils' spiritual development. He meets about 2,000 teachers of religious education every year through courses and conferences. The Department for Education and Skills awarded PCFRE a grant to produce citizenship materials for classroom teachers, based on ideas and themes from religious education. The resulting publication, edited by Lat Blaylock, is *Secondary RE and Citizenship: Towards an Open Frontier* (2002).

Dr David Chidester is Professor of Comparative Religion and Director of the Institute for Comparative Religion in Southern Africa (ICRSA) at the University of Cape Town, South Africa. His recent books include *Patterns of Transcendence: Religion, Death, and Dying* (2002), *Christianity: A Global History* (2000), and *Savage Systems: Colonialism and Comparative Religion in Southern Africa* (1996). In the field of religion and public education ICRSA has developed textbooks, resources for teachers and a book on public policy: David Chidester, Gordon Mitchell, A. Rashied Omar and Isabel Apawo Phiri, *Religion and Public Education: Options for a New South Africa* (1994).

Dr Julia Ipgrave is Assistant Head Teacher at Uplands Junior School, a school of over 400 7–11 year olds in inner-city Leicester, with over 90 per cent children from Muslim homes. She is also Honorary Research Fellow in the Warwick Religions and Education Research Unit, where she completed her M.A. and Ph.D. degrees and where she is involved in on-going research and development. She has been engaged in externally funded research on pupil-to-pupil dialogue in the classroom and is establishing an e-mail network for inter-faith dialogue between pupils of contrasting schools across England. Her publications include 'Issues in the delivery of religious education to Muslim pupils: perspectives from the classroom' (*British Journal of Religious Education*, 1999) and *Pupil-to-*

pupil Dialogue in the Classroom as a Tool for Religious Education (Warwick Religions and Education Research Unit, Working Paper 2, 2001).

Dr Robert Jackson is Professor of Education in the Institute of Education at the University of Warwick and Director of the Warwick Religions and Education Research Unit. His books include *Religious Education: An Interpretive Approach* (1997) and (with Eleanor Nesbitt) *Hindu Children in Britain* (1993). He has directed a number of externally funded research studies funded by the Economic and Social Research Council, the Arts and Humanities Research Board and the Leverhulme Trust. He co-directed the *Warwick RE Project*, a major curriculum series drawing on ethnographic studies of British children from a range of religious and ethnic backgrounds (1994–6). He is Editor-in-chief of the *British Journal of Religious Education* and serves on the editorial boards of several international journals.

Heid Leganger-Krogstad is Associate Professor of Religious Education in the Department of Teacher Education and School Development in the Faculty of Education at the University of Oslo, Norway. After teaching in secondary education she trained teachers of religious education at Finnmark University College in Alta before being appointed to her present post. Her main research interest is the development of a contextual approach to RE. Related publications in English include 'Religious education in a global perspective: a contextual approach' in H-G. Heimbrock, C. T. Scheilke and P. Schreiner (eds) *Towards Religious Competence: Diversity as a Challenge for Education in Europe* (2001).

Dr Sissel Østberg is Associate Professor in the Faculty of Education at Oslo University College. She teaches on graduate and postgraduate programmes in religious education and in multicultural and international education. She also works as a consultant and researcher for the International Centre for Education (LINS) with special responsibility for Pakistan and Bangladesh. She has published numerous articles in Norwegian on RE and articles in English on Muslim children and young people in Norway, including 'Islamic nurture and identity management' (*British Journal of Religious Education*, 2000) and 'Punjabi, Pakistani, Muslim and Norwegian? Self-perceptions and social boundaries among Pakistani children in Oslo' (*International Journal of Punjab Studies*, 2000). Her Ph.D. thesis from the University of Warwick (1999), *Pakistani Children in Oslo: Islamic Nurture in a Secular Context*, was published in 2002.

Dr Geir Skeie is Associate Professor at the Faculty of Humanities, Stavanger University College, Norway, where he teaches religious studies and religious education. His research deals mainly with theoretical issues related to the philosophy of religious education, with particular emphasis on modernity, pluralism and identity issues. His publications in English include 'Plurality and pluralism: a challenge for religious education' (*British Journal for Religious Education*, 1995) and 'Citizenship, identity politics and religious education' in H-G. Heimbrock, C. T. Scheilke and P. Schreiner (eds) *Towards Religious Competence: Diversity as a Challenge for Education in Europe* (2001).

Dr H. Christina Steyn is a Senior Lecturer in the Department of Religious Studies at the University of South Africa (UNISA), where she is responsible for the training of prospective teachers in religious studies. In the field of religious studies her particular interest lies in contemporary and alternative religious movements. Her books include *Worldviews in Transition* (1996), *Religion in Life Orientation* (2000) and (with J. S. Krüger and G. L. A. Lubbe) *The Human Search for Meaning* (1996).

Dr Judy Tobler lectures in the Department of Religious Studies and is a researcher with the Institute for Comparative Religion in Southern Africa at the University of Cape Town. Her particular research and teaching interests are women's studies and feminist theory in the Hindu and Buddhist religious traditions. She co-edited and contributed to D. Ackermann, E. Getman, H. Kotze and J. Tobler, *Claiming our Footprints: South African Women Reflect on Context, Identity and Spirituality* (2000), and contributed to *Women's Spirituality in the Transformation of South Africa*, ed. Azila Reisenberger (2002).

Dr Wolfram Weisse is Professor of Religious Education in the Faculty of Education and Professor of Ecumenical Theology at the University of Hamburg. His main research interests are in religious education in multicultural societies and the role of religions in the transformation process in South Africa. His recent publications include *Vom Monolog zum Dialog. Ansätze einer dialogischen Religionspädagogik* (2nd edn, 1999) and *Religion and Politics in South Africa: From Apartheid to Democracy*, which he edited with Abdulkader Tayob (2000).

Preface

This book results from a seminar conducted under the auspices of the International Network for Inter-religious and Inter-cultural Education and held at the University of Warwick in early September 2001. The Network was set up in 1994, soon after the election of a democratic government in South Africa, and had its first meeting in September in the Faculty of Education at the University of Hamburg, organized by Professor Wolfram Weisse. The aim was to promote links between Southern African and Northern European research groups working in fields connecting religion and education in culturally diverse democratic societies. The seminar brought together Northern European and Southern African members of research and development groups working in the fields of religion, education and cultural diversity in order to share insights and to learn from one another.

The second meeting of the seminar, convened by Professor Trees Andree, was held in 1996 at the University of Utrecht in the Netherlands. The Institute of Comparative Religion in Southern Africa at the University of Cape Town, under the leadership of Professor David Chidester, hosted the third seminar in 1998. Papers from the meetings are published in Weisse (1996), Andree et al. (1997) and Chidester et al. (1999).

Warwick Religions and Education Research Unit was invited to organize the 2001 seminar at the University of Warwick. The seminar topic was prompted by a concern in all of our countries about issues of religious and cultural plurality in relation to citizenship. Such discussions raise issues about the values underpinning democracy, about the rights and obligations associated with membership of society (and of other narrower or wider social groupings), and about balancing respect for diversity with the goal of social cohesion. Questions are also raised about identity – whether national identity or other forms of social or personal identity.

For the UK organizers, the seminar theme was influenced by the fact that in England and Wales in 2002, Citizenship Education was to be introduced as a new subject within the national curriculum for secondary schools. Primary schools would also have the option of including citizenship education in the curriculum. The central issue here was how far and in what ways religious education or studies of religion might contribute to a broadly based education for citizenship. The introduction of this theme to an international seminar prompted a variety of responses, including the fact that the term 'citizenship' has no direct equivalent in some languages and also prompting reflections on the nature of citizenship in late modernity, illustrating relationships and tensions between different modes of global, local, national and transcultural citizenship. The chapters in this volume have been selected because their references to particular national situations illustrate generic issues for the incorporation of studies of religion and culture into education for citizenship, whether that be in the form of a discrete subject, an aspect of several subjects or fields, or a dimension of the whole curriculum.

The seminar finished on 5 September, just six days before the attacks on New York and Washington. In revising their papers for publication, contributors were invited to take account of the implications of these events and their aftermath in their discussions if they wished to do so. Some contributors revised their chapters accordingly.

The introductory chapter sets the scene for discussions of citizenship end education in plural, democratic societies, while the chapters in Part I discuss major themes in the debate, sometimes from the perspective of particular national situations, whilst also addressing generic issues. Part II includes three contributions offering theoretical discussions and practical experience of dialogical approaches to religious education in schools. Here dialogue is seen as a vital contributor to the promotion of good citizenship in schools and beyond. The final chapter reflects on the previous contributions, drawing out ideas and strategies that can make a direct impact on educational practice. Each chapter begins with a synopsis.

All the contributors work in the field of religion, as specialists in religious studies or religious education (or religion education, as our Southern African colleagues designate the subject), and all are involved professionally in education, either in departments of religion or in institutes of teacher education. As such, their work overlaps with other fields, especially in the social sciences, in ethnography and feminist theory, for example. The discourses of multiculturalism, cultural diversity and multi-ethnicity and of citizenship often neglect religion as an issue. This collection deliberately emphasizes religion, not simply because it is the key academic and professional interest of the contributors, but because in all the societies in which we work, religion is a central and controversial issue in debates about cultural diversity and citizenship.

R.J.

References

Andree, T., Bakker, C. and Schreiner, P. (eds) (1997) *Crossing Boundaries: Contributions to Interreligious and Intercultural Education*, Münster: Comenius Institute.

Chidester, D., Stonier, J. and Tobler, J. (eds) (1999) *Diversity as Ethos: Challenges for Interreligious and Intercultural Education*, Cape Town: Institute for Comparative Religion in Southern Africa.

Weisse, W. (ed.) (1996) *Interreligious and Intercultural Education: Methodologies, Conceptions and Pilot Projects in South Africa, Namibia, Great Britain, the Netherlands and Germany*, Münster: Comenius Institute.

Acknowledgements

I am grateful to all the members of the seminar for their participation and collegiality and, in particular, to the contributors to this book for their patience, co-operation and flexibility. I am especially indebted to three Research Fellows in the Warwick Religions and Education Research Unit: Ursula McKenna for her invaluable assistance in organizing the seminar and for checking the references of the contributions to the book; Elisabeth Arweck for her finely tuned linguistic skills; and Ann Henderson for her helpful comments on drafts of several chapters. I am grateful to Eleanor Nesbitt, Judith Everington and Jim Beckford for their on-going support and encouragement. Warm thanks are also due to the British Academy for a grant towards conference expenses. Without it several delegates would have been unable to travel to Warwick.

R.J.

Chapter 1

Citizenship, religious and cultural diversity and education

Robert Jackson

Synopsis The introductory chapter sets the scene for discussions of citizenship education in plural, democratic societies, providing a context for the contributions that follow and highlighting some themes developed in later chapters. The history of the term 'citizenship' is outlined and then related to accounts of plurality and the position of nation-states in the late modern/postmodern world. Using examples from qualitative research, I argue for an understanding of diversity within debates about ethnicity, nationality, religion and culture. Outlining a range of positions within each debate, I argue that internal diversity within groups should be recognized fully, dialogue valued and a model of 'differentiated' citizenship adopted. A section on Islam in Britain and the West picks up an earlier point about the importance of minority involvement in formal structures and demonstrates the role of ethnographic field studies in questioning popular assumptions about Islam and nationality. A brief account of the debates about faith-based schools in Europe precedes a discussion of the roles the study of religion may have in citizenship education in common schools in England and Wales. Interpretive and dialogical pedagogies are seen as especially appropriate for studying religions in ways that offer young people access to the debates about citizenship. These approaches encourage the recognition of social plurality, differentiated citizenship and the experience of individuals.

Citizenship

The topic of citizenship is very much on the agenda of education systems in many democracies. Whether influenced primarily by fears of the young's disengagement with political processes, as in England and Wales, or by concerns about social cohesion in multicultural societies, as in South Africa's commitment to nation building, citizenship education has emerged, either as a curriculum subject in its own right or as a dimension of the wider school curriculum (Paludan and Prinds 1999). In those societies where the *term* 'citizenship' (or its equivalent) is not used, other elements are emphasized such as democratic values, virtues and political literacy (Skeie in Chapter 3 of this volume).

An important element of the citizenship debate concerns issues raised by social plurality, including issues of religious and cultural diversity. So far, discussions of citizenship education have made little reference to issues of religious diversity or to the contribution that the study of religions might make to our understanding of citizenship. This book sets out to explore some of the issues from the point of view of a group of scholars working in the field of religion, and from educationists with a specialism in the study of religions. Perspectives from Britain, Norway, Germany and South Africa illustrate some of the key generic issues for educational theory and pedagogy. Contributors emphasize religious/religion education's contribution to citizenship education, but also deal with wider issues, such as state-funded religious schools and cultural diversity in relation to common citizenship. This introductory chapter provides a context for the discussions that follow.

In its primary meaning, 'citizenship' implies membership of a political society, involving the possession of legal rights, usually including the rights to vote and stand for political office. For many centuries citizenship was a privileged status given only to those fulfilling certain conditions such as owning property. However, in modern states, citizens' rights are usually considered an aspect of nationality, usually granted automatically to all those born in a particular country as well as to others in certain circumstances, such as permanent settlers. Citizenship is a distinctively democratic ideal. Citizens, in contrast to subjects, have legal protection against arbitrary decisions by their governments. At the same time they have the opportunity to play an active role in influencing government policy. Whereas Aristotle considered citizenship (*politeia*) primarily in terms of duties, citizenship, in modern liberal thinking, has tended to be viewed more in terms of rights – citizens have the right to participate in public life, but also the right to put their private commitments before political involvement. Many commentators, including those writing from a communitarian perspective (e.g. Etzioni 1993), argue that citizenship should involve a balance between rights and duties, usually with the latter resulting from a feeling of responsibility and belonging, rather than compulsion.

In T. H. Marshall's often cited discussion, citizenship is a status related specifically to the nation-state, which confers civil rights, political rights and social rights. Civil rights include rights under law to personal liberty, freedom of speech, association, religious toleration and freedom from censorship. Political rights include the right to participate in political processes, while social rights include the right of access to social benefits and resources such as education, economic security and welfare state services (Marshall 1950).

Current discussions about citizenship take place in the context of forms of plurality and diversity that were less evident in Marshall's day. Although the nation-state is the main provider of social rights (including the benefits of the welfare state), its boundaries are challenged in a whole variety of ways, from migration, multinational companies, the press and media, wider federations such as the European Union, international feminist, environmental and human rights movements, international peace courts and websites to bodies such as the United Nations, NATO and the International Monetary Fund. It is not surprising that debates about citizenship and identity are taking place in many Western countries.

As Geir Skeie points out, descriptively, plurality is of at least two types (Skeie 1995; this volume, Chapter 3). The first is what he calls 'traditional' plurality. In this regard, Britain is overtly a religiously plural society partly because migrants, principally in the post-colonial period, came from South Asia, East Africa and the Caribbean, including significant numbers with, for example, Muslim, Hindu and Sikh religious backgrounds and others identifying with other groupings such as Pentecostal Christians and Rastafarians. In countries like South Africa, Norway, Canada or Australia, that religious plurality also includes the ways of life of indigenous peoples. These may have been suppressed or ignored for a variety of reasons, but have come back on the agenda (e.g. Leganger-Krogstad 2001). In all the societies mentioned above, one might add the emergence of new religious movements and various new age phenomena as further elements of religious plurality (Beckford 1985, 1986; Heelas 1996).

Skeie's second sense of plurality relates to the plural intellectual climate of late modernity. In particular, he points to the plurality of modern societies in the sense of being fragmented, with various groups having competing and often contradictory rationalities, and the growth of individualism and the privatization of religion. Critiques of assumptions, ideas and values that characterized the European Enlightenment have led to a plurality in contemporary thought that is often pictured as a move from modernity to late modernity or 'high modernity' (Giddens 1990) or from modernity to postmodernity (e.g. Lyotard 1984). Modern plurality is the context in which traditional plurality now operates; the two are inextricably intertwined in current debates about citizenship.

As theorists argue whether the world is in a condition of late or postmodernity, tangible changes in social, political and economic life make it evident that the traditional idea of the nation-state is being eroded. The globalizing tendencies related to massive advances in information and communications technology have enhanced world trade, yet have also reinforced inequalities, especially between countries of the North and South. Multinational companies can be more wealthy than some individual nation-states and are capable of wielding huge power, sometimes against the interests of the poor or causing long-term damage to the environment. Those committed to universal human rights, to the reduction of inequality or to the conservation of the environment (and some of them are religious voices) can find themselves at odds with government policies perceived as promoting a narrow national interest at the expense of the poor or with policies of multinational companies seeming to show scant regard for the long-term future of the planet. In ways such as these, global concerns can have a reciprocal relationship with concerns of particular local groups within countries, affecting individuals' relationships with and views of the nation-state. For example, there are those who would both act as citizens of particular countries and also argue for global governmental structures beyond the nation-state to eradicate poverty, and to exercise constraint over multinational companies. Moreover, there is the issue of nation-states belonging to wider political and economic groupings (the British and German contributors to this book are automatically citizens of the European Union, for example) and of the potential fragmentation of nation-states through devolution.

Education in citizenship, then, needs to take account of these different but interrelated forms of plurality. There needs to be an informed exploration of the debates about identity and belonging in relation to the nation-state, and also in relation to global and more local issues. These issues are related in a variety of ways, but especially so in 'multicultural' societies where some citizens have transnational links with other family members or co-religionists (see in this volume Chidester, Chapter 2, on social, cultural and global citizenship and Østberg, Chapter 5, on transcultural citizenship).

Religion figures in a number of key interrelated debates that are relevant to discussions about citizenship in relation to plurality, especially in 'multicultural' societies. These include debates about the nation-state (and related concepts such as nationality), ethnicity, culture and about religion itself. The debates show a range of positions from, at one extreme, 'closed' views that reify the concepts to postmodern views, at the other, offering complete deconstructions. The key educational task is to engage learners in a critical analysis of how such terminology is used, both in relation to their own experience (and several contributors to this book would make this the starting point) and with regard to examples from a variety of other sources. By participating in such discussions, students should also be helped to examine their own and their peers' assumptions and reflect upon their own identities. Different positions within the debates (rather than their technical detail) can be used to clarify, challenge or illuminate positions advanced by students. It would be helpful to attempt a brief overview of the main debates about the nation-state, ethnicity, religion and culture.

The nation-state and nationality

The modern nation-state has a relatively short history of around 500 years, with most states being formed within the last century or so. A 'state' is usually regarded as a governed society, supported by a civil service, ruling over a specific area, and whose authority is supported by law and the ability to use force. Thus a 'nation-state' is a variety of modern state in which 'the mass of the population are citizens who know themselves to be part of that nation' (Giddens 1993: 743). Perhaps Giddens's definition should be broadened, for a state can include groups who regard themselves as nations (comprised of one or more ethnic groups) and may aspire to their own statehood, as with Scottish and Welsh nationalism in Britain. Nationality is recognized or denied by each nation-state on its own rules, and usually gives entitlement to citizenship. Disputes about nationality and citizenship are common, in relation to welfare benefits, for example. However, we have already noted the impact of globalizing forces on the nation-state.

Nationalism, the ideology of one or more privileged ethnic categories, regards an essentialized and romanticized culture as the 'heritage' of the national group. Inflexible and narrow views of national, ethnic and religious identity tend to emerge when fixed and bounded views of the nature of cultures are combined with reified views of nationality, ethnicity and religion. Nationalism leads both to 'biological racism' and to what Tariq Modood calls cultural racism. Cultural racism builds on biological racism in order to vilify cultural difference (Modood 1997; see also Steyn's material in Chapter 6 below on the relationship between religious education and citizenship in South Africa during the apartheid period).

However, some nation-states attempt to find ways of incorporating more than one ethnic group through abstracting a romantic idea of 'super-ethnicity', with ideas such as 'the American people' or the idea of assimilation through a melting pot of cultures. However, this notion is in tension with any idea of retaining the distinctive but shifting cultural traditions of minorities. The tension can be there in the rhetoric of a single politician, as in US President George W. Bush's televised references to 'the American people' in one breath while appealing to 'Arab-Americans' in another. Skeie's account (Chapter 3 in this volume) of the production of a new national religious education syllabus finds an attempt to incorporate difference within a sense of a common Norwegian national identity. The resultant tensions manifest themselves through dissatisfaction with the syllabus among religious and non-religious minorities who see it as privileging a view of 'Christian heritage'. Insufficient account is taken, for example, of the subtleties of identity described and analysed by Østberg in her research on Pakistani Muslim young people in Oslo (this volume, Chapter 5).

Another way of accommodating ethnic or religious difference is through finding ways to incorporate different groups through the modification of civil religion or national custom. In Britain, for example, there is a gradual incorporation of the main faiths represented in the country into national and local civic religious life – whether a royal wedding or funeral, a mayoral investiture or hospital or prison chaplaincy (Beckford and Gilliat 1998). The current heir to the throne's declaration that he sees himself not as the future 'Defender of the Faith' but as a 'defender of faith' is another example.

In South Africa the struggles for radical change following the collapse of the apartheid system are seen as a process of 'nation building', and there are new symbols of national identity. Politicians are attempting to rectify injustices in the ways in which religion was used or denied in the previous system, through educational innovation, for example (see Chidester in Chapter 2 and Steyn in Chapter 6 below). What is clear from reflections on civil religion is that each nation-state has its own variety, conditioned by its own particular history. In this sense the nation-state cannot be entirely neutral when dealing with issues of religious and cultural diversity.

Whatever the difficulties, it is crucial that members of different minorities need to be involved directly in the democratic processes of society. Different views as to how this goal may be achieved vary according to the degree to which religions, ethnic groups and cultures are regarded as internally homogeneous. Those taking a 'closed' view (and they may be insiders as well as outsiders) tend to take the line that 'representatives' can speak authoritatively on behalf of their constituencies, while those emphasizing the varied and contested nature of groups look for a much wider range of activities through which many different individuals (including women and children) can participate in dialogue and negotiation with others (see Ipgrave in Chapter 8, Jackson in Chapter 4 and Tobler in Chapter 7 below).

Ethnicity

As well as the on-going debate about ethnicity within academic circles, there is also the question of popular uses of the term (Banks 1996; Baumann 1996). Ethnic groups are popularly thought of as having a common ancestry and descent, marked by some form of cultural continuity which distinguishes them from other groups around them. There is also the common equation of supposedly overt 'racial' difference and ethnic difference. Ethnic differences can also be highlighted by legal definition, as in a judgement made in England by Lord Fraser in 1983, in which he ruled Sikhs to be an ethnic group. Fraser's argument, largely derived from dictionary definitions based on popular usage, hinged on a tight connection (but not identification) between the ethnic and 'racial' character of a group (Bailey *et al.* 1991; Jones and Welengama 2000: 40).

If a person is labelled as being from a certain ethnic group, that person can be stereotyped by certain 'outsiders' or members of the majority culture, 'locked' into a particular identity and expected to behave in certain preconceived ways. 'Insiders' may also sometimes have an interest in presenting a closed view of their own ethnic group. This static view has been criticized especially by those who have recognized the situational character of ethnicity through their field research. Thus Fredrik Barth draws attention to changes that take place across socially constructed ethnic boundaries, where one group influences another, either positively or negatively (Barth

1969, 1981, 2000). Such ethnic re-formation takes place, for example, among groups which have rediscovered religious or ethnic symbols as a result of being marginalized by more powerful groups around them, or groups that have attempted to redefine themselves in response to influences or pressures from other social groups or institutions. Barth's analysis of ethnicity focuses attention on the maintenance of ethnic boundaries. Ethnic identity depends on ascription by both insiders and outsiders; ethnicity is not fixed, but is defined situationally.

In her research on Pakistani Muslim young people in Britain, Jessica Jacobson highlights this shifting nature of ethnic identity. Jacobson observed that a sense of ethnic identity can vary according to context. It could be more related to Pakistani ancestry or be 'British Pakistani' in certain contexts (in the family, for example), and be 'Asian' or 'British Asian' in another (with members of the peer group, for example). Jacobson's research suggests that, in the case of young British Pakistani Muslims, there is evidence that ethnicity is in a state of flux and rapid change, while religion is perceived as stable and having universal applicability (Jacobson 1997).

Some writers also speak of 'hyphenated' ethnic identities (see Østberg, Chapter 5 below). For example, Michael Fischer's analysis of 'Chinese-American' ethnic identity finds a group with an ancestry that goes back ultimately to China (so there is still *some* sense of ancestry). However, he also asserts that ethnicity is dynamic, and not taught and learned, not simply passed on from generation to generation. To be Chinese-American 'is a matter of finding a voice or style that does not violate one's several components of identity' (Fischer 1986: 196). Shared ancestry is still a feature of ethnicity, but the internal variety within an ethnic group is acknowledged, as well as the possibility of ethnic re-formation.

The most radical positions in the debate reject the very idea of ethnicity. These range from the Marxist critique, claiming the only significant category to be social class (Castles and Kosack 1973: 5), to forms of 'super-ethnic' nationalism in which ethnic distinctions are assimilated (the 'melting pot' view, for example), to postmodernist views, seeing ethnicity as an oppressive social construction. On this last view, even the situationist analysis of ethnicity, with its use of terms such as 'group', 'boundary' and 'maintenance', is regarded as potentially enclosing individuals within artificial identities.

Many ethnographic field studies find that 'ethnicity' implies *some* degree of identification with an ancestral tradition or a sense of 'shared peoplehood' (Dashefsky 1972), but it also changes situationally, includes an element of cultural choice and can never be fixed or static (Jackson and Nesbitt 1993). As Gerd Baumann puts it, 'Both wine and ethnicity are . . . creations of human minds, skills and plans – based on some natural ingredients, it is true, but far beyond anything that nature could do by itself' (Baumann 1999: 64).

Religion

Modern Western thinking derives its conceptions of 'religion' and 'religions' mainly from the European post-Enlightenment tradition. During the seventeenth and especially the eighteenth centuries the Protestant Reformist idea of *religio* as personal piety (associated with Zwingli and Calvin, for example) was largely displaced by a concept of religion as systematic, intellectual and 'exterior', in which religions were regarded as belief systems (Smith 1978). This concept reflected and stimulated religious conflict, and was used to delineate groups within Christianity and to classify and encompass what were perceived to be equivalent phenomena in non-Christian cultures encountered by the West in the colonial period. In the main these 'religions' were not yet given specific single-word names but were referred to, for example, as 'the Hindoo religion' (Jackson 1996). As well as reflecting Western intellectual tendencies of the Enlightenment period (looking back to a golden age with key texts, for example), the processes of defining 'other' religions reflected the unequal power relationship between indigenous peoples and European colonialist writers (e.g. Chidester 1996; King 1999; Oberoi 1994; Said 1978).

At the end of the eighteenth century Schleiermacher revived the inward and non-intellectual meaning of religion. During the nineteenth century the term 'religion' also changed to include the history of the 'religions', and most of the modern names for religions were coined. For example, the earliest use of the term 'Hinduism' I can find is 1808 – by an English professional soldier in India (Jackson 1996). By 1817 'Hinduism' was being used by certain 'insiders' and subsequently there have been competing representations by different Hindus of 'true' or 'false' Hinduisms (Jackson and Killingley 1988).

Under Hegel's influence, the reification of 'religion' was taken to its extreme, with the emergence of the idea that 'religion' itself has an essence. This process is exemplified in Ludwig Feuerbach's *The Essence of Religion* (1851). Feuerbach, a former student of Hegel, had earlier written *The Essence of Christianity* (1841). Both 'a religion' and generic 'religion' were held to embody an essence (Smith 1978: 47). This essentialist view of religion was perpetuated in the phenomenology of religion (Chantepie de la Saussaye 1891; Leeuw 1938). Thus a methodology emerged for identifying and classifying 'essences' in particular religions and in religion generally. The phenomenology of religion had a great influence on the development of comparative religion and religious studies in higher education. By the late 1930s, the term 'world religions' was being used occasionally (James 1938: 18) and more widely by the early 1950s (Champion and Short 1951; Finegan 1952) to denote distinct major religions with stable sets of key concepts and beliefs. This way of representing religious material has a growing number of critics who seek more flexible ways of presenting the uniqueness of individuals in the context of religious traditions (Smith 1978) or spiritual movements, or who find other ways of deconstructing religions or forms of academic study that focus on world religions or religion as a generic category (Fitzgerald 2000; McCutcheon 1997). Many ethnographic studies also provide empirical evidence showing the permeability of religious boundaries and the high degree of diversity that exists within religious traditions (e.g. Ashenden 1995; Geaves 1998; Geertz 1968; Nesbitt 2000). Modern religious education in Britain and some other Western countries is deeply influenced by 'world religions' approaches. Some educators aim to find more flexible and personal ways of representing religious material that relate to the concerns of students (e.g. Jackson 1997; see also below Ipgrave in Chapter 8, Leganger-Krogstad in Chapter 9 and Weisse in Chapter 10. Chidester's chapter in this book illustrates how a world religions model, although flawed, can still serve as a useful organizing tool for religion education).

The culture debate

If we look historically at the term 'culture', then, in the fifteenth century, we find it referring to the tending of crops or animal husbandry. During the next two centuries it is used analogically to refer to the human mind (Hobbes, for example, wrote of the culture of minds). During the eighteenth century 'culture' became associated with the arts and scholarship – in philosophy and history, for example – and was considered to be for the wealthy.[1] At about the same time, under the influence of the German philosopher Herder, we get an alternative view, namely the idea of distinct and variable cultures, a view developed in the Romantic movement. An essentialized culture was regarded as the collective 'heritage' of the national group, itself equated with a particular ethnic group.

This closed view of cultures came into early social or cultural anthropology, though not so much with strongly nationalistic overtones. For example, Herder's work influenced Franz Boas and other cultural relativists in the United States. Ruth Benedict, one of Boas's students, thought of each culture as distinct, by analogy with types of living organism. For Benedict, cultures either survived or died out, with no possibility of the formation of new cultural expressions through cultural interaction (Benedict 1935). The idea of uniform, bounded cultures was perpetuated in early work in multicultural education in Britain and is still to be found in the rhetoric of the political right, in popular newspapers and in the writings of some educators (e.g. Tate 1995).

At the opposite extreme there are postmodern deconstructions of the idea of 'a culture', with any idea of continuous tradition being regarded as an imposed and manipulative 'metanarrative'. On this view, the way of life someone adopts is a matter of personal, individual choice with, in one version, the role of education being to filter out 'metanarrical' influences on the young, from traditional forms of authority or from pre-prepared educational materials, in order to allow children to construct their own personal narratives and faith positions (Erricker and Erricker 2000). In between the two poles are intermediary positions, emphasizing the changing and contested nature of cultures over time. These range from Clifford Geertz's view of cultures as internally diverse, but with cultural continuity maintained through inherited conceptions, expressed through symbols (1973: 89) to views emphasizing internal (sometimes inter-generational) conflict or negotiation in creating cultural change (e.g. Clifford 1986; Said 1978). These latter authors also point to the role of the *observer* (whether anthropologist, historian, journalist or student) in constructing 'cultures'. On this view, as with biographies, single definitive accounts are not possible.

There are also those who emphasize process rather than content in making and describing culture. Culture is seen, not so much as an 'entity' (albeit one that is in a constant state of flux), but as an active process through which humans produce change. Instead of having a distinct and fixed cultural identity, individuals and groups identify with elements of culture, or synthesize new culture through bringing different elements together. The emphasis is on people *engaging with* culture, drawing on different cultural resources (e.g. Barth 1994, 1996; Østberg, Chapter 5 below). The emphasis in identity formation is less on descent and inheritance than on a series of identifications through dialogue and communication with others.

Cultural discourse

Qualitative research studies show that there are *both* inflexible *and* highly flexible approaches to nationality, ethnicity, religion and their relationship in cultural discourse (Baumann 1999). In various situations, there are those whose interests may be to present a particular relationship between a fixed view of culture (or cultures) and reified views of nationality, ethnicity and religion. British national identity is often described by the political far right as if it were some kind of fixed entity (usually associated romantically with terms like 'Anglo-Saxon') with its own distinct culture, related to a closed view of ethnicity (usually with 'Britishness' being associated with being white) and religion (Christianity in very particular forms). Such closed views provide simplistic criteria for judging whether someone is 'truly' British.[2] Similarly, both outsiders and insiders may use terminology such as 'the Muslim community' or 'Asian culture' when it suits their purposes. Gerd Baumann calls this tendency to reify, whether from extremist groups, politicians, the media or cultural communities, 'dominant discourse'. 'Demotic discourse', however, is his term for the language of culture *making*, and characteristically becomes used when people from various different backgrounds interact together in approaching topics of common concern. Baumann's conclusion is that 'culture' can be seen as *both* the possession of an ethnic or religious 'community' and also as a dynamic process relying on personal agency, in which, for example, community boundaries may be renegotiated (Baumann 1996).

Multicultural societies

Models of a multicultural society need to acknowledge both forms of discourse. Some views, of multicultural education, for example, are couched *entirely* in terms of dominant discourse, picturing cultures as bounded entities, with subordinate cultures functioning in their own private space, and depending on the values of the dominant culture for their continued existence (e.g. McIntyre 1978). Evidence from qualitative research shows that this idea of a multicultural society is not sustainable. The way we picture a multicultural society needs to be more flexible.

More needs to be made, for example, of the fact that some degree of cultural plurality in a society is not dependent on the presence of ethnic minorities who are descended from migrants, nor on indigenous peoples, but on other forms of local diversity. The anthropological studies of local British communities conducted by Anthony Cohen and his co-writers show no single homogeneous national culture but, rather, many diverse cultures often founded on a sense of local belonging. Cohen illustrates how members of local communities manipulate symbols in sustaining boundaries, with individuals investing common features (from everyday speech to watching television soap operas) with 'local meaning' (Cohen 1982a, b, 1986). For Cohen, 'local experience mediates national identity'; the latter cannot be understood without a knowledge of the former (1982b: 13). It is also evident from some chapters in this book that cultural conditions in different countries result in different views of national identity, and this affects the ways in which multicultural societies are described. (Compare in this volume Chapter 3 by Skeie, Chapter 6 by Steyn and Chapter 10 by Weisse in this respect.)

Also, minority cultures, religions and ethnicities are themselves internally plural, and the symbols and values of their various constituent groups are open to negotiation, contest and change. Moreover, individuals from any background may identify with values associated with a range of sources and may draw eclectically on a variety of resources in creating new culture. A young person may be a 'skilled cultural navigator' (Ballard 1994) or display 'multiple cultural competence' (Jackson and Nesbitt 1993). At the same time, in the context of groups, there will be those claiming a more bounded religious and cultural identity. In Gerd Baumann's words, 'A multicultural society is not a patchwork of five or ten fixed cultural identities, but an elastic web of crosscutting and always mutually situational identifications' (Baumann 1999: 118). Of crucial importance for the maintenance and development of such societies is the provision of mechanisms that raise awareness of the debates and maximize dialogue and communication, identifying common or overlapping ideas and values, but also identifying and addressing difference. There is a need for structures that enable and foster these interactions, including educational structures. (See the ideas described by Ipgrave in Chapter 8, Leganger-Krogstad in Chapter 9 and Weisse in Chapter 10 of this volume, for example.) Such interaction promotes positive cultural development.

Islam in Britain and other Western societies

In order for such dialogue and conversation to take place effectively, there needs to be a willingness by all parties to participate in the democratic process and a wish to 'belong' to society. The events of 11 September 2001 in New York and Washington and the reactions to them from the West have precipitated emotive responses from some Westerners who doubt the commitment of diaspora Muslims to full participation in their societies. Some of these responses show such an ignorance of Islam that, at the very least, reveals the need to include studies of Islam in schools and other educational institutions.

Whatever the rhetoric about the unity of Islam (and there are, of course, strong unifying elements), there needs to be some understanding of its diversity. As one Muslim scholar puts it, 'There are as many Islams as there are situations that sustain it' (Al-Azmeh 1993: 1). One way to get a sense of the unity and diversity of Islam is by using the interpretive methods described below. One can get a framework of key concepts and teachings and a historical sketch as reference points, but these provisional sketches then need to be humanized, challenged and modified through the continuing study of varied individual cases. Alternatively one might start with an individual example and then work out from it in order to get a preliminary and provisional understanding of Islamic tradition. In classes with Muslim students, dialogical methods such as those used by Ipgrave, Leganger-Krogstad and Weisse might be used (Ipgrave 1999 and below, Chapter 8; Leganger-Krogstad below, Chapter 9; Weisse below, Chapter 10).

The work of Edward Said has shown how Western stereotypes of Islam have been perpetuated in Western literature and the media (Said 1978, 1981). The aftermath of the events of 11 September 2001 included a repetition of many of these, especially the reification of Islam as a monolithic and uniform ideology, the association of Islam in general with terror and violence, and the assertion that Muslims cannot be loyal both to Islam and to the civil and legal requirements of a non-Muslim state. Clearly, the debate about citizenship in plural societies needs to pay attention to the position of Muslim minorities within non-Muslim nation-states. In this respect, evidence from qualitative research studies is of help in challenging some common assumptions. The following illustrations question three particular assumptions: that many members of Muslim diasporas in Western societies *choose* not to identify themselves as British, Norwegian or whatever; that any loyalty beyond the nation-state implies disloyalty to the nation-state; and that loyalty to a transnational Islam is inconsistent with adherence to Western democratic practices.

First, *a feeling of identification with a particular nationality is not a matter of personal rational choice, but depends on the degree to which a person feels accepted and affirmed by society.* Jessica Jacobson's research on young British Pakistanis' perceptions of Britishness shows that the degree to which they feel a sense of British national identity is strongly influenced by their interaction with others, and she identifies three different, interrelated and shifting 'boundaries of Britishness' (Jacobson 1998). In a purely civic sense, all of Jacobson's respondents were British citizens, and many of them referred to this sense of being British. However, most of them felt it to be an incomplete way of belonging to a nation, lacking emotional content. Moreover, many had experienced overt racism through which they had found their British identity rejected by some whites on the grounds of 'biological' racism and/or because of perceived cultural difference. Thus 'racial' and cultural boundaries to Britishness, the latter featuring a closed and exclusive view of culture, were constructed mainly by whites. The British Pakistani young people's feelings as to the degree and variety of their *own* Britishness varied according to their personal experiences and encounters, but most felt that ethnic, cultural and religious distinctions should be a healthy and significant part of British life, rather than a threat to national identity.

The extreme consequences of a feeling of rejection by elements of society, especially in a climate of economic deprivation, is the kind of community fragmentation along social, cultural, ethnic and religious lines that has occurred in some northern English towns and cities such as Bradford, and which led to riots in the summer of 2001. Lord Ouseley notes the high degree of ignorance of 'other cultures and lifestyles' and he reports on the 'very worrying drift towards self-segregation' in Bradford, through parental choice of particular schools, for example. His recommended reforms in education (especially citizenship education) and community leadership in order to promote dialogue and communication are at least a move in the right direction (Ouseley 2001). However, as the Runnymede Trust's report *The Future of Multi-ethnic Britain* suggests, the development of a sense of belonging and citizenship requires attention to underlying economic factors affecting cross-sections of the population.

> Rather than concentrate on minorities based on ethnicity or religion, should we not urge Government increasingly to counter the emergence of an underclass, whose deepening exclusion – known to every youth magistrate – is a matter of shame to the whole nation? Of course this underclass has black, Asian (mainly Muslim) and white minorities

within it – but it is the pains, injustices and problems of the underclass as a whole which require fundamental action. It is here that the questions of racism, equalities etc. take on their sharpest edge.

(Runnymede 2000)

Secondly, *the idea that citizenship is only to do with rights and responsibilities granted and expected by the nation-state needs to be revised.* The reality is that many citizens have local and global ties and commitments beyond those to the nation-state. It is important to stress that these can feed into and enhance national democratic debates and practices. We have already noted the research of Anthony Cohen and his colleagues in 'traditional' British settings. This provides evidence of heterogeneous local cultures and a local, rather than purely national, sense of belonging (Cohen 1982a, 1986). Similarly, those embracing global causes through bodies such as Christian Aid, Oxfam or Amnesty International or through the feminist or environmental movements do not confine their commitments and loyalties to the nation-state. (See David Chidester's comments on the relationship between cultural, global and social citizenship, below, Chapter 2, and Judy Tobler's feminist perspective, below, Chapter 7.)

Parallel and further points can be made about members of Muslim diasporas living in Western democracies. Sissel Østberg's Chapter 5 in this book is based on studies of young Pakistani Muslims in Norway and Britain. Her young interviewees in Oslo *do* identify themselves as Norwegian, but their feeling of belonging is less to 'the state' than to the local areas of Oslo where they were born and are growing up. Moreover, they also identify with Pakistani local urban or rural places where members of their family live, showing no strong attachment to Pakistan as a country – a finding also reported by Jacobson (1998). Members of their extended family networks may also live in different parts of the world such as the Middle East, England or the United States, and all are part of a global Islamic 'community' (*umma*), 'transcending time and national borders'. Thus these young people in Norway and Britain live in a trans-territorial world, comprising local and global personal networks of family relations, ethnic background and religion. Østberg therefore describes their citizenship as *transcultural* and their identities as both integrated and plural.

Thirdly, *such transculturalism does not imply that Muslim diasporas are inherently opposed to Western democratic practices.* We have already noted that local and global commitments can feed into and enhance national democratic debates and practices. In the case of British Muslims, Pnina Werbner argues that Muslim mobilizations (even the conflicts surrounding the Rushdie affair and the Gulf War) 'have been key moments in the development of a Muslim British civic consciousness and capacity for active citizenship' (Werbner 2000: 309). She gives an example from her own research that cuts across the standard stereotypes of Islam. Al Masoom is a Pakistani women's association based in Manchester and founded in 1990 with a membership of practising Muslims committed to a view of Islam as an egalitarian religion guaranteeing women's rights. Members of Al Masoom have espoused international human rights causes (some directly connected with Islam and some not) and have mobilized non-Muslims as well as Muslims, including male politicians, gaining a great deal of respect in the wider political community. As Werbner notes:

> The women's transnational activities for causes beyond the British state . . . achieved their civic integration into the ethnic community as equal and legitimate actors in their own right; at the same time, it also facilitated their integration into a broader network of British non-ethnic human rights and philanthropic church and other organisations, as well as the British media and parliamentary representatives.
>
> (Werbner 2000: 321)

Similarly, Werbner argues that male activism for ethnic and Islamic causes, even when a degree of conflict has been involved, has accelerated their integration into British civil politics. For example, the Rushdie affair brought 'a new consciousness of citizenship as a legal struggle for rights and as a subjective commitment to permanent settlement' (Werbner 2000: 315), and it led to discussions of such topics as the role of state-funded religious schools and the blasphemy law which influenced government policy and discussions about legislation to prohibit incitement to religious hatred. One hopes that such activity will precipitate positive responses to the events of 11 September 2001 and their aftermath.[3]

Incidentally, Werbner's work is a good example of an interpretive approach, since she sets her examples of involvement in democratic processes in the wider context of Islamic tradition, specifically in relation to Islamic law. These aspects may be unfamiliar to most Muslims, but they provide a reference point for the reinterpretation of Islamic ideas in order to cater for new situations. Werbner cites the work of Bernard Lewis (1994) in relation to Islamic law on Muslims living in non-Muslim lands. Lewis points out the categories of *dar-el aman* (land of security) and *dar al-ahd* (land of treaty) that were introduced into Islamic law to clarify obligations for travellers and traders residing in non-Muslim countries. Here the condition of stay was the freedom to practise Islam openly. Although different schools of law have interpreted this requirement differently (for example, there are different views about the jurisdiction of Muslim judges), the Hanafi school (to which most British South Asian Muslims relate) is satisfied with tolerance as a condition of stay.

Werbner goes on to discuss the work of Shadid and van Koningsfeld (1996), showing the on-going nature of this legal debate, with past and current arguments contributing to discussions about the status, duties and responsibilities of Muslims living in Western countries. They identify four current positions, of which two, at least, provide the basis for the integration of an Islamic way of life in Western societies. The *pragmatic* approach, for example, takes the view that the religious freedom granted to minorities in democratic societies means that such a country is a *dar al-ahd* (land of treaty), thus making naturalization and settlement permissible. On this interpretation, Muslims should participate actively in political life, perform military service and accept national law. The other three positions identified show the complex and contentious nature of the debate.[4]

Faith-based schools

At the level of schooling, it is vital that young Muslims and non-Muslims should communicate and exchange ideas. Ipgrave, Leganger-Krogstad and Weisse (Chapters 8, 9 and 10 below) have set out to promote such dialogue in publicly funded primary and secondary schools. However, many (though by no means all) Muslims, and especially their community leaders, have argued for separate schooling for Muslims. Clearly there is an issue in relation to debates about citizenship. Educational provision in Norway sets out to cater for all within a uniform system, with a form of religious education designed to meet the needs of all students. Policy determines that there are no religious schools within the state system, although the state gives substantial financial support to private schools, which cater for less than 2 per cent of pupils. Conditions are very different in the Netherlands, where the state education system includes many schools set up by associations of parents and other interested parties (around 65 per cent of schools). These include different types of religious school (Spinder 2000), and there are a few Muslim schools and one joint Christian-Muslim school (Eggert 1997). The approach in most German federal states (*Länder*) is to teach religious education to Protestant, Catholic and occasionally Muslim children in separate religious groups. The system in Hamburg, in which children from different backgrounds learn together, is an exception (see Weisse, below, Chapter 10).

A Muslim school was first incorporated into the state system in England in 1998. From the beginning of the English and Welsh state education system there have been some partially state-funded Church schools. Under the 1944 legislation some Jewish schools were added, with funding mainly from the state.[5] Several Muslim independent schools attempted unsuccessfully to obtain the same status during the 1980s and 1990s. However, since 1997 the Labour government has introduced radical changes, enabling a range of independent religious schools, including one all-female secondary and several primary Muslim schools, to receive state funding.[6]

The key issue in relation to citizenship in culturally diverse societies is whether separate schooling for religious minorities strengthens or erodes social cohesion. Werbner's argument (above) would be to support such schools on the basis that their existence results from the constructive involvement of community leaders and others in national and local democratic processes. Others would question this view on the grounds that community leaders are not representative of the range of religious positions in society and (being usually male) do not represent women's interests or perspectives (Connolly 1992; see also below, Chapters 4 by Jackson and 7 by Tobler).

Proponents argue for state-funded religious schools that help to give a sense of cultural and religious identity to pupils of the school's affiliation and yet are broadly based enough to take some children from a variety of backgrounds while maintaining the distinctive ethos of the school's religious foundation. Arguments for separate Muslim schools also appeal to human rights legislation in relation to the rights of parents (e.g. Felderhof 2000) and for consistency with legislation allowing Christian and Jewish schools. In England and Wales, in addition to the government's stated aim of achieving fairness and good community relations, evidence of higher attainment and a stronger sense of community in some religious schools, an increased demand from parents, lobbying from pressure groups and the requirements of the Human Rights Act[7] have all contributed to current policy.

There are those (from within the religious traditions as well as others, such as many humanists) who argue against state funding for such schools on the grounds that future citizens should learn to live together in society despite their religious and cultural differences. Will Kymlicka makes this point by arguing that the deliberate separation of children by religion for schooling by *definition* militates against education for good citizenship (Kymlicka 1999: 88–90). In England, following unrest and conflict between young people from different ethnic backgrounds in Oldham, Bradford and Leeds, stirred up by the opportunism of far right political groups, the force of this point is clear. Others point out that it is possible for people with particular religio-political agendas to use such schools to promote their own ideologies, and that they have the potential to become seedbeds of social disharmony. The events on 11 September 2001 in New York and their consequences have reinforced doubts about the wisdom of separate schooling for those who hold this view.

The on-going debate is complicated by issues such as the introduction of a form of selection through the ways in which religious schools operate admission procedures, the attainment of black and Asian children, arguments about racism/anti-racism, the view that the state should not subsidize the propagation of religion, and not least by research suggesting that some types of religious schools are ineffective in maintaining allegiance to particular traditions. The debate will go on, but, in practical terms, no British government is likely to phase out state-funded religious schools. The 'dual system' model is likely to stay for the foreseeable future, while the bulk of religious education will continue to be taught to mixed groups in community schools. Ipgrave's plan to extend her dialogical method through linking children from faith-based and non-faith-based schools by e-mail is a welcome innovation (see Ipgrave below, Chapter 8).

Values, religion, spirituality and citizenship

So far we have not dealt directly with the dimension of values within citizenship education. In Britain the Crick report identified social and moral responsibility as one of the three strands running through education for citizenship, and the national curriculum documents on citizenship make reference to the promotion of spiritual, moral and cultural development of students in order to foster self-confidence and responsibility. The wide-ranging international literature in the broad fields of moral and values education debates how far and in what ways publicly funded schools should promote particular values or moral positions and how far they should help pupils to develop their own skills of moral thinking and decision making (Halstead and Taylor 2000). The issue for the contributors to this book is the role that religion might play in either process in state-funded schools that are not religious foundations. The kind of education in religion advocated in the contributions to this book reflects the plurality of late modern democratic societies, which includes diverse religious and secular positions. It is no longer appropriate to promote particular views of religious truth in schools that reflect such a plurality of views and beliefs. The view is taken that schools should help to develop an understanding of religions that is both critical and reflective, with students being given the opportunity to gain insight from their studies as well as knowledge and understanding. The ethical teachings of religions and spiritual movements are thus source material for study and reflection rather than sources of authority which all pupils are expected to follow. In the dialogical approaches to learning advocated by some contributors, pupils' own stances on moral issues – some of them grounded in religion – become source materials for study and reflection, while students from different religious and non-religious backgrounds may work together in exploring and developing stances on particular moral or social issues (Ipgrave in Chapter 8, Leganger-Krogstad in Chapter 9 and Weisse in Chapter 10 of this volume). There is the possibility of pragmatic agreement on moral issues from participants whose values 'overlap'. The school can provide opportunities for 'conversation' and 'negotiation' within a broadly democratic framework.

There is another relevant issue. Whilst it is inappropriate to promote the teachings of any particular religion or philosophy in publicly funded common schools, it is arguable that there are certain generic skills and activities derived from or associated with religions and spiritual movements that may offer an experiential dimension to moral development and citizenship education. Activities such as 'stilling' or sitting quietly whilst concentrating on an idea or value have features in common with some forms of prayer or meditation. There is an argument that such activities can be used legitimately for all pupils, but away from the context of a particular religious worldview. An account of one school's use of such techniques suggests that they can be highly effective in promoting a sense of responsibility, humanity and maturity amongst pupils (Farrer 2000). The fact that some schools adapt materials influenced by religious or spiritual movements to help children to experience calm and stillness or to explore values may also indicate a need for this type of experiential activity (Henderson and Nesbitt 2001).

Pedagogy and dialogue

If citizenship education is to cover issues related to national, religious, ethnic and cultural identity, where in the curriculum may such issues be covered and by what methods may they be explored? As is clear from some of the contributions to this book, some of these topics may already be partially covered in subjects such as religious education, personal and social education and social studies and through outcomes-based approaches to topics such as 'life orientation' in South Africa. The introduction of citizenship education as a separate subject in England and Wales should enable specialists in religion to contribute to programmes and to work collaboratively with others on such topics. This possibility is especially welcome, given the limited amount of time available specifically for religious education and given the marginalization of multicultural education through the introduction of the national curriculum in 1988 and through the policies of former governments.[8]

With regard to pedagogy and didactics, there is a need to employ methods that take account of the debates about culture, nationality, ethnicity and religion and, crucially, that engage students by connecting with their personal experience and concerns. The interpretive approach, for example, employs a flexible model which encourages exploration of the relationship between individuals in relation to religio-cultural groups to which they may belong, using elements of the wider religious tradition as reference points (Jackson 1997). The tradition is seen as a tentative 'whole', but the contested nature of that whole is recognized: for example, different insiders (as well as different outsiders) may have varying understandings of the nature and scope of, say, the Christian or Hindu traditions. The model encourages a view of religions which acknowledges their complexity, internal diversity, permeable boundaries and their varying interactions with culture. It especially emphasizes the personal element in religions, seeing religion as part of lived human experience. However, the approach is not relativistic with regard to truth, acknowledging varying and often competing truth claims.

One element of this interpretive approach is the application of the model of representation outlined above – moving backwards and forwards between case studies of individuals in the context of their groups and aspects of the wider religious tradition so that each can illuminate and inform the other. The method also requires a comparison and contrast between the learner's concepts and those of the insider, with some comparison and contrast between the learner's and the insider's concepts and experiences.

The pedagogy of the approach encourages reflection and constructive criticism. The reflective element provides time for learners to reassess their understanding of their *own* ways of life as a result of their studies, while the critical element enables pupils to make constructive criticisms at a distance and to contribute to critical reviews of methods of study. Clearly, the more the teacher is aware of the religious and ideological backgrounds of students, the more sensitive and focused the teaching can be. Methods are also needed that encourage students to gain insight from their peers and to examine different ideas of truth held within the classroom. Lesson 'content' is not simply data provided by the teacher, but includes the knowledge and experience of the participants and an interactive relationship between the two. If teachers can have the right degree of sensitivity towards their students' own positions, as well as to the material studied, and can develop appropriate teaching strategies, a genuinely conversational form of education can take place which can handle diversity. Indeed, in some contexts, where racism is a problem, for example, there is a strong case for starting with students' own assumptions, awakening their awareness to their own conditioning about the nature of cultures, religions and ethnic groups. (See Jackson below, Chapter 4, for examples of variants on the interpretive approach tailored to specific situations.)

The interpretive approach allows learning to *begin* at any point on the hermeneutic circle. For example, it could start with an overview of key concepts, if that suited the needs of a class, or it could start with the experiences and assumptions of class members. Three approaches advocated in this book, developed by Ipgrave in England, Leganger-Krogstad in Norway, and Weisse and his team in Germany, concentrate on the second option, emphasizing dialogue in the classroom, in which the pupils are the starting point as well as the key resources and actors.

Ipgrave's approach has involved analysis of children's dialogue and the development of approaches and exercises for the promotion of pupil-to-pupil dialogue in primary schools. Her research shows how the children involved drew on their experience of religious plurality in order to seek new joint understandings with their peers in exploring religious language (Ipgrave 2001 and Chapter 8 below; Jackson, Chapter 4 below).

Leganger-Krogstad's contextual approach was developed through her research and work in teacher training in northern Norway in an area with both Sami and Finnish (Kven) minorities, together with a 'hidden' Sami culture within the majority society. Here she found her views about the nature of religion and education challenged and she became convinced that the fundamental resource material for her work should be the children's own life-world and concerns. In this contextual approach, through interacting with each other and a variety of source materials, pupils are encouraged to see themselves in relation to the past and the future, looking 'inwards' to draw upon their own life-worlds and 'outwards' in relation to society. Pupils' individual concerns and questions, raised through their first and second-hand experiences, are related to wider social and cultural issues, with 'local' issues acting as a bridge. The issues of social plurality and identity raised by Skeie are connected with the life-worlds of individual pupils at their own level (Leganger-Krogstad 2001 and Chapter 9 below).

Weisse's approach in Hamburg essentially combines religious education and education for citizenship in a multicultural society. As noted above, the Hamburg approach is unusual in the German system in bringing children from different religious and cultural backgrounds together in the same class for religious education. Where the subject differs from most approaches in England and Wales is in its emphasis on themes of social justice, peace and human rights as well as on understanding and learning from religions and on the exploration of existential questions. There is an overtly political dimension: RE aims to help pupils to come to terms with various religious, ideological and political beliefs. It is also action-oriented, encouraging an 'active acceptance of responsibility towards society'.

The approach is underpinned by both theological and social justifications.[9] The approach unashamedly adopts a value position that is protective of justice and social harmony; there is a distancing from religious and political fundamentalist attitudes, regarded as socially divisive and erosive of good citizenship. The method is dialogical and personal, with young people learning about others' positions, and clarifying their own, by comparing and contrasting their views with one another. The dialogical approach is overtly concerned with helping pupils to form a sense of their own personal identity, but also with key social issues. As in other chapters of this book, the issue of personal identity is seen in relation to wider social and political issues. The starting point of dialogue is the common experience of all as humans, not the similarities and differences of religions. *Personal* encounters are decisive; pupils' own personal views and commitments are the key source materials rather than the religious systems with which they may be associated. The approach acknowledges the inevitability of conflict, and that there will be situations of unsettled difference. There is a deliberate goal of affirming and appreciating difference within society. Much power is devolved to pupils to explore particular issues of concern (Weisse 1996: 275–6 and Chapter 10 below).

One thing that all these approaches have in common is the emphasis they put on the engagement of pupils with their own beliefs and values in relation to understanding others. They do not fit comfortably with national or local syllabuses that specify the systematic coverage of large amounts of information, leaving little or no space for interaction, reflection and criticism. Perhaps one of the main problems for religious education in countries such as Norway and England is the feeling of constraint felt by many teachers and students when it comes to exploring issues raised by children in class when the syllabus requires systematic coverage of too much information. More time needs to be allowed for pupils to initiate ideas, to reflect and to interact without allowing the subject to become too unstructured. The dialogical and interpretive approaches described above encourage the kind of 'differentiated citizenship' advocated by Iris Young (1990), in which she argues for more institutions through which individual voices can be represented.

Conclusion

This chapter has argued that studies of religion have an important part to play in citizenship education, especially in terms of understanding various aspects of social plurality in relation to the experience of individual students. This social plurality combines traditional and modern/postmodern dimensions, connecting national, local and global elements. It has been argued that debates about religion need to be set in the context of complementary debates about the nation-state, ethnicity and culture, and that aspects of these debates can be used to clarify, challenge or illuminate positions adopted by students. By participating in such discussions, students should be helped to examine their own and their peers' assumptions and reflect upon their own identities.

The situation of Islam in Britain and other Western societies was discussed briefly in order to illustrate how data from field studies of religions can be used to illuminate issues relating to the debates about citizenship. Some comments have also been made about the contribution of the study of religions and spiritual movements to elements of values education, often identified as an important dimension of citizenship education.

Over against the view that participation in the democratic processes of society is a matter principally for community representatives working within conventional political structures, the view has been adopted that:

> we require participatory structures in which actual people with their geographical, ethnic, gender and occupational differences, assert their

perspectives on social issues within institutions that encourage the representation of their distinct voices.

(Young 1990: 116)

In promoting this idea of 'differentiated citizenship' the common school is seen as a vitally important forum. The dialogical and interpretive approaches developed by some of the contributors to this book are seen as contributing theoretical and practical ideas for helping students to interact with one another and with a variety of source materials in developing and refining their own stances. The main arguments in the on-going debate about separate faith-based education are noted, but the facilitation of communication and dialogue between pupils from different types of schools has been advocated as a pragmatic strategy in societies maintaining forms of separate education.

I have argued that the religious dimension of citizenship education can be covered in a variety of ways. Pragmatically, religious/religion education on its own may not have sufficient time available to deal with all the relevant issues (Everington 2001), while citizenship education or social studies would need expertise from specialists in religion. Collaborative and inter-disciplinary approaches would seem to be most appropriate for citizenship education. Especially important is the insight from contributors to this book that both religious/religion education and citizenship education should engage students and not be reduced to an externally imposed body of knowledge.

Notes

1 During the twentieth century the term 'popular culture' emerged – mass culture working through the mass media – a notion in tension with 'high culture' (i.e. the eighteenth-century 'high arts' idea of culture).

2 The views of Anthony Coombs, written when he was a British Conservative Member of Parliament, are an example: 'Unless RE is set in a Christian context it cannot fulfil its academic role of ensuring pupils have a sufficient understanding of the British way of life' (Coombs 1988).

3 Werbner notes Philip Lewis's argument that the integration of Irish Catholics into British society was facilitated through a state subsidy given for separate Catholic schools (Lewis 1997).

4 The others are as follows. (1) The *modernist:* this rejects the opposition between *dar al-Islam* (land of Islam) and *dar al-harb* (land of war) as inapplicable today in Muslim and Western countries, attempting to introduce new terms such as the idea of *dar al-dawa* (land of preaching). On this basis, Muslim minorities in the West should ensure Muslim education for their children in order to transmit Islam to the next generation. (2) The *utopian:* this was the position adopted by the late Kalim Siddiqui, who advocated the creation of a unified and legally autonomous Muslim community in Britain and the West, as part of a transnational Islamic *ummah*. On this basis national law was to be obeyed so long as it did not conflict with loyalty to Islam. (3) The *traditionalist:* this is a marginal position

held by a few Muslim clerics in Europe and elsewhere in the Muslim world, maintaining the traditional division between 'land of Islam' and 'land of war'.
Permanent settlement in the West is disapproved of as potentially leading to
assimilation. (Werbner 2000, citing Shadid and van Koningsfeld 1996.)

5 Such schools, with mainly state funding, but with a contribution from the religious
body towards building and maintenance costs, are called Voluntary Aided schools.

6 As Voluntary Aided schools, all staff costs are covered by the state, and, at the time
of writing, 85 per cent of building and maintenance costs.

7 The European Convention of Human Rights was incorporated into British law in
the Human Rights Act (1998) and implemented in October 2000.

8 The British Prime Minister, John Major, declared at the 1992 Conservative Party
Conference that 'primary teachers should learn how to teach children to read,
not waste their time on the politics of gender, race and class'. A year later, the
former Chief Executive of the National Curriculum Council revealed that there
had been specific instructions to remove references to multicultural education
from the National Curriculum (Graham 1993).

9 The theological influence comes especially from the Christian theologian Hans-
Jochen Margull and the Jewish theologian Martin Buber, and biblical themes
such as the idea that all people are children of God are invoked. The socio-political
justification is grounded in the kind of 'humaneness' that is embodied in declarations of human rights, such as the UN Charter on the Rights of Children.

References

Al-Azmeh, Aziz (1993) 'Prologue: Muslim "Culture" and the European Tribe', in
Islams and Modernities, London: Verso, 1–17.

Ashenden, C. (1995) 'Christianity and the Primary School: The Contribution of
Anthropology to Teaching about Christianity', unpublished thesis, University of
Brighton.

Bailey, S. H., Harris, D. J. and Jones, S. L. (1991) *Civil Liberties: Cases and Materials*,
3rd edn, London: Butterworth.

Ballard, R. (ed.) (1994) *Desh Pardesh: The South Asian Presence in Britain*, London:
Hurst.

Banks, M. (1996) *Ethnicity: Anthropological Constructions*, London: Routledge.

Barth, F. (ed.) (1969) *Ethnic Groups and Boundaries*, London: Allen & Unwin.

Barth, F. (1981) 'Ethnic groups and boundaries', in *Process and Forms in Social Life:
Selected Essays*, London: Routledge.

—— (1994) 'A personal view of present tasks and priorities in cultural and social
anthropology', in R. Borofsky (ed.) *Assessing Cultural Anthropology*, New York:
McGraw-Hill, 349–61.

—— (1996) 'How features of the encompassing society set parameters for local
multiculturalism', unpublished paper, conference on 'Multicultultural Competence: a Resource for Tomorrow', Høgskolen i Bergen, August.

—— (2000) 'Boundaries and connections', in Anthony Cohen (ed.) *Signifying
Identities: Anthropological Perspectives on Boundaries and Contested Values*, London:
Routledge, 15–36.

Baumann, G. (1996) *Contesting Culture: Discourses of Identity in Multi-ethnic London*,
Cambridge: Cambridge University Press.

—— (1999) *The Multicultural Riddle: Rethinking National, Ethnic and Religious Identities*, London: Routledge.

Beckford, James A. (1985) *Cult Controversies: The Societal Response to the New Religious Movements*, London: Tavistock.

Beckford, James A. (ed.) (1986) *New Religious Movements and Rapid Social Change*, London: Sage.

Beckford, J. and Gilliat, S. (1998) *Religion in Prisons: Equal Rites in a Multi-faith Society*, Cambridge: Cambridge University Press.

Benedict, R. (1935) *Patterns of Culture*, London: Routledge.

Castles, S. and Kosack, G. (1973) *Immigrant Workers and Class Structure in Western Europe*, London: Oxford University Press for the Institute of Race Relations.

Champion, S. G. and Short, D. (1951) *Reading from World Religions*, London: Watts.

Chantepie de la Saussaye, P. (1891) *Manual of the Science of Religion* (English translation of *Lehrbuch der Religionsgeschichte*, Freiburg, 1887).

Chidester, D. (1996) *Savage Systems: Colonialism and Comparative Religion in Southern Africa*, Charlottesville VA: University Press of Virginia.

Clifford, James (1986) 'Introduction: Partial Truths', in J. Clifford and G. Marcus (eds) *Writing Culture: The Poetics and Politics of Ethnography*, Berkeley CA: University of California Press, 1–26.

Cohen, Anthony (ed.) (1982a) *Belonging: Identity and Social Organization in British Rural Cultures*, Manchester: Manchester University Press.

—— (1982b) 'Belonging: the experience of culture', in Anthony Cohen (ed.) *Belonging: Identity and Social Organization in British Rural Cultures*, Manchester: Manchester University Press.

—— (ed.) (1986) *Symbolizing Boundaries: Identity and Diversity in British Cultures*, Manchester: Manchester University Press.

Connolly, C. (1992) 'Religious schools: refuge or redoubt', in M. Leicester and M. Taylor (eds) *Ethics, Ethnicity and Education*, London: Kogan Page, 137–45.

Coombs, A. (1988) 'Diluting the faith', *Education*, 26 August.

Dashefsky, A. (1972) 'And the search goes on: religio-ethnic identity and identification', *Sociological Analysis*, 33 (4), 239–45.

Eggert, H. (1997) 'The RE model of the Juliana van Stolbergschool in the discussion about interreligious education', in In Trees Andree, Cok Bakker and Peter Schreiner (eds) *Crossing Boundaries: Contributions to Inter-religious and Intercultural Education*, Münster: Comenius Institute, 61–2.

Erricker, C. and Erricker, J. (2000) *Reconstructing Religious, Spiritual and Moral Education*, London: RoutledgeFalmer.

Etzioni, A. (1993) *The Spirit of Community: The Reinvention of American Society*, New York: Touchstone.

Everington, J. (2001) 'Dreams, difficulties and dilemmas: the relationship between citizenship and religious education in English schools', unpublished paper, international seminar on 'Citizenship and Education: International Perspectives on Cultural and Religious Diversity', University of Warwick.

Farrer, F. (2000) *A Quiet Revolution: Encouraging Positive Values in our Children*, London: Rider.

Felderhof, M. (2000) 'Religious education and human rights', in N. Holm (ed.) *Islam and Christianity in School Religious Education*, Åbo (Finland): Åbo Akademi University, 21–39.

Finegan, J. (1952) *The Archaeology of World Religions*, Princeton, NJ: Princeton University Press.

Fischer, Michael M. J. (1986) 'Ethnicity and the postmodern arts of memory', in James Clifford and George Marcus (eds) *Writing Culture: The Poetics and Politics of Ethnography*, Berkeley CA: University of California Press, 194–233.

Fitzgerald, T. (2000) *The Ideology of Religious Studies*, New York: Oxford University Press.

Geaves, R. (1998) 'The borders between religions: a challenge to the world religions approach to religious education', *British Journal of Religious Education*, 21 (1), 20–31.

Geertz, Clifford (1968) *Islam Observed: Religious Development in Morocco and Indonesia*, Chicago: University of Chicago Press.

—— (1973) *The Interpretation of Cultures*, New York: Basic Books.

Giddens, A. (1990) *The Consequences of Modernity*, Cambridge: Polity Press.

—— (1993) *Sociology*, 2nd edn, Cambridge: Polity Press.

Graham, D. (1993) *A Lesson for Us All: The Making of the National Curriculum*, London: Routledge.

Halstead, J. M. and Taylor, M. (2000) *The Development of Values, Attitudes and Personal Qualities: A Review of Recent Research*, Slough: National Foundation for Educational Research.

Heelas, P. (1996) *The New Age Movement: The Celebration of Self and the Sacralization of Modernity*, Oxford: Blackwell.

Henderson, A. and Nesbitt, E. M. (2001) 'Citizenship education and smaller religious organisations in the UK', unpublished paper, international seminar on 'Citizenship and Education: International Perspectives on Cultural and Religious Diversity', University of Warwick.

Ipgrave, J. (1999) 'Issues in the delivery of religious education to Muslim pupils: perspectives from the classroom', *British Journal of Religious Education*, 21 (3), 147–58.

—— (2001) *Pupil-to-pupil Dialogue in the Classroom as a Tool for Religious Education*, Warwick Religions and Education Research Unit, Working Paper 2, Coventry: Institute of Education, University of Warwick.

Jackson, R. (1996) 'The construction of "Hinduism" and its impact on religious education in England and Wales', *Panorama: International Journal of Comparative Religious Education and Values*, 8 (1), 86–104.

—— (1997) *Religious Education: An Interpretive Approach*, London: Hodder & Stoughton.

Jackson, R. and Killingley, D. (1988) *Approaches to Hinduism*, London: John Murray.

Jackson, R. and Nesbitt, E. M. (1993) *Hindu Children in Britain*, Stoke on Trent: Trentham.

Jacobson, J. (1997) 'Religion and ethnicity: dual and alternative sources of identity among young British Pakistanis', *Ethnic and Racial Studies*, 20 (2), 238–56.

Jacobson, J. (1998) *Islam in Transition: Religion and Identity among British Pakistani Youth*, London: Routledge.

James, E. O. (1938) *Comparative Religion: An Introductory and Historical Study*, London: Methuen.

Jones, R. and Welengama, G. (2000) *Ethnic Minorities in English Law*, Stoke on Trent: Trentham.

King, R. (1999) *Orientalism and Religion: Postcolonial Theory, India and 'the Mystic East'*, London: Routledge.

Kymlicka, Will (1999) 'Education for citizenship', in J. M. Halstead and T. H. McLaughlin (eds) *Education in Morality*, London: Routledge.

Leeuw, G. van der (1938) *Religion in Essence and Manifestation*, London: Allen & Unwin.

Leganger-Krogstad, H. (2001) 'Religious education in a global perspective: a contextual approach', in H-G. Heimbrock, P. Schreiner and C. Sheilke (eds) *Towards Religious Competence: Diversity as a Challenge for Education in Europe*, Hamburg: Lit Verlag, 53–73.

Lewis, B. (1994) 'Legal and historical reflections on the position of Muslim populations under non-Muslim rule', in B. Lewis and D. Schnapper (eds) *Muslims in Europe*, London: Pinter.

Lewis, P. (1997) 'Arenas of ethnic negotiation: co-operation and conflict in Bradford', in T. Modood and P. Werbner (eds) *The Politics of Multiculturalism in the New Europe: Racism, Identity and Community*, London: Zed Books.

Lyotard, Jean-François (1984) *The Postmodern Condition: A Report on Knowledge*, trans. Geoff Bennington and Brian Massumi, Manchester: Manchester University Press.

McCutcheon, R. (1997) *Manufacturing Religion*, Oxford: Oxford University Press.

McIntyre, J. (1978) *Multi-culture and Multifaith Societies: Some Examinable Assumptions*, Occasional Papers, Oxford: Farmington Institute for Christian Studies.

Marshall, T. H. (1950) *Citizenship and Social Class*, Cambridge: Cambridge University Press.

Modood, T. (1997) '"Difference", cultural racism and antiracism', in P. Werbner and T. Modood (eds) *Debating Cultural Hybridity*, London: Zed Books, 154–72.

Nesbitt, E. M. (2000) *The Religious Lives of Sikh Children: A Coventry Based Study*, Monograph Series, Leeds: University of Leeds, Community Religions Project.

Oberoi, H. (1994) *The Construction of Religious Boundaries: Culture, Identity and Diversity in the Sikh Tradition*, Delhi: Oxford University Press.

Ouseley, H. (ed.) (2001) *Community Pride not Prejudice: Making Diversity Work in Bradford*, Bradford: Bradford Vision.

Paludan, P. and Prinds, E. (1999) *Evaluation of Education in Citizenship and Moral Judgement*, Copenhagen: Danish Ministry of Education.

Runnymede (2000) *The Report of the Commission on the Future of Multi-ethnic Britain*, London: Runnymede Trust.

Said, E. (1978) *Orientalism*, London: Routledge.

—— (1981) *Covering Islam*, London: Routledge.

Shadid, W. A. R. and van Koningsfeld, S. (1996) 'Loyalty to a non-Muslim government: an analysis of Islamic normative discussions and the views of some contemporary Islamists', in W. A. R. Shadid and S. van Koningsfeld (eds) *Political Participation and Identities of Muslims in non-Muslim Countries*, Kampen (Netherlands): Kok Pharos.

Skeie, G. (1995) 'Plurality and pluralism: a challenge for religious education', *British Journal of Religious Education*, 17 (2), 84–91.

Smith, W. C. (1978) *The Meaning and End of Religion*, London: SPCK.

Spinder, H. (2000) 'The Netherlands', in P. Schreiner (ed.) *Religious Education in Europe*, Münster: Comenius Institute, 117–22.

Tate, N. (1995) 'Cultural Identity and Education', address to Shropshire Secondary Heads Conference, 13 July, London: School Curriculum and Assessment Authority.

Weisse, Wolfram (1996) 'Christianity and its neighbour-religions: a question of tolerance?' *Scriptura: International Journal of Bible, Religion and Theology*, 55 (4), 263–76.

Werbner, P. (2000) 'Divided loyalties, empowered citizenship? Muslims in Britain', *Citizenship Studies*, 4 (3), 307–24.

Young, Iris Marion (1990) *Justice and the Politics of Difference*, Princeton NJ: Princeton University Press.

Part I

Issues in citizenship, education and diversity

Chapter 2

Global citizenship, cultural citizenship and world religions in religion education

David Chidester

Synopsis As a rationale for the study of religion and religions, citizenship has advantages over earlier, imperial justifications that recommended this field of inquiry for providing useful information for trading with, conquering or administering people of foreign lands. Based on the recognition of shared rights and responsibilities within a common society, citizenship offers a more inclusive framework. However, the nature of this inclusivity needs to be clarified in relation to our understanding of both religion and citizenship. With respect to religion, the notion of 'world religions', which is apparently comprehensive, but actually quite arbitrary, has tended to exclude indigenous and other forms of religious life from consideration. Within various national projects in religion and public education, the notion of 'world religions' has been regarded differently, sometimes criticized for reifying difference, other times adopted as a way of celebrating diversity. At the same time, the notion of citizenship has been undergoing dramatic transformations through transnational initiatives in global and local citizenship. While feminist, environmentalist, human rights and other movements have been advocating new types of global citizenship, many local forms of cultural citizenship have been advanced to make claims about public rights and responsibilities based on the public recognition of difference. In both cases, citizenship calls upon loyalties that are not exclusively defined by national citizenship. By exploring the problem of 'world religions' in relation to these new forms of global and cultural citizenship, I hope to highlight some of the challenges and possibilities for teaching and learning about religion, religions and religious diversity within an inclusive educational practice.

Why study religion and religions? Why should we be involved as educators, students, parents, or administrators in the process of teaching and learning about religious diversity? In this chapter, I want to test one possible answer: citizenship. As I hope to show, the validity of this answer depends less upon what we mean by religion than upon what we mean by citizenship, although both terms will have to be brought into focus. Without exhausting all possible avenues of exploration, at the very least I hope to suggest that the study of religion, religions, and religious diversity can be usefully brought into conversation with recent research on new formations of citizenship.

Conventionally, the modern notion of citizenship has combined political-legal rights and responsibilities with symbolic-affective loyalties and values into a public status of full inclusion and participation within a society. Located within the constitutional frameworks of modern states, social citizenship has generally been defined as national citizenship. Although the second half of the twentieth century certainly produced declarations of transnational rights and social movements with transnational loyalties, social citizenship formally remained national citizenship. According to many analysts, however, the increasing scope and pace of globalization since the 1990s have generated new forms of 'post-national citizenship', which have appeared in both local assertions of different kinds of 'cultural citizenship' and transnational assertions of a planetary 'global citizenship'. In order to test my answer, therefore, I will need to consider how these changing forms of citizenship affect the terms of inclusion and the conditions of participation in public educational programmes in the study of religion, religions, and religious diversity. In spite of its conceptual and practical problems, I will propose, citizenship provides a useful rationale for the study of religion and religions.

Imperialists and idiots

Why should we study religion and religions? In an essay published in the *Guide to the Study of Religion*, I criticized imperial answers, from nineteenth-century British imperialism to twentieth-century American neo-imperialism, which have been based on the assumption that the study of religion and religions is good for maintaining a certain kind of transnational order (Chidester 2000a). For example, in a series of lectures on *The Religions of the World* published in 1847, the British theologian F. D. Maurice proposed that the study of religions provided knowledge that was useful for a nation that was currently 'engaged in trading with other countries, or in conquering them, or in keeping possession of them' (Maurice 1847: 255; see Chidester 1996: 131–2). Over a century later, in the first edition of his popular survey of world religions published in 1958, *The Religions of Man*, the American scholar of religion Huston Smith reported that his series of lectures to officers of the US Air Force provided useful knowledge because 'someday they were likely to be dealing with the peoples they were studying as allies, antagonists, or subjects of military occupation' (Smith 1958: 7–8; see McCutcheon 1997: 180–1). Certainly, these recommendations for the study of religion suggest a remarkable continuity from British imperialism to American neo-imperialism in justifying the field of study as an intellectual instrument of international trade, military conquest, and political administration of alien subjects.

In case we think that such strategic justifications for the study of religion and religions have disappeared, we can refer to the introductory course

offered by Chaplain Ken Stice at the US Army John F. Kennedy Special Warfare Center and School. In the syllabus for that course on 'Religious Factors
in Special Operations', Chaplain Stice identified the 'terminal learning
objective' as enabling a Special Operations soldier to brief his or her
commander on the impact of religion and religions on a mission and its
forces. 'Why do Special Operations soldiers need to study religion at all?'
Chaplain Stice asked. 'Primarily, because of the truth of Special Operations
Imperative No. 1: Understand the Operational Environment!' As an adjunct
to military strategy and tactics, the study of religion and religions can be
useful in gaining the co-operation or submission of adherents of foreign,
unfamiliar religions that Chaplain Stice could characterize as 'different
from our own' (Stice 1997).

By contrast to this imperial strategy, a different rationale for studying
religion and religions has emerged under conditions of increased religious,
cultural, and linguistic diversity within urban centres of the West. Increasingly, people encounter adherents of other religions not only in international business, military operations, or foreign missions but also at
home. To illustrate this local rationale for studying religious diversity, I
refer to a popular text, *The Complete Idiot's Guide to the World's Religions*.
Addressing the reader, the authors reformulate my initial question as
'Why Bother to Learn?' As the authors explain:

> At one point or another, just about everyone has felt some form of
> anxiety about encountering an unfamiliar religious tradition. This book
> will not only help you reduce the likelihood of embarrassing missteps,
> it will also clue you in about the guiding ideas behind just about every
> religious tradition you're likely to encounter in today's world.
>
> (Toropov and Buckles 1997: *frontis*)

Notice the personal reasons for studying religion and religions: we need to
deal with personal feelings of anxiety about the unfamiliar; to avoid personal
embarrassment in dealing with others; and to live knowledgeably, comfortably, and confidently in a multicultural, multi-religious world. Ultimately,
the study of religion and religions is recommended as an antidote to fear
of the unknown. 'Perhaps the most important reason to study faiths
beyond one's own,' the authors advise, 'is that it is a marvelous way to
replace fear with experience and insight. It's hard to be frightened of something you really understand' (Toropov and Buckles 1997: 8). The study of
religion and religions, therefore, emerges as a kind of therapy for fear.
'The more you know about other faiths,' the authors promise, 'the less
fear will be a factor in your dealings with people who practice those
faiths' (Toropov and Buckles 1997: 10).

Although the *Idiot's Guide* observes in passing that these personal accom-
plishments are always useful for tourists visiting strange and distant places,

the authors repeatedly stress that the problems of anxiety, embarrassment, and ignorance urgently need to be resolved at home. In the workplace, the neighbourhood, the school, and even the family, religious diversity is a local fact of life. Accordingly, the study of religion and religions is not a strategy for dealing with foreign subjects, but a therapy for dealing with fears that arise in on-going and regular relations with fellow citizens who live and work in the same operational environment.

As any idiot knows, structural and historical causes can be identified for local religious diversity. Addressing an American audience, the authors of the *Idiot's Guide* point to the framework of the US constitution as a legal structure that ensures religious diversity. By ensuring freedom from any religious establishment and guaranteeing freedom for all religious exercise, the First Amendment to the US constitution created 'a pluralistic religious environment'. Recent history of population movements, immigration, and diaspora, however, has expanded the scope of diversity. As a result, the authors observe, 'We live in a society in which true religious diversity, guaranteed by the Constitution of the United States, is finally becoming a reality' (Toropov and Buckles 1997: *frontis*). In structural terms, the reality of religious diversity can be understood as working out the terms and conditions of the US constitutional framework, 'Catching Up with the Constitution', as the authors put it. However, the historical dynamics in and through which people, money, technology, images, and ideas move around the world have clearly accelerated the pace of this race to catch up with the US constitution. 'In an earlier era, unfamiliar religious systems could be dismissed as "foreign" and left for the scholars to explore,' the authors note. 'In this era, that is usually not a realistic option' (Toropov and Buckles 1997: 5). Learning about religion and religions has become a necessity for everyone, 'even if you don't have an advanced degree in comparative religion', they urge, adding the tantalizing question: 'Why leave all the excitement to academics?' (Toropov and Buckles 1997: 7).

By treating adherents of different religions as local citizens rather than as foreign subjects, *The Complete Idiot's Guide to the World's Religions* represents a significant alternative to the imperial study of religion. Although the guide does not directly address citizenship, the basic ingredients are there in politico-legal rights and responsibilities and the symbolic-affective terms for group identification and shared values. Recognizing a citizen's right to religious worship, the guide spends less time on rights than on responsibilities – the responsibility to exercise religious tolerance, the duty to respect religious diversity, and the civic obligation to ensure that no one is disadvantaged on the basis of religious difference – that implicitly recognize the reality of an inter-religious citizenry. In an aside, the *Idiot's Guide* urges employers to avoid discriminating against employees on the basis of religion. Not merely a matter of etiquette, this freedom from religious discrimination in public is a legal right held by all citizens. As the authors warn:

Watch It! Just a reminder: It is completely inappropriate (and usually illegal) to question someone who reports to you about the whys and wherefores of his or her religion as it relates to workplace performance. Stay on the right side of the law; do not give even the barest impression that you are judging someone's performance, or potential for a job opening, on his or her religious beliefs.

(Toropov and Buckles 1997: 23)

While asserting the legal rights and responsibilities of an inter-religious citizenry, the guide also promotes an inter-religious basis for group identification and shared values in which no one is defined as 'the "Other" on the basis of religion' (Toropov and Buckles 1997: 9) and all religions are found to hold in common the same elemental truths of humanity's relation with the eternal, the interconnectedness of all creation, and the limits of the logical mind (Toropov and Buckles 1997: 11–19). Although this common ground of shared religious values must seem very thin, the *Idiot's Guide* nevertheless develops a rationale for the study of religions that is based on the mutual recognition of citizens, for all their religious diversity, in a common inter-religious society.

World religions

Although I have been busy so far appreciating and applauding *The Complete Idiot's Guide to the World's Religions* for advancing the study of religion and religions within an inclusive framework of inter-religious citizenship, the text certainly must also come in for some criticism. In many respects, the *Idiot's Guide* is more symptom than solution of the problem of teaching and learning about religious diversity in a common society. Researchers and educators in the study of religion will certainly object to many of its guiding premises, especially its overheated diagnosis of anxiety, its reduction of the field of study to personal therapy, and its superficial assimilation of religious diversity into a common core of beliefs supposedly shared by all religions of the world.

Certainly, as the *Idiot's Guide* suggests, we cannot leave all the excitement of studying religion and religions to academics, but we also cannot simply ignore academic theory and method in the field. In this regard, the most serious problem with *The Complete Idiot's Guide to the World's Religions* is its adherence to the very notion of 'world religions'. The book's substantive chapters consist of simple reviews of the history, beliefs, and practices of 'world religions' as if they were separate systems, continuous with the past and uniform in the present. Among academics, considerable excitement in the study of religion and religions in recent years has been generated by rejecting, for many good reasons, the organizing framework of 'world religions'.

First, the framework is arbitrary. How many 'world religions' are there in the world? In the 1590s, when the word 'religions' first appeared in English, there were two, Protestant and Catholic (Harrison 1990: 39). During the eighteenth century, there were four, Christianity, Judaism, Islam, and Paganism (Pailin 1984). In 1870 the putative founder of the scientific study of religion, F. Max Müller, identified eight –Christianity, Judaism, Islam, Hinduism, Buddhism, Zoroastrianism, Confucianism, and Taoism (Müller 1873). As the study of religion developed in the twentieth century, Max Müller's list of major 'world religions' was altered on account of contingent historical factors to remove Zoroastrianism and add Shintoism. Although a recent survey has identified thirty-three principal 'world religions' (Eliade *et al.* 2000), common usage of the framework has generally settled on a kind of G8 of major religions in the world.

Secondly, the framework is exclusionary. By privileging the religions that emerged from urban, agricultural civilizations of the Middle East, India, and the Far East, the model of 'world religions' implicitly excludes all forms of indigenous religious life. When not ignored entirely (Burke 1995; Sharma 1993), indigenous religions are incorporated in the model as 'nature and tribal' (Küng and Kuschel 1995), 'basic' (Hopfe 1994), 'primal' (Richards 1997; Smith 1994), or 'non-literate' (Coogan 1998). Consistent with this general practice, the *Idiot's Guide* includes a brief chapter on 'Non-scriptural nature religions' of Africa and Native America (Toropov and Buckles 1997: 193–9). Although it might be assumed that the term 'world religions' stands in contrast to either non-religion or religions from other planets, it actually operates in opposition to the indigenous religions of colonized people all over the world. In general surveys of 'world religions', indigenous religions are rarely referred to as 'indigenous', as William Pietz has observed, because that term would imply 'the right to land, territories, and place' associated with the kind of indigenous national autonomy asserted by the International Covenant on the Rights of Indigenous Nations (Martin and Stahnke 1998: 133–7; Pietz 1999: 7–8). By rendering indigenous religions as a residual category, the framework of 'world religions' excludes them from such claims to identity and place in the world.

Thirdly, the framework is readily available for the ideological work of asserting conceptual control over the entire world. In the case of Max Müller, who adopted the aphorism 'Classify and conquer', the division of the world into 'world religions' promised conceptual control over religious diversity in the service of the British imperial project. Arguably, recent systems of classification, such as Samuel Huntington's eight 'world civilizations', which can be easily mapped as 'world religions', continues this ideological work of asserting global conceptual control (Huntington 1993, 1998). Organized within the framework of 'world religions', clashing civilizations can be not only understood but also managed from the imperial centre.

Although more could be said against the notion of 'world religions', let this suffice for the moment. Whether arbitrarily or strategically constructed, the power of the category 'world religions' is derived from the implicit assertion of control over the complex, changing world of religious diversity. During the 1990s, despite criticisms within the academic study of religion, the notion of 'world religions' underwent a revival on two fronts, global and local, especially as evidenced by the changing role of religion in public education.

On the global front, a range of inter-religious initiatives – the Global Ethic, the Parliament for the World's Religions, the World Conference on Religion and Peace, and so on – promoted the major 'world religions' as if they were a kind of security council in a religious United Nations (Chidester 2000b: 598–600). Although they might not agree on matters of religious doctrines, myths, and rituals, the 'world religions' could be invoked to underwrite a global religious consensus on questions of ethics, social justice, and shared values. However, as Eleanor Nesbitt has argued, these projects in distilling 'shared values' from all the religions of the world are 'always initiated from a western/"host" cultural position'. In the very process of identifying key moral issues, such as sexual relationships, abortion, euthanasia, social justice, or environmentalism, 'dominant western concerns and conceptualization shape the agenda for examining . . . all the faiths' (Nesbitt 1999: 125). Similarly, Wolfram Weisse, Ursula Neumann, and Thorsten Knauth have expressed serious reservations about any 'global ethic' based on the assertion of shared religious values that might be 'imposed from above' (Neumann and Weisse 1999: 138; see Weisse and Knauth 1997: 36–8). Clearly, when representatives of the 'world religions' are brought around the same table, it makes a difference who owns the table.

Locally, in many countries, the category of 'world religions' was revived in response to new demographic situations. In the context of the increasing religious, cultural, and linguistic diversity of British society, as Eleanor Nesbitt has observed, educational policy was marked by the 'shift in the content of religious education towards "world religions" and also towards an internally differentiated Christian tradition' (Nesbitt 1999: 116). In particular, the growing presence of South Asians of Hindu, Sikh, or Muslim religious backgrounds has led to the development of new curricula in religious education based not on Christianity alone but also on 'world religions' (Nesbitt 1999: 118). Of course, not all British educators see this as a progressive development, not because they do not want to be inclusive, but because they want to avoid the arbitrary, exclusionary, and ideological limits of this model. In the on-going research of the Warwick project, the model of 'world religions' has been consistently rejected as an illegitimate point of departure for research, teaching, and learning about religious diversity (e.g. Jackson 1997a). As a global framework, it falsely reifies religions; as a local framework, it inevitably alienates adherents of the religions it reifies. Based on intensive ethnographic fieldwork among British Hindus, Robert Jackson and Eleanor Nesbitt have found that the 'juxtaposition of children with perceptions of their cultural background based on home and community experience and teachers having a "world religion" conception of Hinduism can lead to misunderstandings' (Jackson and Nesbitt 1997: 94). Accordingly, researchers in the Warwick project have developed methods of local ethnography that depart from the static framework of 'world religions'.

In Germany, as Ursula Neumann and Wolfram Weisse have noted, attention to religious diversity has also been motivated by demographic changes resulting from 'the growing number of migrants entering Germany from South Europe, Turkey, Asia, South America and Africa; and in more recent years, from the eastern European countries' (Neumann and Weisse 1999: 136). The challenge of religious diversity, however, seems to have been primarily raised by the increasing presence of Muslim immigrants. Arguably, the challenge of working out new Christian–Muslim relations has made the model of 'world religions' less attractive for educators in Germany. Similarly, in the Netherlands and Norway, religious diversity seems to have registered locally in relations between Christians and Muslims (Van de Wetering 1997; Østberg 1997). Under these changing conditions of religious demography, the global framework of 'world religions' has had less salience. As Neumann and Weisse have argued, the educational task is 'not to define "world religions" as abstract systems, but rather to define them through personal experiences evolving out of dialogue with people who perceive themselves as members of a particular religion' (Neumann and Weisse 1999: 136). Accordingly, educators in the Hamburg project have developed methods of inter-religious dialogue that do not depend upon the model of 'world religions'.

In Namibia and South Africa, however, the framework of 'world religions' has assumed an entirely different significance, not as an instrument for controlling foreign subjects or assimilating alien immigrants, but as a new model of inclusion for nation building. In post-independence Namibia, educators in the field of religious education sought new terms for overcoming the political, social, and economic divisions of the past by searching for a common moral ground on which to build a new nation. As Christo Lombard has observed, educational programmes in the study of religion, religions, and religious diversity were directly linked with moral education. Accordingly, approaches to the study of religion that distilled a 'common morality' (Outka and Reeder 1993) or a 'global ethic' (Küng and Kuschel 1995) were attractive for educators struggling to overcome differences and facilitate reconciliation in an independent Namibia. 'In the Namibian

RME programmes,' as Lombard has reported, 'we have taken this emphasis seriously by linking religious and moral education, and by allowing learners to discover common values through their own discussions and explorations' (Lombard 1997: 120). Although more sophisticated than the prescriptions of the *Idiot's Guide*, this educational undertaking to explore and discover 'common values' has reinforced the framework of 'world religions' in teaching and learning about religious diversity.

Similarly, in South Africa, the model of 'world religions' has increasingly appeared as an inclusive construction. As a world in one country, according to the tourist propaganda, the new, democratic South Africa has been struggling to define new terms of inclusion in a common society. Ongoing debates over the role of religion in South African public education have helped to clarify the ways in which religious diversity, even if that diversity is framed in terms of 'world religions', can be translated into national unity. In a draft submission to the Minister of Education that grew out of a Consulting Workshop on Religion in Education in May 2000, a proposed policy sought to recognize religious diversity but also to affirm the rights and responsibilities of a common citizenship. 'With a deep and enduring African religious heritage, South Africa is a country that embraces all the major "world religions"' (Consulting Workshop 2000: 4). Given this diversity of religion, a national policy must be consistent with the constitutional framework that defines the rights and responsibilities of citizens. As the draft submission recommended, 'Policy for the role of religion in public schools in South Africa must flow directly from core constitutional values of citizenship, human rights, equality, freedom from discrimination, and freedom for conscience, religion, thought, belief, and opinion' (Consulting Workshop 2000: 2). In a society in which citizenship was systematically denied to the majority of the population, the promise of national citizenship has represented not only new terms of inclusion but also new possibilities of empowerment. Although the vocabulary of 'world religions' has often been used, the on-going negotiations over the future of religion in South African public schools have been driven by new requirements of citizenship.

As suggested by research in these different countries, 'world religions' can signify different things – an alienating framework to be rejected, an inclusive framework to be embraced – depending upon the aims and objectives of specific national projects. Nationalism, of course, is not what it used to be. In the South African case, a new, democratic nation was born in 1994 just when nations seemed to be going out of style. In a globalizing world, citizenship is no longer necessarily contained within the political-legal framework of states or symbolic-affective loyalties to nations. Recent research has identified new developments in global and cultural citizenship that must be taken seriously in thinking through relations between citizenship and religion education.

Global citizenship, cultural citizenship

There has always been a tension between the political-legal and symbolic-affective sides of any definition of citizenship, perhaps even a basic contradiction between general rights and distinct social, cultural, and religious identities (Soysal 1994). Nationalism, it may be argued, has been an experiment in resolving that tension by fusing the community of rights and responsibilities with the community of affective loyalty. In the classic formulation by T. H. Marshall, 'social citizenship' signifies the 'full membership' of an individual in 'the community' (Marshall 1950; Marshall and Bottomore 1992). Articulating personal subjectivity and social collectivity, social citizenship, in Marshall's terms, presumes the harmonious integration of the individual within the overlapping social structures of civil society, the nation, and the state. While it is unlikely that those structures have ever actually overlapped in any society, their disjuncture in the present is particularly evident (Hall and Held 1989). Since 1989, as many analysts have observed, new forms of 'post-national citizenship' have dissolved any necessary link between the rights of citizenship and loyalty to the nation-state. Post-national citizenship has been developing on two mutually constitutive planes, global and local, which I will characterize here for purposes of discussion as global citizenship and cultural citizenship.

Global citizenship, which is formed on the basis of universal rights and transnational loyalties, has been promoted by an array of social movements, non-governmental organizations, and international initiatives. In the field of education, global citizenship is receiving increasing attention as an essential component of citizenship education to prepare students for a globalizing world. Although the clearest assertion of global citizenship has emerged in the human rights movement, with its claims to basic rights that transcend the sovereignty of individual states, global citizenship has also appeared in recent formations of transnational identities with their own rights, responsibilities, loyalties, and values that cut across the territorial boundaries of states (Bauböck 1994). In feminist analysis, for example, new forms of women's citizenship have assumed global scope, asserting transnational rights and loyalties on the basis of gender (Berkovitch 1999; Lister 1997; Tobler, Chapter 7 below). Likewise, ecological citizenship has asserted the global rights of nature and responsibilities of human beings towards the environment (Batty and Gray 1996; Hansen 1993; van Steenbergen 1994; Szersynski and Toogood 2000). Other constellations of transnational rights and identities, such as consumer citizenship (Murdock 1992; Stevenson 1997), media citizenship (Ohmae 1990), sexual citizenship (Evans 1993), mobility citizenship (Urry 1990), flexible citizenship (Ong 1999), and cosmopolitan citizenship (Held 1995; Hutchings and Dannreuther 1999), have been identified as new forms of global citizenship. In all of these cases, the very notion of citizenship has been transformed by the increased scope and pace of the global flows of people, capital, technology, images of human possibility, and ideals of human solidarity that Arjun Appadurai identified as the defining features of globalization (Appadurai 1996).

Cultural citizenship, which is formed on the basis of distinctive, often local, loyalties, has been asserting claims on group, collective, or cultural rights. Like the new transnational variants of global citizenship, cultural citizenship cannot be easily assimilated into conventional models of national, political, or social citizenship. The conventional Western liberal definition of citizenship, as S. James Anaya has observed,

> acknowledges the rights of the individual on the one hand, and the sovereignty of the total social collective on the other, but it is not alive to the rich variety of intermediate or alternative associational groupings actually found in human cultures, nor is it prepared to ascribe to such groups any rights not reducible either to the liberties of the citizen or to the prerogative of the state.
>
> (Anaya 1995: 326)

Instead of assuming universal rights and responsibilities, cultural citizenship affirms the distinct cultural identity of citizens and asserts claims for the recognition and protection of that identity. As Renato Rosaldo has proposed, cultural citizenship is premised on the 'right to be different and to belong in a participatory democratic sense' (Rosaldo 1994: 402; see Rosaldo 1997).

Not only a matter of belonging to a particular cultural group, cultural citizenship raises questions of rights. In the subtitle to a collection of essays on Latino cultural citizenship in the United States, the editors identify the task of cultural citizenship as 'reclaiming identity, space, and rights' (Flores and Benmayor 1997). Such claims for rights, even universal human rights, for cultural difference suggests that cultural citizenship has emerged not in opposition but in counterpoint to the transnational identities of global citizenship. Frequently, claims for 'full membership' within the national community have been asserted on the basis of both global and cultural citizenship. For example, as Pnina Werbner has observed, British Muslims have been making claims for inclusion as citizens simultaneously on the basis of cultural difference and universal human rights (Werbner 2000: 319–20). Likewise, in researching Turkish immigrants in France, Yasimin Soysal found that Muslim organizations 'do not justify their demands by simply reaching back to religious treachings or traditions but through a language of rights, thus, citizenship' (Soysal 2000: 9). In this merger of cultural resources and global rights, the constitution of national citizenship is being transformed by post-national citizenship, resulting in what Nira Yuval-Davis has called the 'multi-layered citizen' (Yuval-Davis 1999).

What does any of this have to do with the study of religion, religions, and religious diversity? Religious resonances of the very notion of citizenship could certainly be pursued. On the political-legal side, the idea of human rights is directly related to religion, whether we want to argue that inherent, inalienable, and essentially 'sacred' human rights require some kind of religious grounding (Perry 1998: 11–41), represent competing, conflicting claims in relation to religious obligations (Gustafson and Juviler 1999), or stand in necessary counterpoint to religious loyalties (An'naim 1992). In all of these ways, the rights of citizenship are entangled with religion. On the symbolic-affective side, the sense of belonging, loyalty to the collective, and shared values of citizenship represent a kind of religious work, even if we do not want to use the term 'civil religion' to represent the religious character of the imagined communities (Anderson 1991), invented traditions (Hobsbawm and Ranger 1985), political mythologies (Thompson 1985), and political rituals of citizenship (Kertzer 1988).

Although these hints of a religious genealogy of citizenship could be elaborated, I am not interested in attempting that task here. Instead, I want to suggest that recent formations of global and cultural citizenship, with their multiple identities, shifting locations, and new media, can chart the terrain for resituating the study of religion. As I have suggested elsewhere, the study of religion might be reconceived as disciplined inquiry into the dynamics of human identity, spatial and temporal location, and the medium through which identity and location are negotiated (Chidester 2000c). Put differently, we might understand the study of religion as the creative and critical investigation of the multiple, situated and contested mediations of what it is to be a human person in a human place. Citizenship, particularly 'multi-layered' citizenship, brings those issues into a particularly intense focus. At the intersection of global and local identities, this multiple citizenship, as James Clifford has observed, results in 'forms of community consciousness and solidarity that maintain identifications outside of the national time/space in order to live inside, with a difference' (Clifford 1994: 308). In that politics of difference, as Nira Yuval-Davis has argued, citizenship is a 'constant process of struggle and negotiation' (Yuval-Davis 1997: 193–94). Like religion, citizenship is a process of negotiating human identity in time and space.

If we take seriously these new formations of global and cultural citizenship, then we can no longer think of relations between religious meaning and political power in terms of conventional models, which are basically managerial models, for dealing with religious diversity. Within modern states, models for managing religious diversity have been based upon the distinction either between the public and the private or between the one and the many. For example, while the US constitution has managed diversity by reinforcing the principled separation of private religion from the public apparatuses of the state, the new South Africa has sought to mobilize all of the many religious constituencies within its borders into the service of the one national interest. Given the changing formations and fluctuations of national, global, and cultural citizenship, however, we can no longer be confident that religious diversity can be absorbed into either of these formulas. Beyond the managerial model for dealing with religious diversity, we are faced with new challenges of understanding religious identity, location, and media as negotiated.

By locating the study of religion within the 'constant process of struggle and negotiation' over citizenship, we might find new ways to revitalize our on-going attention to the religious meanings of being human, in all its diversity, within specific times, places, global exchanges, local situations, and power relations. At the very least, citizenship, however it may be negotiated, inevitably raises the stakes in questions of human meaning by translating the meaning of being human into the political dynamics of the inclusion, enfranchisement, and empowerment of human beings. In other words, citizenship conventionally, but also practically, stands for the power of meaning, the power of rights and responsibilities merging with the meaning of affective loyalties and shared values, articulating the powerful, meaningful intersection of personal subjectivity and social collectivity. In these terms, the problems and prospects of citizenship, for all their conceptual ambiguity, global extensions, and local differentiations, may very well be a good place to think about religion, especially within the sphere of public education. In conclusion, I want to reflect briefly on some of the implications of this positioning of the study of religion for teaching and learning about religion, religions, and religious diversity in publicly funded schools.

Religion education

In state schools, the process of teaching and learning about religion has often, if not inevitably, been invested with a public purpose that can be formulated in the service of citizenship. Sometimes, advocates of religious education have enunciated their public intent as facilitating global citizenship. For example, invoking the utopian ideal of a global village, Trees Andree proposed that inter-religious and intercultural education was essential because 'the citizens of that global village, who are all neighbours, have to learn to live together' (Andree 1997: 18). In this formulation, religious education, designed for diversity, promises to make learners into good global citizens of the world. By contrast, many national systems of religious education have been fashioned around more provincial goals of cultivating a certain kind of homogeneous national citizenship. 'In the Norwegian curriculum,' as Breidlid and Nicolaisen have observed, 'construction of cultural identity is regarded as a main task, and the RE subject (among others) is seen as a suitable tool for fulfilling this purpose' (Breidlid and Nicolaisen

1999: 143). From this perspective, public education in religion can serve the goal of initiating pupils into a citizenship that is both national and cultural. However, Muslim immigrants in Norway, accounting for roughly 25 per cent of the pupils in Norwegian public schools in Oslo, have introduced a new challenge to this assumed equivalence between cultural citizenship and national citizenship in Norway (Østberg, Chapter 5 below). As we have seen, however, the disjunctures among national, cultural, and global formations of citizenship are everywhere a feature of public life. If education in religion, religions, and religious diversity in public schools is public, we need to think through what we mean by 'religion' and by 'public'.

Once again, attention to citizenship brings the notion of 'public' into a particular kind of focus. Established by rights and responsibilities, enabled by collective loyalties and shared values, citizenship is actualized in and through public participation. How do we participate as citizens in public? Following Jürgen Habermas, we might imagine a 'public sphere' that is constituted by a certain kind of consensual communication (Habermas 1989). However, as the advocates of both global and cultural citizenship demonstrate, public spheres are multiple. In the Northern Province of South Africa, for example, a citizen may participate in the different public spheres of the national government of the African National Congress (ANC), the regional branch of comrades of the ruling party, a local civic association, a traditional religio-political authority, and a local traditional administrative authority. Documenting these multiple spheres of citizen participation, Isak Niehaus has observed that a 'woman can, for instance, appeal to ANC leaders for information about national politics, ask Comrades to apprehend stock thieves, inform the Civic that a tap is without water, divorce her husband at the chief's *kgoro* and ask the local headman to allocate her a new residential site'. Manoeuvring within and among these different public spheres, any citizen can actualize his or her citizenship by asserting rights, obeying responsibilities, serving obligations, and affirming shared values within multiple contexts. As Niehaus concludes, a citizen operating in these diverse public spheres 'would not perceive these actions as contradictory' (Niehaus 2001: 156).

At the same time, again following Habermas, we might assume the public sphere demands a certain kind of 'public reason', based not on violence, force, or coercion, but on rational persuasion. In the context of global and cultural citizenship, however, public reason requires new mediations of persuasion that are based, not only on assertions about national interest, but also on a kind of public participation that moves in, through, and across differences in order 'to see how issues look from the point of view of those with differing religious commitments and cultural backgrounds' (Kymlicka 1998: 188). Public reason, however, is only a small part of public participation opened up by the new forms of global and cultural citizenship. As Paul Gilroy has observed, alternative public spheres are constantly being opened, not through the rational deliberations of 'public reason', but also through the performances of 'story-telling and music-making' (Gilroy 1993: 200). In a world of global mass media, with its proliferating images, stories, and music, the 'public' character of the public sphere has mutated in ways that validate both global and cultural constructions of human identity.

Situated in these multiple, shifting, and changing landscapes, the study of religion in public institutions, especially in public schools, has to come to terms with citizenship. Whether constructed nationally or transnationally, citizenship is inevitably a matter of identity. Identity, as we have seen, is urgently at stake. If the academic study of religion is concerned with human identity, it will have to attend to all the permutations of invented, emergent, contested, and negotiated identities that have claimed citizenship, whether that citizenship is asserted in national, cultural, or global terms. In public schools, space needs to be created for teaching and learning about religion in ways that recognize, affirm, and explore, creatively and critically, this multiplicity of identity. Fortunately, the educational work is already happening. In Norway, for example, despite the national mandate to cultivate a particular kind of cultural citizenry, educators in the field of religion education have been able to explore the ways in which their pupils identify with multiple cultures, both global and local, and form multiple identities. As Breidlid and Nicolaisen have found, religion education reveals not only religious diversity in the social collectivity but also 'plural identity in the same individual' (Breidlid and Nicolaisen 1999: 148–9). While each pupil may have multiple religious loyalties, the classroom is inevitably a site of religious diversity. In the on-going research of Wolfram Weisse and his colleagues in Hamburg, the classroom has been opened up as a space for the articulation of diversity through the dialogue of pupils from the 'multi-perspective view of the participants' (Weisse 1999: 155). In the study of religion, identity is crucial. As the historian of religions Bruce Lincoln has argued, the study of religion is constantly confronted with the challenge of making sense of the discourses and forces through which any first person plural – any 'us' – is constructed (Lincoln 1987: 74). Religion education in public institutions of learning is also confronted with this problem. Given the multiplying demands of multiple citizenships, however, teaching and learning about religion must respond to the multiplicity of personal and collective identity.

In pedagogical practice, international projects in religion education have developed methods that are responsive to these challenges. Methods have been tested in the classroom – the ethnographic method of Warwick (Jackson 1997a, b), the dialogical method of Hamburg (Weisse and Knauth 1997), the structured exchange of Utrecht (Bakker 1997: 145), the multiple narratives of Norway (Breidlid and Nicolaisen 1999), the moral inquiry of Namibia (Lombard 1997), the participatory pedagogy of Cape Town (Chidester 1997;

Stonier 1997), and so on. For all of their differences, these international projects have agreed on a student-centred, participatory, engaging, multiple, relational, dynamic, and open approach to teaching and learning about religion, religions, and religious diversity. At the same time, each of these projects has struggled to mediate between the national agendas in their working environments and all of the different kinds of cultural and global citizenship that we have considered. As I have tried to suggest, this mediation between the academic study of religion and the multiple political demands of citizenship can be a creative, productive tension for teaching and learning about religion. Although we might not be able to achieve such unity in any other public sphere, the religion education classroom can be a public place, in its own right, in which we can work towards creating an 'us' with no 'them'. Global citizenship, as John Urry has observed, may represent a radical departure from conventional constructions of national citizenship that have inevitably marked out a terrain of insiders and outsiders, 'identifying the non-citizens, the other, the enemy' (Urry 1999: 322). Following the *Complete Idiot's Guide to the World's Religions*, the religion education classroom can be a space for such an inclusive citizenship in which 'no one is defined as "other" on the basis of religion' (Toporov and Buckles 1997: 9). If education is about making citizens, then at the very least we want to develop programmes in religion education that prepare pupils for the national, cultural, and global terrains in which they will negotiate their citizenship in a rapidly changing world.

References

Anaya, S. James (1995) 'The capacity of international law to advance ethnic or nationality rights claims', in Will Kymlicka (ed.) *The Rights of Minority Cultures*, Oxford: Oxford University Press, 321–30.

Anderson, Benedict (1991) *Imagined Communities: Reflections on the Origin and Spread of Nationalism*, 2nd edn, London: Verso.

Andree, Trees (1997) 'From Hamburg to Utrecht', in Trees Andree, Cok Bakker and Peter Schreiner (eds) *Crossing Boundaries: Contributions to Inter-religious and Intercultural Education*, Münster and Berlin: Comenius Institute, 17–21.

An'naim, Abdullah (ed.) (1992) *Human Rights in Crosscultural Perspective*, Philadelphia: University of Pennsylvania Press.

Appadurai, Arjun (1996) *Modernity at Large: Cultural Dimensions of Globalization*, Minneapolis MN: University of Minnesota Press, 27–47.

Bakker, Cok (1997) 'Learning in different worlds: how to match them? A case and some reflection from the perspective of educational psychology', in Trees Andree, Cok Bakker and Peter Schreiner (eds) *Crossing Boundaries: Contributions to Interreligious and Intercultural Education*, Münster and Berlin: Comenius Institute, 141–6.

Batty, Helen and Gray, Tim (1996) 'Environmental rights and national sovereignty', in Simon Caney, David George and Peter Jones (eds) *National Rights, International Obligations*, Boulder CO: Westview Press, 149–65.

Bauböck, Ranier (1994) *Transnational Citizenship*, Aldershot: Edward Elgar.

Berkovitch, Nitza (1999) *From Motherhood to Citizenship: Women's Rights and International Organizations*, Baltimore MD: Johns Hopkins University Press.

Breidlid, Halldis and Nicolaisen, Tove (1999) 'Stories and storytelling in religious education in Norway', in David Chidester, Janet Stonier and Judy Tobler (eds) *Diversity as Ethos: Challenges for Inter-religious and Intercultural Education*, Cape Town: Institute for Comparative Religion in Southern Africa, 140–54.

Burke, T. Patrick (1995) *The Major Religions: An Introduction with Texts*, Oxford: Blackwell.

Chidester, David (1996) *Savage Systems: Colonialism and Comparative Religion in Southern Africa*, Charlottesville VA: University Press of Virginia.

—— (1997) 'Man, God, beast, heaven, light, burning fire', in Trees Andree, Cok Bakker and Peter Schreiner (eds) *Crossing Boundaries: Contributions to Inter-religious and Intercultural Education*, Münster and Berlin: Comenius Institute, 161–7.

—— (2000a) 'Colonialism', in Willi Braun and Russell T. McCutcheon (eds) *Guide to the Study of Religion*, London: Cassell, 423–37.

—— (2000b) *Christianity: A Global History*, London: Allen Lane the Penguin Press.

—— (2000c) 'History of religions, Durban 2000: situating the programmatic interests of the history of religions in South Africa', plenary address, International Association for the History of Religions.

Clifford, James (1994) 'Diasporas', *Cultural Anthropology*, 9, 302–38.

Consulting Workshop (2000) 'Religion, education, and democracy: draft Submission to the Minister of Education for the Consulting Workshop on Religion in Education, May 2000', Pretoria: Department of Education.

Coogan, Michael D. (ed.) (1998) *The Illustrated Guide to World Religions*, New York: Oxford University Press.

Eliade, Mircea, Culianu, Ion P. and Wiesner, Hillary S. (2000) *The HarperCollins Concise Guide to World Religions*, San Francisco: HarperCollins.

Evans, David T. (1993) *Sexual Citizenship: The Material Construction of Sexualities*, London and New York: Routledge.

Flores, William Vincent and Benmayor, Rina (1997) *Latino Cultural Citizenship: Claiming Identity, Space, and Rights*, Boston MA: Beacon Press.

Gilroy, Paul (1993) *The Black Atlantic: Modernity and Double Consciousness*, London: Verso.

Gustafson, Carrie and Juviler, Peter (eds) (1999) *Religion and Human Rights: Conflicting Claims*, Armonk NY: Sharpe.

Habermas, Jurgen (1989) *The Structural Transformation of the Public Sphere*, trans. T. Burger and F. Lawrence, Cambridge MA: MIT Press.

Hall, Stuart and Held, David (1989) 'Citizens and citizenship', in Stuart Hall and Martin Jacques (eds) *New Times: The Changing Face of Politics in the 1990s*, London: Lawrence & Wishart, 171–88.

Hansen, Anders (ed.) (1993) *The Mass Media and Environmental Issues*, Leicester: Leicester University Press.

Harrison, Peter (1990) 'Religion' and the Religions in the English Enlightenment, Cambridge: Cambridge University Press.

Held, David (1995) Democracy and the Global Order, Cambridge: Polity Press.

Hobsbawm, Eric and Ranger, Terence (eds) (1985) The Invention of Tradition, Cambridge: Cambridge University Press.

Hopfe, Lewis M. (1994) Religions of the World, 6th edn, Upper Saddle River NJ: Prentice Hall.

Huntington, Samuel (1993) 'The clash of civilizations?' Foreign Affairs, 72 (3), 22–49.

—— (1998) The Clash of Civilizations, New York: Simon & Schuster.

Hutchings, Kimberly and Dannreuther, Roland (eds) (1999) Cosmopolitan Citizenship, New York: St Martin's Press.

Jackson, Robert (1997a) Religious Education: An Interpretive Approach, London: Hodder & Stoughton.

—— (1997b) 'Ethnographic studies of children and interpretive methods for religious education', in Trees Andree, Cok Bakker and Peter Schreiner (eds) Crossing Boundaries: Contributions to Inter-religious and Intercultural Education, Münster and Berlin: Comenius Institute, 65–73.

Jackson, Robert and Nesbitt, Eleanor (1997) 'From fieldwork to school text: studying and representing British Hindu children', in Trees Andree, Cok Bakker and Peter Schreiner (eds) Crossing Boundaries: Contributions to Inter-religious and Intercultural Education, Münster and Berlin: Comenius Institute, 89–99.

Kertzer, David I. (1988) Ritual, Politics, and Power, New Haven CT: Yale University Press.

Küng, Hans and Kuschel, Karl-Joseph (eds) (1995) A Global Ethic: The Declaration of the Parliament of the World's Religions, New York: Continuum.

Kymlicka, Will (1998) 'Ethnic associations and democratic citizenship', in Amy Gutman (ed.) Freedom of Association, Princeton NJ: Princeton University Press, 177–213.

Lincoln, Bruce (1987) Discourse and the Construction of Society: Comparative Studies of Myth, Ritual, and Classification, New York: Oxford University Press.

Lister, Ruth (1997) Citizenship: Feminist Perspectives, New York: New York University Press.

Lombard, Christo (1997) 'Contextual and theoretical considerations in the Namibian curricular process', in Trees Andree, Cok Bakker and Peter Schreiner (eds) Crossing Boundaries: Contributions to Inter-religious and Intercultural Education, Münster and Berlin: Comenius Institute, 111–23.

Marshall, T. H. (1950) Citizenship and Social Class, Cambridge: Cambridge University Press.

Marshall, T. H. and Bottomore, Tom (1992) Citizenship and Social Class, London: Pluto Press.

Martin, J. Paul and Stahnke, Tad (eds) (1998) Religion and Human Rights: Basic Documents, New York: Center for the Study of Human Rights, Columbia University.

Maurice, Frederick D. (1847) The Religions of the World and their Relation to Christianity, London: Parker.

McCutcheon, Russell T. (1997) Manufacturing Religion: The Discourse of Sui Generis Religion and the Politics of Nostalgia, New York and Oxford: Oxford University Press.

Müller, F. Max. (1873) An Introduction to the Science of Religion, London: Longman.

Murdock, Graham (1992) 'Citizens, consumers, and public culture', in Michael Shovmand and Kim Christian Shrøder (eds) *Media Cultures*, London: Routledge, 17–41.

Nesbitt, Eleanor (1999) 'Diversity as ethos in society: negotiating power relations', in David Chidester, Janet Stonier and Judy Tobler (eds) *Diversity as Ethos: Challenges for Inter-religious and Intercultural Education*, Cape Town: Institute for Comparative Religion in Southern Africa, 116–32.

Neumann, Ursula and Weisse, Wolfram (1999) 'Running into an ethnocentric trap: response to the contribution of Eleanor Nesbitt', in David Chidester, Janet Stonier and Judy Tobler (eds) *Diversity as Ethos: Challenges for Inter-religious and Inter-cultural Education*, Cape Town: Institute for Comparative Religion in Southern Africa, 133–9.

Niehaus, Isak (2001) *Witchcraft, Power, and Politics: Exploring the Occult in the South African Lowveld*, London: Pluto Press.

Ohmae, Kenichi (1990) *The Borderless World*, New York: HarperCollins.

Ong, Aihwa (1999) *Flexible Citizenship: The Cultural Logics of Transnationality*, Durham NC: Duke University Press.

Outka, Gene and Reeder, John P. (eds) (1993) *Prospects for a Common Morality*, Princeton NJ: Princeton University Press.

Pailin, David A. (1984) *Attitudes to other Religions: Comparative Religion in Seventeenth and Eighteenth Century Britain*, Manchester: Manchester University Press.

Perry, Michael J. (1998) *The Idea of Human Rights: Four Inquiries*, New York: Oxford University Press.

Pietz, William (1999) 'Colonial forensics and hybrid rights: reconceiving magic, religion, and knowledge to accommodate an imperial market in British and US law', unpublished paper, Ford Foundation lecture series World Religions as Colonial Formations, Chapel Hill NC: University of North Carolina.

Richards, Chris (ed.) (1997) *Illustrated Encyclopedia of World Religions*, Rockport MA: Element.

Rosaldo, Renato (1994) 'Cultural citizenship and educational democracy', *Cultural Anthropology*, 9 (3), 402–11.

—— (1997) 'Cultural citizenship, inequality, and multiculturalism', in W. V. Flores and R. Benmayor (eds) *Latino Cultural Citizenship: Reclaiming Identity, Space, and Rights*, Boston MA: Beacon Press, 27–38.

Sharma, Arvind (ed.) (1993) *Our Religions: The Seven World Religions introduced by Preeminent Scholars from each Tradition*, New York: HarperCollins.

Smith, Huston (1958) *The Religions of Man*, New York: Harper & Row.

—— (1994) *The Illustrated World's Religions: A Guide to our Wisdom Traditions*, New York: HarperCollins.

Soysal, Yasemin (1994) *Limits of Citizenship: Migrants and Postnational Membership in Europe*, Chicago: University of Chicago Press.

—— (2000) 'Citizenship and identity: living in diasporas in post-war Europe?' *Ethnic and Racial Studies*, 23 (1), 1–15.

Stevenson, Nick (1997) 'Globalization, national cultures, and cultural citizenship', *Sociological Quarterly*, 38, 41–66.

Stice, Ken (1997) 'Religious factors in special operations'. Online. Available HTTP: <http://www-cgsc.army.mil/chap/COURSES/W-REL/STICE/sf-relig.doc>

Stonier, Janet (1997) 'A chorus of voices', in Trees Andree, Cok Bakker and Peter Schreiner (eds) *Crossing Boundaries: Contributions to Inter-religious and Intercultural Education*, Münster and Berlin: Comenius Institute, 169–74.

Szerszynski, Bronislaw and Toogood, Mark (2000) 'Global citizenship, the environment, and the mass media', in Stuart Allen, Barbara Adam and Cynthia Carter (eds) *The Media Politics of Environmental Risks*, London: Routledge, 218–28.

Thompson, Leonard (1985) *The Political Mythology of Apartheid*, New Haven CT: Yale University Press.

Toropov, Brandon and Buckles, Luke (1997) *The Complete Idiot's Guide to the World's Religions*, New York: Alpha Books.

Urry, John (1990) *The Tourist Gaze*, London: Sage.

—— (1999) 'Globalization and citizenship', *Journal of World-Systems Research*, 5(2), 311–24.

Van de Wetering, Stella (1997) 'The life-views of Muslim pupils of an inter-religious (Christian–Islamic) and an Islamic school', in Trees Andree, Cok Bakker and Peter Schreiner (eds) *Crossing Boundaries: Contributions to Inter-religious and Intercultural Education*, Münster and Berlin: Comenius Institute, 127–30.

Van Steenbergen, Bart (1994) 'Towards a global ecological citizen', in Bart van Steenbergen (ed.) *The Condition of Citizenship*, London: Sage, 141–52.

Weisse, Wolfram (1999) 'Religious education in the multiperspective view of the participants: introduction', in David Chidester, Janet Stonier and Judy Tobler (eds) *Diversity as Ethos: Challenges for Inter-religious and Intercultural Education*, Cape Town: Institute for Comparative Religion in Southern Africa, 155–8.

Weisse, Wolfram and Knauth, Thorsten (1997) 'Dialogical religious education: theoretical framework and conceptual conclusions', in Trees Andree, Cok Bakker and Peter Schreiner (eds) *Crossing Boundaries: Contributions to Inter-religious and Intercultural Education*, Münster and Berlin: Comenius Institute, 33–44.

Werbner, Pnina (2000) 'Divided loyalties, empowered citizenship? Muslims in Britain', *Citizenship Studies*, 4 (3), 307–24.

Yuval-Davis, Nira (1997) 'Ethnicity, gender relations, and multiculturalism', in Pnina Werbner and Tariq Modood (eds) *Debating Cultural Hybridity*, London: Zed Books, 191–208.

—— (1999) 'The "multi-layered citizen": citizenship in the age of "glocalization"', *International Feminist Journal of Politics*, 1 (1), 119–36.

Østberg, Sissel (1997) 'Religious education in a multi-cultural society: the quest for identity and dialogue', in Trees Andree, Cok Bakker and Peter Schreiner (eds) *Crossing Boundaries: Contributions to Inter-religious and Intercultural Education*, Münster and Berlin: Comenius Institute, 147–53.

Chapter 3

Nationalism, religiosity and citizenship in Norwegian majority and minority discourses

Geir Skeie

Synopsis The concept of citizenship covers issues related to rights and duties as well as questions of character. Thus it reflects the interdependence of individual and society. This relationship is complex and is conceived differently. Issues of difference related to generation, gender, ethnic background, cultural group and religion play a role in how citizenship is understood and performed. The example of Norway illustrates both that the word 'citizenship' itself has no obvious parallel in Norwegian, and that the issue is intertwined with questions about belonging, integration and ideological aspects of the welfare state. In Norwegian schools, citizenship issues are raised at various points within the curriculum, but there is no separate subject of 'citizenship education'. Reforms in religious education (RE) in the late 1990s have made the subject much broader in terms of content, but at the same time have used the Christian religion as part of a national heritage programme without acknowledging that this may be seen as a threat to religious minorities. It is suggested that this inherent contradiction in the RE curriculum may be understood as a confusion of two separate but related debates about citizenship; the 'minority rights–multiculturalism debate' and the 'citizenship–civic virtue debate'. At the same time this issue reveals the closeness of the relationship between the religious education and citizenship debates, not least because both are concerned with the question of identity.

The concept of citizenship has in recent years become increasingly important in the debate about modern Western democracy, and this is reflected in publications and international conferences dealing with issues such as politics, culture and education.[1] This does not mean that everyone is discussing exactly the same issues. In their introduction to the book *Citizenship in Diverse Societies*, Will Kymlicka and Wayne Norman (2000a: 1) argue that this theme includes two different debates among political philosophers that have been developing more or less independently of each other: 'the rights and status of ethnocultural minorities in multi-ethnic societies (the "minority rights–multiculturalism" debate), and the virtues, practices, and responsibilities of democratic citizenship (the "citizenship–civic virtue" debate)'.

The two debates may be seen as reflections of two different perspectives on present Western society, both based on the interpretation of difference. As the concept of social class seems to fade into the background of political analysis, other forms of difference come into focus, most of which may be labelled 'socio-cultural'. This socio-cultural plurality of Western societies can be described as twofold: traditional plurality and modern plurality. The two are complementary in the sense that they do not exclude each other, but may appear in different combinations (Skeie 2001). Traditional plurality forms the background of the 'minority rights–multiculturalism debate', while modern plurality is the background of the 'citizenship–civic virtue debate'. With Kymlicka and Norman (2000b), I think these two debates should be seen in relation to each other, but first it is necessary to appreciate their differences and the confusions and conflicts that may arise between them. In this chapter I will take examples from Norway, focusing on the relation between education and cultural diversity. I will make particular reference to the recent reforms in Norwegian religious education.

Locating the citizenship issue

For minority groups the questions of inclusion and exclusion are vital. The question of being a citizen has to do with membership, especially in terms of national citizenship. In spite of globalization, the nation-state is still the framework used globally to secure citizenship as membership of a society. At the same time the rights that are connected with being a citizen seem to become universalized and are to some extent anchored in super-national institutions such as the United Nations (Soysal 1996). This creates a tension between the universality of rights and the particularity of the institution that primarily is seen to secure these rights. If citizenship is seen primarily in terms of formal rights or as a certain status in society, it is important to note that this refers particularly to the minority/majority debate. The question of minority rights is relevant not only for immigrant groups but also for indigenous national groups like the Sami population in Norway in their claims for territorial authority. Membership of different minority or majority groups may be a question of ethnicity, but it can also relate to religion, gender or sexual preference. Thus questions of citizenship are inseparable from issues of identity. *Webster's Encyclopaedic Dictionary* refers indirectly to this double aspect in its definition of citizenship;

> 1. The state of being vested with the rights, privileges, and duties of a citizen. 2. The character of an individual viewed as a member of society; behaviour in terms of the duties, obligations, and functions of a citizen.
> (Webster 1994: 270)

Both these perspectives are relevant within the debates referred to earlier, even if they may seem to have drifted apart. One way of holding them together is reflected in F. Twine's assessment of T. H. Marshall's work on citizenship:

> Thus Marshall's (1950) three elements of citizenship – namely, civil, political and social rights – can best be seen as directed to the development of the 'social self'; or, in Mill's terms, 'to the kinds of people we might be'.
>
> (Twine 1994: 13)

What Twine underlines is that citizenship should be seen as part of an interdependence of self and society. Humans are made by society and they are makers of society, therefore citizenship should be seen as a potential, not only as an acquired state or as a result of social evolution. The struggles for democracy, social justice and individual freedom are all examples of how such potential is put into practice. But these struggles should also be a reminder that difference, conflict and power are permanent aspects of what a society is.[2] At the same time conflict and issues of power are linked with the role of the state, one important instrument for managing differences. However, the state, so important for the establishment of democratic institutions, is often under attack in contemporary Western societies. Many question the extent of the need for state interference. The state can be seen more as a threat to individual freedom than a defender of it.[3] This does not necessarily mean that the welfare state is losing support, but it does show that the established existence of the welfare state forms a new basis for how people choose to live their lives. This basis is different from the cultural and socio-political background of those who took part in the introduction and implementation of welfare politics. In this way a generation gap is part of the context for public debate about citizenship. While we see this in Norway, when politicians and other adults voice their worries about young people's lack of interest in political issues and their passivity towards democratic institutions, it is not a purely Norwegian concern (Dahrendorf 1996: 32).

These worries probably do not reflect serious doubts about the legal basis and formal rights and obligations of a citizen, but seem to arise from a perceived lack of certain virtues within parts of the population. A solution to this may be to introduce citizenship into the school curriculum in order to foster the desired virtues. Although the dynamics and effects of education are themselves complex, it is easier to manipulate schooling than the entire social fabric. The approach to educational change, however, depends on how the relationship between education and citizenship is understood. One broad approach is to see the whole education system as an introduction to what it means to be a citizen.

If education is seen as an introduction to what it means to be a citizen (cf. Marshall 1950: 67–8), a perceived decline in the virtues of the citizen can be interpreted either as a failure on the part of the whole education system or as a sign that there has been, in practice, a decline in education's role as a stimulus for critical analysis of society at large. From this perspective, educational change is seen as part of a wider agenda. If education, more modestly, is seen as a tool for the improvement of virtues that may be lacking among the members of a given society, it may be enough simply to suggest changes in the curriculum in order to improve the situation.

Discussion about civic virtues and how to promote them is not restricted to the role of education. It also includes reflection on the basic questions about power and inclusion/exclusion in wider society. This forms the background to Kymlicka and Norman's argument in favour of an 'integrated theory of diverse citizenship' (Kymlicka and Norman 2000b). The horizon of the chapters in their anthology is limited mainly to the Western world, but the perspectives of 'diverse citizenship' and 'citizenship in diverse societies' are relevant globally. Their intention is to relate citizenship to how societies deal with differences and to the dialectic of inclusion and exclusion of individuals and groups.

On the societal level there are good reasons for treating the issues of citizenship in terms of relations between groups, with a specific focus on minority groups in all their diversity (Kymlicka and Norman 2000b: 18–24). Cultural groups are highly complex (see Chapters 1 and 5 in this book) and there are important questions dealing with how group identities are formed and understood, and whether it is possible to develop a common citizenship identity among the members of society without compromising different group identities. This opens up an additional dimension of the citizenship issue, linking it with equally complex questions about identity. The Canadian scholars Isin and Wood (1999) address this problem by introducing the concept of 'radical citizenship'. In their view it is important to distinguish between two aspects of modern society – fragmentation and pluralization.

> The challenge we face today is to conceive of a new way of governing ourselves, a new way of being political under advanced capitalism. Both fragmentation and pluralization are inextricably associated with advanced capitalism . . . The task for radical democrats is to harness the contradictory but democratising tendencies of advanced capitalism towards new political arrangements and recognition of group rights.
>
> (Isin and Wood 1999: 154–5)

The opponents of radical citizenship are defined as 'new orthodoxies of unity', advancing the view that 'any identity is as good as any other and accessible to any and all'. Against this, Isin and Wood want to maintain 'the right to have rights', as well as 'the ability to make promises and commitments' (Isin and Wood 1999: 160–1). In this way they are able to combine the two aspects of citizenship referred to earlier and as defined by Webster's *Dictionary*: the state of being a member of a society and the character of the individual acting as a member of a society. However, equally important is the recognition of citizenship as both a contested and a fragile issue. This is true of citizenship understood both as a state of being vested with particular rights and obligations, and in terms of certain civic virtues. The continuing debate on citizenship itself seems to be woven into the socio-cultural, economic, legal and political features of modern plural society. In what follows, I will explore how this is displayed in a particular society, using Norway as an example.

The Norwegian context

At the conceptual level, the English words 'citizen' and 'civic' lack good synonyms in the Norwegian language. The most common translation, *borger*, denotes meanings like 'city dweller', *bourgeois* (as opposed to 'peasant' or 'worker') and 'politically conservative'. To overcome these problems the word *medborger* (co-citizen) seems to be gaining ground (Østerud 2000a, b).[4] To the extent that *medborger* colours the understanding of the concept, it probably gives more attention to the relational or collective elements.

To an international readership it may seem somewhat narrow-minded to go into linguistic details, but there are reasons to believe that the concepts (not) in use also reveal something about historical developments and cultural values. In the case of Norway, it has been argued that the combination of equality and sameness are important keys if one wants to understand basic values in Norwegian society and culture (Gullestad 1992). A critical reflection on citizenship in Norway needs to take into account how 'the welfare state' and 'nationality' are understood. In both cases, earlier issues of conflict ('difference') have been transformed into a hegemonic and harmonizing ideology in the post-war era. The welfare state is interpreted as the harmonious resolution of earlier sharp social conflicts, and the Norwegian view of nationality is coloured by the struggle for independence from Sweden (1905) and from German occupation (1945). Many commentators would also include the two referendums which both voted 'no' to membership of the European Union.

The tendency towards the harmonization of diversity in daily life since the 1950s has, since the early 1970s, been challenged by the increasingly visible presence of cultural diversity. At the analytical level, the hegemony of ideas about socio-cultural harmony has been challenged by historical and social science research as well as by public debate. At the popular level there is a tendency to see irreducible differences that threaten to undermine the dominant ideology of harmony which may be seen as a significant part of 'Norwegian culture'.[5] An important factor here is 'visibility', in the sense that diversity is experienced both as a part of daily life and as abstract knowledge through public debate and academic work.

When such a 'visible plurality' becomes an issue of public debate, it can be seen as forming a collective reflection on changes in society. Sometimes the debate focuses on differences related to ethnic or religious cultures, and at other times the focus is on subcultural or 'modern' differences. But, in both cases, participants tend to group themselves as proponents or as opponents to diversity. Much less frequently do we find a genuine interest in the features of difference.

One example of the public debates featuring issues of citizenship is that of the Norwegian politics of immigration and the situation of immigrants in Norway. In official Norwegian immigration politics the main goal is 'integration', which is defined in opposition to 'segregation' and 'assimilation'. But, in these debates, there is rarely any clarification of what it means 'to be integrated' and of who has the power of definition. Even if this should be resolved, it is for the minority to decide their approach to determining the socio-cultural result of the integration policy. No one becomes integrated unless they accept to be so. It seems that a particular challenge is the Norwegian construction of nationality as an expression of communality and sameness. Both the ideology of the welfare state and the cultural construction of Norwegianness play down differences or see them as problems to be solved. Those faced with the challenges of multicultural difference seem to invoke welfare and national strategies supported by the ruling majority in order to accomplish 'integration'. This may be interpreted as a view of citizenship based on national integration rather than on recognition of difference. Such a view can be seen in recent educational reforms. These do not introduce citizenship education as a discrete subject, but introduce ideas through the broader curriculum, especially through social studies and religious education.

Citizenship and reforms in education

A search of the internet shows citizenship education to be a worldwide focus of attention, with the websites emanating from institutions such as universities, schools, NGOs and Departments of Education. One interesting example is, of course, the decision in England and Wales to make citizenship education a compulsory school subject from 2002. However, whether or not particular countries have or are planning to have such a subject, the issues are being widely debated (Kennedy 1997).

Even though citizenship is a 'hot issue' in international education, this should not overshadow the fact that modern nation-states have had a long-standing interest in schooling as a means of fostering the kind of citizens who will contribute to the processes of production and reproduction (Lundgren 1998). This general function of education is, however, always set in a particular context, and that context has changed in recent decades. It seems that political developments in the 1980s have made governments in many countries more aware of the importance of knowledge and values related to citizenship. In some countries this was connected with the establishment of more democratic structures of government. In others it was related to the decline in voter participation. At the same time, political activism found new channels outside the established parties. The renewed focus on citizenship also included a debate about and large-scale research into the role of education in this respect (Hébert and Pagé 2000; Heath 2000; Torney-Purta 2000; Torney-Purta *et al.* 2001).

A comparison of the situation in Norway and England shows how differently these issues are dealt with in the two countries, in spite of the fact that both have many economic, political and cultural similarities, as well as numerous contacts in connection with education. In England the introduction of citizenship education as a school subject has been achieved with a broad political consensus, even if the motivation has been somewhat different among the political parties (Kerr 2000).[6] According to government sources, citizenship education has three strands: social and moral responsibility, community involvement, and political literacy. These all contribute appropriate knowledge, skills and understanding so that pupils can play an effective role in society (DfEE 2001). It is difficult to pass judgement on a subject not yet being taught, but certainly one challenge will be how it will relate to other parts of the curriculum. A study of citizenship education carried out in twenty-eight countries in 2001 emphasizes the general practice of the school more than the teaching of one specific subject (Torney-Purta *et al.* 2001: 176). The study shows differences between countries as well as general tendencies that may indicate global developments. Interestingly, Norwegian and English students come out quite differently in the study (Torney-Purta *et al.* 2001: 179). So what is the situation with regard to Norwegian citizenship education?

Even though there is no specific subject called 'citizenship education', citizenship issues are well represented in the latest Norwegian national curriculum, especially in the subject 'social studies'. This includes history and geography, where the aims of the combined subject include social and political awareness and participation (C-97). Compared with the aims of the forthcoming English and Welsh citizenship education, Norwegian social studies seems to cover many of the aims associated with 'social and moral responsibility' and 'political literacy'. In Norwegian schools there is also a subject called 'home economics' with aims that cover much of what is called the 'community involvement' aspect of the English and Welsh citizenship education, focusing on local community, family, health and environment (C-97). In addition, issues connected with the body, health and sexuality are part of the curriculum in the subjects 'science and the environment' and 'physical education'. In addition RE, which in Norway is called 'Christian knowledge and religious and ethical education', takes up citizenship issues, especially the 'ethics' element.[7]

This overview indicates that many of the issues associated with citizenship education are well integrated into the Norwegian national curriculum. This is probably one reason why the idea of citizenship education as a separate subject has not been developed in Norway. Nevertheless, this does not mean that the debate about citizenship issues has been absent from Norwegian discourse on education. Analysis of the present national curriculum shows that it promotes civic virtues strongly, and that RE is given a special role to play in underpinning these virtues.

The role of religious education

To understand the relationship between RE and citizenship it is important to understand how politically sensitive RE is, (even) in a secular country with an overwhelmingly Lutheran population (about 85 per cent). The last educational reform included a significant shift in religious education based on consensus in the central political establishment more than through negotiation between interest groups. A general curriculum passed through Parliament as early as 1993 and formed the basis of reform in upper secondary education (implemented in 1994), and in primary and lower secondary school (implemented in 1997). This general curriculum is understood as a 'common core curriculum' and includes formulations of the kind of civic virtues and citizenship which education is intended to promote, such as good manners, democracy, national identity, and international awareness. It emphasizes the moral contract as the basis of the welfare state and the mutual responsibility needed in society (C-97). The general curriculum was also the basis of the White Paper commission which dealt with RE in the whole school system (NOU 1995: 9). We therefore find the same ethos reflected both in the White Paper and in the final curriculum for a new RE subject.

Throughout the general curriculum there is a clear recognition of the problem of integration in a modern society. After covering different dimensions of the human being that will be fostered through education (spiritual, creative, working, liberally educated, social and environmentally aware) the last paragraph turns to 'the integrated human being'. Here, the problems of integration are conceived as a question of 'balance' between individual and society, between national (and local) heritage and 'other cultures'.

In spite of this ideal of 'balance', the overall impression given by the text is that the plurality of society (difference) basically challenges its cohesion. There is a suggestion that because of this there is a need to enforce what is common over and against society's diversity:

When transitions are massive and changes rapid, it becomes even more pressing to emphasize historical orientation, national distinctiveness and local variation to safeguard our identity – and to sustain a global environment with breadth and vigour. A good general education must contribute to national identity and solidarity by impressing the common stamp of local communities on language, tradition, and learning. This will also make it easier for pupils who move to find their footing anew, as migration will mean relocation within a familiar commonality. The bonds between generations will be closer when they share experiences and insights, stories, songs, and legends. Newcomers are more easily incorporated into our society when implicit features of our culture are made clear and exposed to view.

(C-97: general section)

The forces related to diversity are many, but can be summarized as modernization and immigration. Both these driving forces are seen in the curriculum as normal parts of society's development; they are not lamented or criticized. These are the same two aspects of diversity that I have called the 'traditional' and the 'modern' at the beginning of this chapter. In recent literature on citizenship these elements are seen as common ground for the investigation of modern society from different disciplines. However, there is also a normative perspective: how should we as a society deal with plurality? These are political questions that are dealt with both theoretically and in political practice, and one important arena, as I have indicated, is educational policy. What we see exemplified in the Norwegian context is the ways politicians try to solve difficult and long-term societal challenges by means of the educational system, the idea probably being that schooling can change *people*, and not only structures or processes.

A close reading of the Norwegian general curriculum shows that the spiritual dimension of the human being is thought to play a central part in the social integration process. The inspiration behind this thinking is not romanticist in the sense that inner (spiritual) growth may result in more harmonious human beings, nor is it the introduction of a common religious belief into the tradition of the absolutist state. At the same time, it is difficult to deny that there is a hint of both these tendencies, with an almost postmodern will to combine opposites in a mixture that, it is hoped, will cure some problems of society. However, it is probably fair to say that the dominant tendency in the curriculum is another mixture of opposites, namely of rationalism on the one hand and religion as 'cultural heritage' on the other:

The Christian faith and tradition constitute a deep current in our history – a heritage that unites us as a people across religious persuasions. It has imprinted itself on the norms, worldview, concepts and art of the people. It bonds us to other peoples in the rhythm of the week and in common holidays, but is also an abiding presence in our own national traits: in architecture and music, in style and conventions, in ideas, idioms and identity.

Our Christian and humanistic tradition places equality, human rights and rationality to the fore. Social progress is sought in reason and enlightenment, and in man's ability to create, appreciate and communicate. Education shall be based on fundamental Christian and humanistic values. It should uphold and renew our cultural heritage to provide perspective and guidance for the future.

(C-97: general section)

Even if this is formulated within the context of the general section of the curriculum, there is no doubt that the formulations are particularly related to the subject of RE (Christian knowledge and religious and ethical education). When this was launched in 1997, it meant for the first time in Norway that religious education was explicitly intended to be 'for all'. From a citizenship perspective it is of interest to note that RE was given a particular double role. Partly it was supposed to counter the problematic aspects of (post)modern plurality by giving the younger generation a common reference to the national cultural heritage. In addition RE was also expected to counter problematic aspects of (multi)cultural plurality by bringing students from the different religions together in classrooms to learn from each other, and by giving all students a general knowledge of religions and life-stances. The RE subject had as its mission to deal with diversity through integration, on both the social and the individual level.

There are, of course, other analytical perspectives available from a citizenship perspective if one wants to investigate the general background and the consequences of the Norwegian decisions on RE of 1997. There are interesting problems related to the power play between different actors in the process, the content of the subject, the relationship between aims and content, the regulations of exemption, the name of the subject, etc. Several of these issues have been debated and investigated, and a research-based evaluation has been carried out at the behest of the Ministry of Education (Hagesæther et al. 2000; Johannesen et al. 2000).

In the context of citizenship education, a key question would be: which role does RE play in relation to the basic issues of citizenship? My reading of the Norwegian curriculum is that RE is intended to contribute to the integration of socio-cultural diversity through establishing a common pool of knowledge about the Norwegian cultural heritage, mainly as it is shaped by Christianity. This knowledge is considered an important part of a common identity in the majority population, and a tool for integration on the part of minorities. With a common knowledge of the cultural 'canon' as its basis, the idea seems to be that diversity can be dealt with on rational grounds. The 'cultural canon' is related not only to RE but also to subjects like Norwegian and social studies. The knowledge-based strategy for integration is supposed to work together with the face-to-face interaction between students from different religious backgrounds in the class.

Much of the discourse in Norway on these issues can be understood with the help of the two debates referred to by Kymlicka and Norman. One of them is related to the differences in 'cultures', but often with a rather closed (or essentialist) understanding of 'culture'. The emphasis tends to be on the differences between cultures and how they can be diminished or bridged. The other debate is related to the differences between generations or sub-groups. Here the emphasis tends to be on how different the young are from the older generation or from young people of earlier days, and what can be done to overcome these disturbing differences. This points towards a particular deficit in the Norwegian debate, namely the full recognition of diversity. The dominant underlying view seems to be of the rationalistic type. Diversity is perceived as real, but somehow superficial. This approach considers diversity to be something that may be overcome with the help of enlightenment and rationality, often as communicated by school. Based on this understanding, the former connections between RE and the Church of Norway have been removed from the curriculum, presenting RE as 'broad', 'neutral' and 'pluralist', even if Christianity still plays a dominant role. One could call this a 'culturalization' of religion, turning it into national heritage. It is combined with a vitalization of the subject by expanding the content towards other religions and worldviews, and by the introduction of new methods of teaching, such as narrative and aesthetic approaches.

Behind these curricular decisions I detect a rationalist view of human nature, where rationality is seen as more fundamental and stronger than culture. Culture may be tamed or improved by means of rationality to ensure that cultural diversity does not cause too many problems of integration. The problems of diversity, on this view, can best be overcome by appealing to a common rationality, and this rationality is fostered through education.

Influenced still by rationalism, a somewhat different view of the human situation is inspired also by the romantic and naturalist tradition, claiming that cultural diversity can be deep-seated and not easily overcome by rationality. This view of culture is more dynamic and floating, and sees diversity less as a problem than as a value and expression of creativity. Seen from this more diversity-sensitive point of view, the discourse about citizenship should start from mutual recognition of socio-cultural plurality and its expression in religion, values, traditions and lifestyle.[8]

The analysis of recent reforms in Norwegian RE shows how close the issues of citizenship are to the concerns of religious educators. In particular, the debate on citizenship is important because it focuses on the questions of

diversity that are also important in RE. This makes RE a competent partici-
pator in the debate about citizenship, but it is also a challenge to draw some
borders between subject areas. More than other school subjects, RE has
been preoccupied with issues of identity, which are also central to the
new debate on citizenship. Identity is a multi-faceted phenomenon; civic
identity is not the same as religious identity or personal identity, even if
they overlap. Here there is space for 'integrated theories' about 'integrated
diverse identities' both in the field of citizenship and in that of religion.[9]
The concept of 'spirituality' also seems to be an arena of mutual interest,
but at the same time one which is in need of closer investigation. There
are issues, for example, about the possible discontinuities between human
spirituality and religious belief and the ways in which these might be represented in school.

In addition to the challenges related to separation, localization and definition, there is a need to re-examine the role and meaning of RE within a
wider theory of education and society. There has been a long history of
tension between knowledge-oriented and student-oriented religious education coupled with different educational theories. The Norwegian example
illustrates an international tendency to focus more on the political or civilizing aspects of education. It also illustrates the problems connected with this.
What are the civilizing aspects of RE, and what are the religious aspects of
citizenship?

Conclusion

Investigation into the recent literature on citizenship has shown that this
issue covers a broad area, including both the perspective of individual
virtues and that of legal rights. Both these perspectives open up new hori-
zons of inquiry rather than limiting the area of interest. It has sometimes
been said of the current debate on identity that the posing of the question
is in itself a sign of crisis in the understanding of what identity is and how
it is formed. Something of the same could probably be said about citizenship. On the one hand, there is a worldwide interest in issues of democracy,
human rights and civic virtues. On the other, many Western countries that
proudly carry the historical legacy of early democratic constitutions struggle
with a lack of political interest among parts of their population both on the
local and the national level.

A crisis of citizenship seems to coincide with a crisis of identity in many
Western countries, thereby posing important questions about the foundations of these societies. This happens at a time in history when Western
capitalist civilization seems to be drawing ever more parts of the world
into its sphere of influence. The driving forces of the economy as well as
politics, often in the form of professional public management, both fall
short when it comes to providing basic meaning in people's lives. At the

same time (post)modern society depends heavily on people finding and producing meaning in their daily life. These meaning-producing processes are going on everywhere, and religion is part of them, but largely out of control when seen from a management point of view. When there is talk about a crisis of citizenship and identity it may therefore be interpreted as a sign of the disintegration of society. However, it can also be more of a crisis in the *understanding* of citizenship and identity. This points towards diversity as a major challenge. Cultural diversity, in the widest sense, is serving the needs of modern society by contributing products, markets and 'creativity'. At the same time, diversity is challenging the very same society by producing values that are 'different' and 'inefficient'. Religion is part of this contradictory dynamic, if often marginalized or vulgarized in public discourse, but the study of marginalized phenomena is often instructive in understanding the greater whole. Researchers in religious education are therefore in a good position to research these issues and bring them to the attention of the wider public.

Notes

1 Books on this include: Turner (1993); Twine (1994); Cesarani and Fulbrook (1996); Bulmer and Rees (1996); Torres *et al.* (1999); Kymlicka and Norman (2000a). Recent and forthcoming conferences are well publicised on the internet.
2 'It is clear then that citizenship has changed the quality of the modern social conflict. Remnants of class in the old sense continue to be with us and may even provide the underlying pattern of social and political antagonism for some time to come. . . . Often, a farewell to class is coupled with an overly idyllic picture of things to come. But if one retains the concept of class after citizenship, one has to qualify it and spell out the difference. For purposes of analysis, it is sufficient to note that the days of entitlement conflicts are not over' (Dahrendorf 1996: 46).
3 Sometimes this is a 'meeting place' for right and left politics. When the left wing criticizes immigration policy, both regulations and practice, this may have a broadly similar effect on the public attitude towards state institutions, as when the right wing complains about bureaucratization.
4 A leading Norwegian professor of political science (Øyvind Østerud) has used *medborger* as a translation of 'citizen' in a newspaper article which was based on his keynote lecture at a large international conference (Østerud 2000a, b). For religious educators it may be interesting to know that the Norwegian Humanist Association also used the word when they introduced their 'civic confirmation' ritual in the early 1950s. This was regarded as an alternative to church confirmation and was preceded by 'a course in good citizenship' (*et kurs i godt medborgerskap*). The word *medborger* may have been imported from Sweden, since it seems to be the equivalent of 'citizen' in Swedish and is widely used there, covering both the descriptive and the normative aspects. In Denmark too there are signs, judging from recent publications, that *medborger* is coming to be used in the Norwegian sense.

5 There is a complex relationship here, but my main point is that there is a connection between 'Norwegian culture', understood as everyday life, and the political agendas.
6 'definitions of citizenship are very much a product of the spirit and concerns of the age. In the 1980s and early 1990s, the Conservative Government championed the individualism of the free market and placed an emphasis on the importance of civic obligation or "active citizenship". The term "active citizenship" was part of a wider Conservative philosophy based on the privacy of the rights and responsibilities of the individual over those of the state. . . . The Conservative Government urged individuals to take up actively their civic responsibilities rather than leave it to the government to carry them out. It backed up the call with policies that encouraged greater private ownership and the privacy of consumer rights in all areas of life, including education' (Kerr 2000: 3–4).
7 The 'ethics' part the curriculum includes issues such as racism, multicultural questions, sexuality, peace, responsibility for others, rich and poor, environmental issues, equality and consumerism (http://skolenettet3.ls.no/L97_eng/Curriculum/).
8 There is an implicit reference here to the 'politics of recognition' and the discussion of the views of Charles Taylor. See Taylor and Gutmann (1992). This is an example of the debates about diversity and citizenship. To use the term 'recognition' does not, however, have to indicate a communitarian view. Defenders of a liberal perspective on citizenship with rationalist leanings are also aware of the challenges of fostering common civic virtues in a plural society. See, for example, Callan (1997: 222).
9 See Østberg (1999: 251 ff.) on 'integrated plural identities' and Kymlicka and Norman (2000b: 10 ff.) on 'integrated theory of diverse citizenship'.

References

Bulmer, M. and Rees, A. M. (eds) (1996) *Citizenship Today: The Contemporary Relevance of T. H. Marshall*, London: UCL Press.
C-97: The Curriculum for the Ten Years' Compulsory School (1997) Official English version of the Norwegian national curriculum. Online. Available HTTP: <http://skolenettet3.ls.no/L97_eng/Curriculum/> (accessed 27 July 2001).
Callan, E. (1997) *Creating Citizens: Political Education and Liberal Democracy*, Oxford: Clarendon Press.
Cesarani, D. and Fulbrook, M. (1996) *Citizenship, Nationality and Migration in Europe*, London: Routledge.
Dahrendorf, R. (1996) 'Citizenship and social class', in M. Bulmer and A. M. Rees (eds) *Citizenship Today: The Contemporary Relevance of T. H. Marshall*, London: UCL Press.
DfEE (2001) A–Z Citizenship Education, London: DfEE. Online. Available HTTP: <http://www.dfee.gov.uk/a-z/CITIZENSHIP_EDUCATION.html> (accessed 27 July 2001).
Gullestad, M. (1992) 'Egalitarian individualism', in M. Gullestad (1992a) *The Art of Social Relations: Essays on Culture, Social Action and Everyday Life in Modern Norway*, Oslo: Scandinavian University Press.
Hagesæther, G., Sandsmark, S. and Bleka, D-A. (2000) *Foreldres, elevers og læreres erfaringer med KRL-faget*, Bergen: NLA-forlaget.

Heath, P. (2000) 'Education as citizenship', *Higher Education Research and Development*, 19 (1), 43–57.

Hebert, Y. and Pagé, M. (2000) 'Research initiatives in citizenship education', *Education Canada*, 40 (3), 24–7.

Isin, E. F. and Wood, P. K. (1999) *Citizenship and Identity*, London: Sage.

Johannessen, K. I. and Aadnanes, P. M. (2000) *Et fag for enhver smak? En evaluering av KRL-faget*, Oslo: Diaforsk.

Kennedy, K. J. (1997) *Citizenship, Education and the Modern State*, London: Falmer Press.

Kerr, D. (2000) *The Making of Citizenship in the National Curriculum (England): Issues and Challenges*, European Conference on Educational Research (ECER), University of Edinburgh. Online. Available HTTP:<http://www.nfer.ac.uk/research/papers/ecer.kerr.doc> (accessed 14 August 2002).

Kymlicka, W. and Norman, W. (eds) (2000a) *Citizenship in Diverse Societies*, Oxford: Oxford University Press.

Kymlicka, W. and Norman, W. (2000b) 'Citizenship in culturally diverse societies: issues, contexts, concepts', in W. Kymlicka and W. Norman (eds) *Citizenship in Diverse Societies*, Oxford: Oxford University Press.

Lundgren, U. P. (1998) 'Culture, reproduction and education', in H. Johansson (ed.) *Challenge the Future through your Culture: Proceedings of the Symposium in Pedagogics, 12–15 June 1988, Luleå, Sweden*, Luleå: Centek.

Marshall, T. H. (1950) *Citizenship and Social Class, and other Essays*, Cambridge: Cambridge University Press.

NOU (1995) *Identitet og dialog*. Kristendomskunnskap, livssynskunnskap og religionsundervisning. Utredning fra et utvalg oppnevnt av Kirke-, undervisnings- og forskningsdepartementet. (White Paper addressing questions about RE on all levels in the school system.)

Skeie, G. (2001) 'Citizenship, identity politics and religious education', in H. G. Heimbrock, C. T. Scheilke and P. Schreiner (eds) *Towards Religious Competence: Diversity as a Challenge for Education in Europe*, Münster: Lit Verlag.

Soysal, Y. N. (1996) 'Changing citizenship in Europe', in D. Cesarani and M. Fulbrook (eds) *Citizenship, Nationality and Migration in Europe*, London: Routledge.

Taylor, C. and Gutmann, A. (1992) *Multiculturalism and the Politics of Recognition: An Essay*, Princeton NJ: Princeton University Press.

Torney-Purta, J. (2000) 'Comparative perspectives on political socialisation and civic education', *Comparative Education Review*, 44 (1), 88–95.

Torney-Purta, J., Lehmann, R. and Schultz, W. (2001) *Citizenship and Education in Twenty-eight Countries: Civic Knowledge and Engagement at Age Fourteen*, Amsterdam: IEA. Online. Available HTTP: <http:www.wam.umd.edu/~iea/interreport.htm> (accessed 27 July 2001).

Torres, R. D., Mirón, L. F. and Inda, J. X. (1999) *Race, Identity, and Citizenship: A Reader*, Oxford: Blackwell.

Turner, B. S. (1993) *Citizenship and Social Theory*, London: Sage.

Twine, F. (1994) *Citizenship and Social Rights: The Interdependence of Self and Society*, London: Sage.

Webster's (1994) *Webster's Encyclopedic Unabridged Dictionary of the English Language*, New York: Gramercy Books.

Østberg, S. (1999) 'Pakistani Children in Oslo: Islamic Nurture in a Secular Context', unpublished Ph.D. thesis, Coventry: University of Warwick.

Østerud, Ø. (2000a) Demokratiets rystelser. Kronikk i Aftenposten. Column in the newspaper *Aftenposten* published on the internet 23 September 2000. Online. HTTP: <http://tux1.aftenposten.no/meninger/kronikker/d163831.htm> (accessed 24 July 2001).

—— (2000b) 'Democracy and the transformation of politics', keynote speech at the seventh conference of the Society for the Study of European Ideas (ISSEI), 14–18 August 2000. Available on CD-ROM, published by the HIT Centre, University of Bergen.

Chapter 4

Citizenship as a replacement for religious education or RE as complementary to citizenship education?

Robert Jackson

Synopsis   The argument that, in schools in England and Wales, religious education and citizenship education are complementary is developed, using insights from the study of religions and cultures in three stages. First, the view that they are mutually exclusive is rejected in a detailed critique of David Hargreaves' position (that social cohesion is best fostered within state education through the provision of citizenship education in secular/common schools and religious education in religious schools). I argue that Hargreaves works with a limited view of citizenship education, a dated concept of religious education as using a religion to inculcate morality, a mistaken definition of secular and an inadequate account of pluralism throughout all society, including religious groupings. Consequently, Hargreaves does not acknowledge that in common schools, citizenship education should include debates on issues connected with pluralism or that religious education can and should support these. Secondly, links between contemporary religious education and citizenship education can easily be demonstrated. There are pedagogies that provide analyses and skills to help pupils in common schools to respond to the difficulties encountered in understanding diverse identities in Britain. The work of three practising teachers demonstrates ways in which the interpretive approach in religious education can meet the needs of particular school communities. Thirdly, consideration of aspects of the religions themselves suggests that religious traditions have the potential to enable schools to move beyond Crick's nation–state citizenship to incorporate global ideas of citizenship. Religious education in common schools, in other words, complements citizenship education through the process of helping children debate issues relevant to a plural society.

The turn of the millennium (at least for users of the Gregorian calendar) has prompted many a reflection on social and political change in relation to education. Some of the old 'certainties' about values that helped to define and form individual and social identities have gone or are questioned in the context of the social and intellectual plurality of late modernity. It is hardly surprising that there are lively debates and shifting policies in relation to moral and religious education and education for citizenship. All these are contested fields.

In England and Wales, at least until the late 1950s, religious education, moral education and civic education were seen as closely related. Religious education was equated with Christian education, a form of nurture that had moral and civic goals, although these were often tacitly expressed. In the atmosphere of moral and social renewal following World War II the British government associated civic education with Christian education, seeing Christian faith as the basis of morality and citizenship, and as an integrating principle for all education. A report by the Institute of Christian Education refers to the government position of the day:

> The Ministry's Education Pamphlet No. 16, *Citizens Growing Up*, plainly says (p. 10) that Christian belief and practice are the most secure foundations for the building of a true and enduring citizenship. It goes on to show how religion should inspire and integrate the teaching of the basic subjects in the curriculum.
>
> (ICE 1954: 8)

The combined forces of secularization, plurality and globalization have made this association of Christian, moral and civic education no longer sustainable for public education. Indeed, by the late 1960s religious education was changing in character, while moral and political education emerged as independent fields. In religious education in Britain there has been a good deal of thinking about how the subject should change in relation to these forces, with the work of Ninian Smart and his colleagues probably being the earliest to introduce a global dimension into a secularized religious education (Smart 1968; Schools Council 1971). Starting with the pioneering work of John Wilson and his collaborators in the 1960s (Wilson *et al.* 1967), much work in the field of moral education has also taken account of a secular and pluralist climate, as indicated over the years in various books (e.g. Downey and Kelly 1978; Hirst 1974; Loukes 1973; McPhail *et al.* 1972) and numerous contributions to the *Journal of Moral Education*, which first appeared in 1971. In the field of civic education, by the late 1960s, Bernard Crick was arguing for education for political literacy in the secondary school (1969: 3–4) and later set up a curriculum project on political education that produced the report *Political Education and Political Literacy* (Crick and Porter 1978). It is not well known that this work influenced writing on religious education through Richard Tames's work on Islam and political education (Tames 1982).

The advent of the Thatcher government in 1979 put paid to any further developments in political education or any political dimension to citizenship education and, not surprisingly, the national curriculum that was introduced via the 1988 Education Reform Act stuck to traditional subjects, marginalizing fields such as multicultural and anti-racist education and social studies (Tomlinson and Craft 1995). Citizenship was included as a non-statutory cross-curricular theme (NCC 1990), but with an overloaded compulsory curriculum there was little chance of its development.

Thus the debate about the relationship between religious, moral and citizenship education was put on ice. It was not until the 1990s that the debate reopened in earnest (Heater 1990). The election of a Labour government in 1997 facilitated the resuscitation of political education as an aspect of citizenship education, and it was Bernard Crick who chaired the Advisory Group on Citizenship that produced the Crick Report (QCA 1998), heralding the introduction of the subject as part of the revised national curriculum for secondary schools. The report states:

> We aim at no less than a change in the political culture of this country . . . for people to think of themselves as active citizens, willing, able and equipped to have an influence in public life . . . There are worrying levels of apathy, ignorance and cynicism about political and public life and also involvement in neighbourhood and community affairs.

The Crick Report urged that the statutory order should declare citizenship to be:

> the knowledge, skills and values relevant to the nature and practices of participative democracy; the duties, responsibilities, rights and development of pupils into citizens; and the value to individuals, schools and society of involvement in the local and wider community . . . both national and local and an awareness of world affairs and global issues, and of the economic realities of adult life.
>
> (QCA 1998)

The report identifies three strands which should run through education for citizenship at local, regional and national levels: social and moral responsibility, community involvement and political literacy.[1] These strands are evident in the curriculum which was prepared for introduction in secondary schools in 2002 as part of the national curriculum.[2]

The Crick Report and the national curriculum orders do not attempt to discuss the relationship between education for citizenship and religious education. However, there was an important contribution in the mid-1990s to the debate about citizenship in relation to issues of religion and education from David Hargreaves, at that time Professor of Education at Cambridge University and, until 2001, Chief Executive of the Qualifications and Curriculum Authority. In this discussion, Hargreaves relates his arguments directly to specific recommendations for policy change (Hargreaves 1994). Hargreaves' views on education have been highly influential on the policies of the 1997 Labour government. His ideas about educational research, his advocacy of the expansion of state-funded religious schools and his plea for the introduction of citizenship education have all contributed to government policy. His views about religious education have not been adopted, although some commentators are concerned that they could be in the future (Gay 2001). It is thus important that Hargreaves' arguments should be considered.

Hargreaves' arguments

Hargreaves recognizes that, in a secular and plural society, religion can no longer be the basis of a socially cohesive civic education. He points out that 'the problem of Britain as a pluralistic society is how to find some social cement to ensure that people with different moral, religious, and ethical values as well as social, cultural and linguistic traditions can live together with a degree of harmony' (Hargreaves 1994: 31). Hargreaves proposes a threefold solution.

First, there should be an expansion of religious schools within the state system. These should have a distinct ethos, asserting the links between religious faith and morality, and should express a joint commitment by home and school to 'the transmission and living experience of a shared moral and religious culture'.

Secondly, religious education should be abolished in all other schools – what Hargreaves calls 'secular schools'. Hargreaves argues that, since religious education has a moral purpose, there is no point in attempting to provide it in schools reflecting a secularized, religiously diverse society where there is no consensus about the relationship between religion and morality. As Hargreaves puts it, 'The notion of a non-denominational core RE to be offered in all schools as a buttress to moral education is becoming less and less viable and should now be abandoned' (Hargreaves 1994: 34). Multi-faith religious education is no answer, according to Hargreaves.

> The multi-faith pick 'n' mix tour of religions easily trivialises each faith's claims to truth. As an academic discipline, it has little appeal to most children and comes before they are mature enough to engage in the necessary historical and philosophical analysis.
>
> (Hargreaves 1994: 34)

For Hargreaves, religion is no longer a 'first language' in society. It is a 'second language', to be spoken in the home and the faith community (including the faith-based school). However, argues Hargreaves, religious and cultural groups do build bridges between the individual and the state, and are thus vitally important. Such groups should express themselves through the participation of representatives in a range of public institutions.

Thirdly, religious education in 'secular' schools should be replaced by citizenship education. Hargreaves' argument is that, whereas Christianity formerly provided a moral basis for civic life, now the 'public language of citizenship' provides the necessary social cement, also functioning as a bridge to the 'second languages' of the distinct moralities of the various religions now actively present in society. The first language of religion is thus replaced by the first language of common values associated with citizenship. Hargreaves also argues for citizenship education in religious schools, as a complement to religious education.

Hargreaves thus sees more or less homogeneous religious communities providing state-supported faith-based education in which their children inherit the beliefs and values of particular religions. Meanwhile, key adults from the communities participate in the democratic process, representing the beliefs and values of their constituents, and identifying values shared with other members of society in order to promote social cohesion.

A critique of Hargreaves

In this section I will argue that Hargreaves' analysis is flawed through its particular assumptions about the homogeneity of religions (and implicitly cultures and ethnic groups), about the nature of secularity in society and (a related point) about the nature of social plurality. I will argue that, rather than being an outmoded subject, to be replaced by citizenship education, religious education (though not as understood by Hargreaves) has a vital contribution to make to various aspects of education for citizenship in the common school.[3]

How far do community leaders and faith-based schools represent religious communities?

First, there are problems with Hargreaves' view of the homogeneity of religions. This creates difficulties for his view of the role of faith-based schools and his claim that community representatives should act as the bridge between the 'second languages' of faith groups and the 'first language' of public institutions through which democracy functions. Religious schools are seen by Hargreaves as havens for particular moralities, in which home and school are jointly committed to 'the transmission and living experience of a shared moral and religious culture', while key adult members of religious communities are regarded as their spokespersons and negotiators. This view exhibits an over-uniform view of the nature of religious or religio-cultural groups. Many ethnographic field studies confirm the diversity of belief and practice within religions that appear superficially to be monolithic, often challenging conventional views of religious boundaries (e.g. Geaves 1998; Nesbitt 1990a, b, 1998a, 2000). This diversity is not simply the product of different cultural influences on homogeneous belief systems. A considerable body of scholarship in cultural history (e.g. Marshall 1970; Said 1978) and the study of religions (e.g. Chidester 1996; Fitzgerald 1990; Jackson 1996; King 1999; Oberoi 1994; Smith 1978) provides evidence that the representation of religions as bounded systems with an essential core of beliefs is a product of the rationalism of the European Enlightenment coupled with and shaped by encounters during the colonial period.[4]

Moreover, ethnographic field studies of children and young people also reveal how religious and cultural elements interact and change over time. Young people may draw on the religious and cultural resources of their historical family traditions, but they are likely also to import elements from a variety of sources, thereby generating new religious and cultural positions. This is especially evident in situations where families have migrated from one society to another (e.g. Barth 1996; Jackson and Nesbitt 1993) and in which influences on the formation of identity are plural and complex (e.g. Østberg 1999, 2000a, b). The riots in Oldham, Burnley, Bradford and Leeds in England in 2001 provide a graphic example of the gap in perceptions of personal and social identity that can exist between community leaders and groups of young people ostensibly from the same religious or ethnic 'communities'. Putting the point another way, treating religious and cultural groups as homogeneous allows the possibility for 'leaders' to invoke traditional authorities and practices in order to impose restrictions on their own members – a point often made by feminist writers in relation to discussions of women (Kassam 1997; Lister 1997: 37; Tobler, this volume, Chapter 7), but equally relevant to other groups such as children or those whose traditions diverge from an abstracted norm.

The difficulty for individuals seeking to speak and negotiate authentically on behalf of those who identify themselves with a particular religion is clear. Individuals may act in the interests of a particular sub-group, perhaps to promote a particular ideological viewpoint, or in their own interests. Furthermore, the issue of representation in this context raises an issue of gender. As feminist discussions of citizenship have pointed out, the political institutions associated with such formal representation in the public arena have been traditionally understood as male domains (Chapter 7, this volume). For example, it is perhaps no coincidence that the faith group representing different elements of 'the Hindu community' in advising on the content of national model syllabuses for religious education in England had an entirely male membership (SCAA 1994).

Gerd Baumann's reflections on his field studies in Southall, west London, are helpful in unpacking the discourse of religion, culture, ethnicity and community. Baumann describes the processes of cultural negotiation and change in terms of the interaction of two kinds of discourse, creating ambiguities in the use of terms such as 'community' and 'culture'. Baumann identifies these as 'dominant discourse' and 'demotic discourse'. 'Dominant discourse' reifies cultures, seeing 'communities' as defined by ethnic and religious identity. This is the kind of language used by politicians and the media, but also by 'insiders' when it suits their interests, for example when engaging in contests regarding group rights. 'Demotic discourse', however, is the language of cultural interaction on the ground, so to speak. It is the language of culture making, and characteristically becomes used when people from a range of backgrounds focus together on topics of common concern or interest. Thus 'culture' can be seen as both the possession of an ethnic or religious 'community' and as a dynamic process relying on personal agency, in which community boundaries are renegotiated and there is the possibility of redefinition of the meaning of 'community' in particular situations (Baumann 1996).

When Hargreaves' points are considered in the light of this analysis, it is clear that he focuses *entirely* on 'dominant discourse', reinforcing the idea of bounded and homogeneous cultures and religions. In doing so he is simply doing what politicians and the media often do. As Baumann puts it:

> the civil religion and political culture of Britain encourages so-called minorities to strive for emancipation as if they were sports teams: They are approached as so-called 'communities', and politicians, the media and almost everybody else thinks of them as tightly knit 'cultural groups' held together by the same traditions, value system and history.
> (Baumann 1999: 76)

Baumann goes on to point out that groups collude with this, since they can hope to achieve civil emancipation only by accepting such reifications when state agencies try to 'help' them and, anyway, co-operation may suit the personal agenda of some of those identified as community leaders. This compounds the problem with regard to the reification of cultures and communities. Baumann identifies the stages in the encounter between the state and minority communities in Britain. First, a group is identified (it could be a temple, mosque or association of some kind) as the representative of a community of culture. Next, the state provides resources and therefore assists in forming new, more tightly bounded groups. Thirdly, the state devolves some of its functions to the 'community'. This is exactly the cycle that Hargreaves recommends in relation to faith-based schools, and which is now being applied as government policy. In pointing this out I am not condemning the idea of faith-based schools in principle, but am attempting to raise awareness of the dangers attendant on the processes through which they are often established. Similarly, I am arguing not for the marginalization or exclusion of community leaders or representatives, but for a more 'differentiated' approach to dialogue and citizenship (see above, Chapter 1).

The key point is that dialogue should not be *confined to* the participation of official representatives of groups in public arenas. As Baumann's research shows, there are many possibilities for dialogue, exchange and negotiation in social life. However, what Hargreaves especially misses by wanting to shunt religious education *only* into faith-based schools is the opportunity for dialogue and interaction between young people from different backgrounds in the common school (Ipgrave 2001; Jackson 1997). The community school is a rare, structured social forum for debates about religion and culture, and for bringing different perspectives to bear on religions or issues of common concern, such as the environment, gender and the rights of children or prisoners – topics that cut across reified views of religions or cultures.

The issue of the homogeneity of religions applies also when considering faith-based schools. Rather than being clear partners with families, promoting shared community values, faith-based schools could set out to promote a particular view of orthodoxy or the views of the school's sponsors rather than reflecting the diversity of tradition to be found on the ground. Since there is as yet no state-supported Hindu school in Britain, let us consider, by way of illustration, a possible scenario in relation to the Hindu tradition. The rise of the religious political right in India has had a deep effect on the way 'Hinduism' is represented by those with political power (e.g. Smith 1996). A strand of militancy and intolerance has emerged from the most tolerant and flexible of religious traditions. This tendency in India is reflected to a degree in the diaspora, especially through the activities of particular organized groups such as the Vishwa Hindu Parishad. Members of this group in Britain wrote a textbook on Hinduism for use in religious education (Prinja 1996). This generalizes the authors' ideological stance to a whole tradition. At one point the text claims that Buddhism and Sikhism 'may be taught as separate religions, but both should be treated as branches of Hinduism' (Prinja 1996: 47). The book presents as uncontroversial the view that Buddhists, Sikhs and Jains are all Hindus, and that there is a common 'racial' origin for these groups (Prinja 1996: 60). The assumption gives offence to many whose self-designation would be different and could be interpreted as being implicitly anti-Muslim. The book has been attacked very strenuously by a British Indian academic (Mukta 1997). The reply by the editor of *Explaining Hindu Dharma* and other members of the Vishwa Hindu Parishad is equally vituperative (Prinja *et al.* 1998). The story illustrates the fact that members of powerful groups can set themselves up as spokespersons for a religion and yet promote a viewpoint different from that of many others from a broadly similar religious background. Such 'community representatives' may equally claim to represent 'Hinduism' in public institutions or make a bid to become sponsors of a state-funded religious school. In these cases, community leaders would not genuinely represent the diversity of Hindu practice and values in Britain. This example should make it clear that Hargreaves' view of religions as close-knit communities with shared values is, at the very least, an over-simplification.

It is equally clear that, while religious schools may have some very positive features, there can equally be a down side, a point reinforced by the negative effects on community relations of separate schooling for Catholics in Northern Ireland (Barnes 2000). Separate religious schools can have a role in imposing identities on children and reinforcing boundaries between different groups in society (Humanist Philosophers' Group 2001).[5] In this respect, some commentators argue that separate religious schools militate *against* education for good citizenship, precisely because of their deliberate physical separation of children of one religious group from others of different background (Kymlicka 1999: 88–90). It is interesting, in the wake of the terrible acts of genocide in the former Yugoslavia, that educators in Bosnia-Herzegovina are attempting to promote dialogue between young people from groups for which conflict has promoted a perception of identities that equate stereotypical representations of religion and ethnicity (Orthodox Serbs, Catholic Croats, Bosnian Muslims). The aim is to introduce a new subject, 'Culture of Religions', in order to give a critical analysis of such representations and to promote tolerance, reconciliation and mutual understanding between groups (ICCS 2001: 2–3).

The nature of religious education

Hargreaves' key reason for dismissing religious education from the curricula of common schools is that the subject has ceased to be relevant to issues of morality and citizenship for the majority of members of a largely secular society in which there is no consensus about the relationship between religion and morality. This view is based on his assumption that religious education has a moral purpose achieved through the promotion of a religious view of life. In maintaining this view of the subject, Hargreaves ignores over thirty years of British scholarship in the field of religious education in which alternative models of the subject have been advanced that take account of secularization (from Cox 1966 onwards) and religious plurality both globally (from Smart 1967, 1968 onwards) and locally (from Cole 1972 onwards). The only alternative to a religious and moral formation model Hargreaves countenances is what he calls a 'multi-faith pick 'n' mix tour of religions', which he regards as trivializing claims to truth and as inappropriate for those who have not reached a state of intellectual maturity. This glib dismissal of multi-faith religious education echoes – in word as well as sentiment – attacks on the subject by lobbyists from the political radical right in the late 1980s (Burn and Hart 1988; Hull 1991; Jackson 1992, 2000a), and ignores discussions informed by scholarship and research (Jackson 2001a). There is some evidence that Hargreaves' view is largely based on his experience as Chief Inspector of the Inner London Education Authority (Hargreaves 1986). At the time, ILEA had a heavily content-laden religious education syllabus with little reflective and critical work built into it, and it is not surprising that he was sceptical about the effectiveness of this highly diluted version of phenomenology, and found the subject to be unpopular with young people in schools. His view also seems to be coloured by the on-going political debate about the nature and purpose of RE, and he is clearly irritated with the various fudges and compromises that have weakened legislation and non-statutory advice. One can but sympathize.

Yet Hargreaves fails to offer convincing evidence for rejecting the possibility of a genuinely open and plural religious education that promotes dialogue and communication across boundaries, that takes issues of truth seriously, that is appropriate to the age, aptitude and family background of pupils and that engages them intellectually and emotionally. There are several approaches that succeed in providing this combination of elements, and there is evidence of teachers employing them, or variants on them, with a high degree of success. I will mention three from Britain by way of illustration: Michael Grimmitt's earlier work, combining elements of phenomenology and humanist psychology (Grimmitt 1987), his work with John Hull and others on the Gift to the Child project (Hull 1996) and his more recent work utilizing pedagogical ideas from constructivism (Grimmitt 2000); Andrew Wright's work on the development of religious literacy (e.g. Wright 1993, 1998); and the interpretive approach developed by myself and my colleagues at Warwick, aiming to balance the skills of interpretation with reflective and critical activities appropriate to the age of children and often drawing on ethnographic studies of young people in Britain (Jackson 1997, 2000b). All these approaches have resulted in good or excellent practice in schools.[6] There are thus strong grounds for rejecting Hargreaves' easy dismissal of multi-faith religious education.[7]

Secular schools or plural schools?

In Hargreaves' scheme of things there would be religious schools and secular schools, with religious education confined to the first. The assumption is that secular schools would reflect the secular climate of the greater part of society. There would be an interest in moral education in secular schools (which, says Hargreaves, could be dealt with by subjects such as English) and there would be civic education. However, Hargreaves' characterization of the common school as secular in contrast to religious schools misunderstands the plurality of community schools.

First, there are plenty of individuals, families and groups practising religion who do not favour separate education for children. Some of them see real dangers in separate schooling, and wish their children to learn with others from a range of backgrounds in the community school (see, for example, Connolly 1992; Humanist Philosophers' Group 2001; Jackson 1987; Jackson and Nesbitt 1993). Secondly, Hargreaves assumes that young people not practising religion in a formal way have little or no interest in religious or spiritual issues or in being informed about religion (see

Blaylock 2001 for a report of evidence to the contrary;[8] see also the survey of secondary pupils in Pocock 2000). Thirdly he assumes (because of his view of the nature of religious and moral education as forms of socialization) that religious education hi-jacks moral education rather than complementing it (see Hawke 1982 for a different analysis). Fourthly, his view of plurality in society is limited to overt religious diversity and secularity. He largely omits the dimension of what Geir Skeie has called 'modern plurality', the intellectual climate of late modernity or postmodernity that provides the context of religious and ethnic diversity and provides a backdrop for all education (Skeie 1995). Skeie is not stating a normative position on the modernity/postmodernity debate but pointing out that any education in religious and cultural diversity needs to take account of the social frag-mentation, globalizing tendencies and alternative rationalities that are characteristic of late modernity, exemplified in debates about truth and meaning, knowledge and power and personal and social identity. When different positions on modern plurality are brought together with religious diversity, a wide variety of spiritual and moral responses and syntheses become possible, many not being directly identifiable with orthodoxies of the major religions. Similarly, the debate about citizenship is broadened when modern plurality is taken into account, to take on board the debates about rights and duties at local and global levels as well as the level of the nation-state. It is Hargreaves' restricted view of plurality that mainly accounts for his sharp distinction between the religious and the secular. This is also probably true of his view of citizenship, seen purely as a set of duties and rights related to one's place within the state rather than as a wider debate about the relation of the individual to a broader range of collectivities, including global responsibilities and rights.

The common school should not be secular in the sense that Hargreaves uses, that is, as the direct opposite of 'religious'. Rather, community schools should be secular in the Indian constitutional sense of 'secular' – that is, maintaining impartiality towards different religious and non-religious truth positions. The community school can provide a genuine forum for dialogue between students and teachers from different religious and non-religious backgrounds and for learning the skills to interpret, reflect upon and gain insight from different worldviews. However, community schools should make room for the exploration of debates, whether about religion, culture, morality or citizenship or about modernity and postmodernity, as well as opportunities for encounter and exchange with people having differ-ent views and commitments. In this sense, the common school should be a microcosm of a democratic society, and is therefore the ideal place to explore and practise ideas of citizenship. The knowledge, understanding and skills that can be provided by religious education have a vital contribution to make to this process.

The contribution of religious education to education for citizenship

Fortunately, the national curriculum for citizenship is not seen by the government as a replacement for religious education or any other subject area. Rather, it envisages a core of topics covered as 'citizenship', with a range of contributions from other subjects, including religious education. It is a pity that the cross-references to contributory subjects omit religious education, again because the references are specifically to the national curriculum.[9] However, the guidance documents refer clearly to RE's potential contribution, as does Bernard Crick in his personal reflections on the citizenship curriculum, emphasizing its flexibility (Crick 2000). Moreover Estelle Morris, the Secretary of State for Education and Skills at the time of writing, has stated clearly that 'Citizenship education complements RE; it does not replace it' (personal communication 2001).

In this section I will offer a few illustrations of how religious education might contribute to education for citizenship in the common school. I shall also argue that the application of general pedagogical principles needs to take close account of the particular contexts in which teachers work. For the purpose of this discussion I will consider some ways in which the interpretive approach to religious education, in particular, may lend insight to some of the elements listed in the curriculum for citizenship.

The requirements for citizenship at both Key Stage 3 and Key Stage 4 require knowledge and understanding of 'the diversity of national, regional, religious and ethnic identities in the United Kingdom and the need for mutual respect and understanding' (DfEE/QCA 1999a), while the non-statutory advice for Key Stages 1 and 2 encourages children to 'appreciate the range of national, regional, religious and ethnic identities in the United Kingdom' (DfEE/QCA 1999b). These are not easy tasks. The critique of early work in multicultural education in the 1970s by anti-racist writers (e.g. Troyna 1983) shows the very real dangers of superficial treatment of this topic, of giving a simplistic portrayal of 'cultures' and of inadvertently manufacturing stereotypical identities and confirming them in young people. I have already referred to ethnographic research in various religio-cultural settings that points up the complexity of identity formation in relation to religion, ethnicity, community, culture and nationality as well as the contestability of these concepts (see Chapter 1 and, for example, Baumann 1996; Jackson and Nesbitt 1993; Jacobson 1998; Nesbitt 2000; Østberg 1999). The interpretive approach to religious education uses insights from this and related research in order to promote a flexible approach to debates about these issues and to portrayals of multicultural societies, and therefore has a good deal to offer citizenship education (Jackson 1997: chapters 3–4).

The interpretive approach aims to develop an understanding of the grammar – the language and wider symbolic patterns – found in religious traditions, and the skills of interpretation necessary to gain that understanding. The achievement of this aim necessitates the development of critical skills which would open up issues of the representation of religions and the interpretation of religious material as well as questions of truth and meaning. The interpretive approach emphasizes the inseparability of the processes of understanding and reflection, suggesting that 'edification' (the deepening of one's own personal understanding), engagement in constructive criticism and the involvement of students in the design and review of study methods should be further goals for the subject (Jackson 1997: 133–4, 2000b). The combined principles associated with representation, interpretation and reflexivity in relation to religious positions provide many of the skills of inquiry, communication, participation and responsible action required by the national curriculum for citizenship (DfEE/QCA 1999a), and are convertible into practical methods for use in religious education. However, the shift from pedagogical principles to practical strategies needs to take account of the context in which learning takes place.

I have suggested that the common/community school is ideally placed for dialogue and communication between different positions, whether between children and others beyond the school or between children from different backgrounds within the school. However, community schools themselves are diverse in character, and some of them present particular challenges to teachers attempting to cater for the needs of the school's population. Current policy, and the policies of previous governments with regard to parental choice in schooling in England and Wales, have led to some community schools almost becoming ghettoes for particular groups of young people. Some inner-city schools have a predominant population from an 'Asian' or African-Caribbean ethnic or religio-ethnic group, while others have a majority of white children, often from impoverished backgrounds. Some analysts regard the presence of a young economically deprived underclass (Runnymede 2000) and *de facto* separate schooling (Ouseley 2001) as major contributory factors in the division and unrest that led to riots in the north of England, and the government needs to address the issue with urgency.

Some teachers of religious education have employed particular strategies in order to take account of their particular situations. To take a first example, the mainly white, predominantly secular and working-class setting described by Sarah Edwards, in her discussion of religious education and cultural development in her comprehensive school, prompted her to synthesize ideas from the interpretive approach to religious education with ideas from a range of sources such as critical theory, Paulo Freire's educational ideas and liberation theology. Edwards utilizes her own pupils' various negative attitudes towards religion by making them the focus of debate in RE lessons. Through raising their awareness of cultural choices, her approach seeks to challenge pupils' assumptions about religions. She does this by engaging them in critical debate, potentially releasing them from confinement within static cultural identities. At the heart of what she calls 'Emancipatory RE' lie some key values such as respect for one's students and the commitment to principles of humanization and justice.

> Emancipatory RE has the potential to prevent pupils from being locked into a particular and static cultural identity, or even to release pupils to consider critically the cultural material upon which they draw. If, as many will, such pupils choose to re-enter and continue to draw from the same range of cultural materials as before, then at least they may do so in a new light, having been edified in some way by their experience of RE such that their choice becomes more completely their own rather than an imposition. However, some pupils will be inspired with new visions through exposure to new cultural material, and, having had the opportunity for critical thought concerning these new stimuli, may include them in their cultural 'heritage'.
>
> (Edwards 1999: 53–4)

Edwards's method focuses on questions that pupils select for investigation *prior to* the detailed planning of the scheme of work. The pedagogical skill of the teacher is used to select appropriate material from the Agreed Syllabus that can be covered as part of the exploration of the questions raised by students, with the teacher taking the role of 'critical co-investigator'. The basic requirements of the syllabus are met, but the 'content' becomes secondary to the exploration of issues.

As can be seen in more detail in Chapter 8 of this book, Julia Ipgrave, in her Leicester primary school with an 85 per cent Muslim majority, has conducted research into children's influence upon one another and introduced strategies to promote dialogue and communication between children from different religious and non-religious backgrounds within and beyond the school (Ipgrave 2001). Her research identifies shifting boundaries between groups of children, which at times may be reinforced through conflict. On other occasions, boundaries are crossed as children filter and rework one another's religious languages in formulating their own ideas. Ipgrave's work illustrates that, in plural contexts, children are able to draw on a variety of religio-cultural resources in addition to their parental traditions in creating their own culture (cf. Jackson 1997: chapter 4). Ipgrave's analysis of children's language illustrates graphically how these processes occur in her school – through interaction with others, reflection on others' language and meanings, and through disagreement with or through the adaptation or adoption of others' words. Her research gives concrete examples of both Baumann's 'demotic' and 'dominant' discourses. Ipgrave's on-going work is seminal in appreciating the potential of RE in the state-funded school as a site for inter-religious and intercultural dialogue and interaction, and provides an alternative model to that envisaged by Hargreaves, in which key adults are seen as the representatives of religious groups in dialogue and negotiation with others. It also demonstrates (*contra* Hargreaves) that 'multi-faith' religious education can be successful with children of primary age. Ipgrave's earlier research pointed up the need for awareness of the distinct forms of Islam represented in the school in contrast to the reifications presented in many textbooks and often internalized by teachers (1999). Her recent research on dialogue opens up further possibilities for using the experience of children in school as source material for religious education. One element of this, which will be developed further in a new project, is the linking of children from different schools together by e-mail in order to participate in dialogue (Ipgrave 2001: 27–31). This work includes contact between children in community schools and others in voluntary aided religious schools. There is potential here for increasing understanding across different worldviews and for reducing the negative effects of separate religious schooling referred to earlier.

A third example is Elizabeth Bassett's systematic application of pedagogical principles from the interpretive approach to her work as a teacher in a culturally fairly 'monochrome' community primary school, using outside visits and visitors to the school as a means to maximize contact between her pupils and people from different religious backgrounds (Bassett 2001). Bassett trains her pupils in ethnographic methods, such as interviewing and participant observation, paying particular attention to activities intended to sensitize children to the study of the culturally unfamiliar and to interpretive and critical skills. Following this preparatory activity, religion is studied through particular examples involving visits to religious locations, such as the Krishna Consciousness Centre at Bhaktivedanta Manor, or interviews with visitors to the school.

> By talking to people first-hand, the problem of distancing is partly solved, and it allows people to talk about a tradition from their own perspective, explaining the aspects which are important to them and why. It also enables pupils to gain an inside view of why religion is important for those particular individuals and the flexibility to follow up their interests and concerns as they interact with people directly. Just as important, it provides the opening for those pupils who practise a religion themselves, to feel included and able to add their own individual, unique picture into the equation.
>
> (Bassett 2001: 29)

By setting up an interplay between an individual case and a broader understanding of tradition, and a comparison of the visitor's concepts and experiences with some of those of the children, Bassett goes on to explain how the method attempts to avoid stereotyping, promoting dialogue and reflection, in this case in relation to meetings with a female Jewish visitor to her class.

> Using a visitor would aid the pupils' understanding of Judaism as a tradition to which individuals relate in a variety of ways, rather than a set system of beliefs . . . It would enable them to engage dialogically with an insider, providing an opportunity to compare their own experiences of commitment with someone else's, thus engaging critically with the overall concept. Interpretation and reflexivity can be seen here to be inseparable or dependent on each other. In order to begin to interpret, children must be given opportunities to move between the gaining of some knowledge of the wider religious tradition, a personalised account from within the tradition and their own understanding of certain concepts.
>
> (Bassett 2001: 39)

These examples of moving from pedagogical principles to strategies appropriate in particular educational settings all illustrate the interpretive approach to religious education's strong contribution to aspects of citizenship as understood in the national curriculum documents and the non-statutory guidance for primary schools. However, they by no means exhaust the possibilities of alternative or complementary approaches (see e.g. Wright 2001) or of new developments.

Religious education and global citizenship

So far, the emphasis in this discussion has been upon citizenship as conventionally understood in political thought. In T. H. Marshall's classic discussion, for example, citizenship is a status related specifically to the nation-state, which confers rights under at least the headings of:

- civil rights (rights under law to personal liberty, freedom of speech, association, religious toleration and freedom from censorship);
- political rights (rights to participation in political processes);
- social rights (rights of access to social benefits and resources: education, economic security, the services of the welfare state) (Marshall 1950).

Other analysts emphasize equally the responsibilities and duties that accompany such rights within the state. Despite their occasional references to international and global issues, both Crick and Hargreaves see education for citizenship as relating essentially to rights and duties within the democratic nation-state. It also seems likely that politicians' interest in citizenship education is linked more with voter apathy than with international issues of human rights, poverty, peace and conflict or with major ecological issues related to global warming or sustainable development. In this final section I will argue that the tensions between ideas of state citizenship and global citizenship constitute a set of debates to which religious education can make a significant contribution.

One product of globalization is a growing debate about rights and responsibilities on a global scale, and many would argue for particular views of global citizenship. For example, one educational publication sees the global citizen as 'someone who: is aware of the wider world and has a sense of their own role as a world citizen; respects and values diversity; is willing to act to make the world a more equitable and sustainable place; (and) takes responsibility for their actions' (Oxfam n.d.).[10] There is a growing amount of literature supporting this perspective as an educational goal, including government publications. For example, non-statutory guidance expresses the hope that pupils will gain 'the knowledge, skills and understanding necessary to become informed, active, responsible global citizens' and to explore the concepts of citizenship, sustainable development, social justice, diversity, interdependence, conflict resolution and human rights, 'developing a critical evaluation of images of the developing world and an appreciation of the effect these have on people's attitudes and values' (DfEE 2000). Even the national curriculum for citizenship expects young people to be aware of 'the wider issues and challenges of global interdependence and responsibility, including sustainable development'.

Whereas Crick's approach to education for citizenship is rooted in his earlier work on political education, educational material promoting considerations of global citizenship tends to emerge from the Development Education and World Studies movements. There are obvious tensions between citizenship in relation to the state and ideas of global citizenship, as is exemplified by the vilification of even the most peaceful protestors at the 2001 G8 summit in Genoa by some British politicians, or by the hostile attitude to asylum seekers promoted by elements of the British press. Thus there is a debate about the nature and parameters of citizenship, complicated further by the fact of dual or multiple allegiances of citizens whose sense of identity relates to several localities in more than one country (see the discussion of Islam in Western countries in Chapter 1; Jacobson 1998; Østberg 1999 and Chapter 5 below).

Religions have obvious relevance to the debates about the relation between different forms of citizenship. Bodies representing individual religions or inter-religious groupings are active in promoting the idea of global citizenship. For example, the Alliance of Religions and Conservation (ARC) is an international religious environmental organization, linking eleven faiths – Christians, Muslims, Jews, Hindus, Buddhists, Jains, Sikhs, Zoroastrians, Bahais, followers of Taoism and Shintoism – with environmental programmes.[11] With regard to the *study* of religions, the programme of the eighteenth quinquennial world congress of the International Association for the History of Religions illustrates a shift away from an earlier emphasis on dispassionate phenomenological analyses to studies with social import: no fewer than three workshops dealt with different aspects of religion and human rights, others focusing on freedom of religion, religion and nature activism, religion and feminism and religious education (Hackett 2000).

With reference to educational material published in Britain, the Oxfam *Curriculum for Global Citizenship* includes a range of activities for religious education. The *RE Curriculum for Global Citizenship* (Christian Aid 2000) regards a responsible global citizen as 'an individual with rights and responsibilities whose actions are based on his/her developing beliefs and values in relationship with others within interdependent local, national and global communities'. John Hull, in his introduction to this booklet, is blunt about the tensions between education for national and for global citizenship:

> Those wealthy countries, with about two-sevenths of the world's population, are surrounded by a money curtain which keeps the rest of the world outside. Our world is deeply divided into the rich and the poor, the well fed and the hungry, those with a long expectancy of life and those whose life expectancy grows less each year . . . Global citizenship suggests that we should regard ourselves not only as belonging to our own nation, or the group of nations which we call our natural competitors, but to the world, to human beings, to all life. Our education system seems intent upon producing citizens of the UK who can help to make this country more successful as a competitor with other nations. This can mean building up the money curtain. Global citizenship implies the tearing down of the money curtain. Nevertheless, if we allow ourselves to be drawn into the remorseless international competition, we will all ultimately fail. We must look to a world beyond the money curtain, one in which everyone will share in life.

The cyclical model of learning presented in the sample units of work, covering Key Stages 1–5 and special schools, moves from 'enquiry' to 'reflection' to 'identification' to 'action'. At the level of 'action' the pupil 'acts inwardly and outwardly in response to events and people in ways that express personal values and identity' and 'negotiates, decides and takes part responsibly in community activities at local, national and global levels'.

Others point out religious education's lack of attention specifically to issues of human rights. For example, Liam Gearon considers the implications of concern for human rights for religious education, partly deriving from the Human Rights Act in the United Kingdom and from other international codes or legislation. He draws on post-colonial theory in arguing that religious education needs to take more account of the political implications of teaching and learning in the representation of religious traditions. In particular, he argues for a heightened awareness and practical implementation of human rights education within the subject. This involves examining not only the positive contributions of religious people to human rights but also the role of religious traditions and religious people in the denial of human rights, 'especially in the repression of women and indigenous peoples, a process particularly notable in the history of imperialism' (Gearon 2002). Others emphasize the rights of particular groups such as parents, children and teachers in relation to religious education as a subject. For example, Marius Felderhof considers the parental rights (as understood in the UN's Declaration of the Rights of the Child, the Convention on the Rights of the Child and the Protocol to the European Convention on Human Rights) in relation to religious education, arguing that 'parents are entitled to share their religious and philosophical convictions through schooling' (Felderhof 2000: 37).

Conclusion

In this chapter I have argued that David Hargreaves' arguments for replacing religious education with education for citizenship are flawed. I have attempted to show, conversely, that religious education has a great deal to offer to citizenship education, for example in offering sophisticated analyses of 'religion' in relation to concepts such as ethnicity, community and nationality and in providing a range of skills relevant to understanding social plurality. Moreover, religious education has some distinct contributions to offer the debates about the parameters of citizenship and, specifically, the tensions between perceptions of national and global citizenship.

Earlier I referred to Geir Skeie's view of religious education. This takes account of modern plurality, integrates the social and the personal, and sees religious education, not as a set body of knowledge, but as a series of debates in which pupils are encouraged to participate, with a personal stake related to their own developing sense of identity (Skeie 1995). The identity of the child and the social context are seen as part of the same cultural process. The aim of education in general and of religious education in particular should be 'to make us become increasingly conscious participants in this process' (Skeie 1995: 90).

Rather than being confronted with a particular view on religions, secularization, plurality or on citizenship, children and young people, at their own level, need to be helped to *participate* in the relevant debates as part of their religious education (Jackson 2000b). This is a condition for the kind of inter-cultural and inter-religious communication that is necessary to the health of plural democracies. The common school is an appropriate setting for such explorations, embracing pluralism in an *epistemologically open* way (Jackson 1997: 126).[12]

This has the aim of giving children and young people competence so that they can move:

> between the different arenas and perspectives of religious and modern plurality. They are the subjects in their own culture, representing and presenting traditions and innovations. Religious education has the possibility of going deeper into both the religious and the modern plurality of which these children and young people are part, and developing their abilities both as observers and participants. This would mean working with pluralism rather than against it.
>
> (Skeie 1995: 90)

The debates about citizenship are an entirely appropriate terrain for such an exploration.

Notes

1 The Crick Report identifies the benefits of citizenship education as: (1) for pupils – an entitlement in schools that will empower them to participate in society as active, informed, critical and responsible citizens, (2) for teachers – advice and guidance in making citizenship provision coherent intellectually and in curriculum terms, (3) for schools – to relate positively to their local communities, (4) for society – an active and politically literate citizenry convinced they can influence government and community affairs at all levels.

2 'Citizenship gives pupils the knowledge, skills and understanding to play an effective role in society at local, national and international levels. It helps them to become informed, thoughtful and responsible citizens who are aware of their duties and rights. It promotes their spiritual, moral and cultural development, making them more self-confident and responsible both in and beyond the classroom. It encourages pupils to play a helpful part in the lives of their schools, neighbourhoods, communities and the wider world. It also teaches them about our economy and democratic institutions and values; encourages respect for different national, religious and ethnic identities; and develops pupils' ability to reflect on issues and take part in discussions' (DfEE/QCA 1999a: preface).

3 Until September 1999 (when the School Standards and Framework Act 1998 was implemented) 'common schools', that is, schools *fully* funded by the state, were designated by law as 'county schools'. Such schools are now known as 'community schools'.

4 Jackson (1997: chapter 3) discusses some of the literature challenging conventional representations of religions as bounded systems with a core of essential beliefs.

5 Eleanor Nesbitt points out that the growing number of 'mixed' religious marriages suggests that, increasingly, membership of a particular religious group by descent cannot be assumed (Nesbitt 1998b).

6 In relation to Grimmitt's work see Grimmitt (2000); in relation to Wright's work see Hookway (2002); in relation to the Warwick-based work (including primary) see Bassett (2001); Bennett (1999); Edwards (1999); Ipgrave (1999, 2001); Jackson (2000b, 2001b).

7 One problem with regard to religious education in England and Wales is that the rather cumbersome way of producing local syllabuses and developing programmes of study from them makes it difficult for syllabus conferences to incorporate ideas from new or recent projects. New pedagogical ideas tend to be tried out as a result of continuing professional development programmes or as an element of partnerships between researchers and teachers, more than through official syllabuses.

8 'New research by the Professional Council for RE has found that among secondary pupils aged 11–18 those who enjoy the subject and see benefit for their own lives from studying religion outnumber those who are negative about RE by four to one' (Blaylock 2001).

9 Although RE is an entitlement of all children, it is a part of the basic curriculum and not the national curriculum. The national curriculum plus RE makes up the basic curriculum.

10 The Oxfam Curriculum for Global Citizenship reports research on children and global issues: 'Research among 11–16 year olds carried out in 1998 by MORI for the Development Education Association provides evidence that the vast majority of children (81%) are interested in global issues and feel it is important to learn about them at school. They think that young people need to understand global matters in order to make choices about how they want to lead their lives. However, over half say they feel powerless to do anything to change the world (54%).' See http://www.oxfam.org.uk/coolplanet/teachers/globciti/globciti.htm.

11 Details of the Alliance of Religions and Conservation can be found at http://www.religionsandconservation.org/.

12 In different contexts I have heard Denise Cush and David Chidester use the expression being 'epistemologically humble' in teaching religious studies and religious education.

References

Barnes, L. P. (2000) 'Religious education in Northern Ireland', in P. Schreiner (ed.) *Religious Education in Europe*, Münster: ICCS and Comenius Institute, 60–7.

Barth, F. (1996) 'How features of the encompassing society set parameters for local multiculturalism', unpublished paper, conference on 'Multicultural Competence: a Resource for Tomorrow', Høgskolen i Bergen, August.

Bassett, E. (2001) 'Implementing the Principles of the Interpretive Approach', unpublished M.A. dissertation, Coventry: Institute of Education, University of Warwick.

Baumann, G. (1996) *Contesting Culture: Discourses of Identity in Multi-ethnic London*, Cambridge: Cambridge University Press.

—— (1999) *The Multicultural Riddle*, London: Routledge.

Bennett, S. (1999) 'Can the Interpretive Approach to Religious Education be Delivered by Flexible Methods in Secondary Schools?', unpublished M.A. dissertation, Coventry: Institute of Education, University of Warwick.

Blaylock, L. (2001) 'Answers and clues', *Times Educational Supplement*, Curriculum Special, 29 June.

Burn, J. and Hart, C. (1988) *The Crisis in Religious Education*, London: Educational Research Trust.

Chidester, D. (1996) *Savage Systems: Colonialism and Comparative Religion in Southern Africa*, Charlottesville VA: University Press of Virginia.

Christian Aid (2000) *An RE Curriculum for Global Citizenship*, London: Christian Aid in association with the Association of Religious Education Inspectors, Advisers and Consultants, CAFOD, the ClearVison Trust, the Development Education Association and the Department for International Development.

Cole, W. O. (1972) *Religion in the Multifaith School*, 1st edn, Leeds: Yorkshire Committee for Community Relations.

Connolly, C. (1992) 'Religious schools: refuge or redoubt', in M. Leicester and M. Taylor (eds) *Ethics, Ethnicity and Education*, London: Kogan Page, 137–45.

Cox, Edwin (1966) *Changing Aims in Religious Education*, London: Routledge.

Crick, B. (1969) *The Teaching of Politics*, Harmondsworth: Penguin.

—— (2000) 'Introduction to the new curriculum', in D. Lawton, J. Cairns and R. Gardner (eds) *Education for Citizenship*, London: Continuum, 3–8.

Crick, B. and Porter, A. (eds) (1978) *Political Education and Political Literacy*, London: Longman.

DfEE/QCA (1999a) *The National Curriculum for England: Citizenship*, London: Department for Education and Employment and Qualifications and Curriculum Authority.

—— (1999b) *The National Curriculum for England: Non-statutory Frameworks for Personal, Social and Health Education and Citizenship at Key Stages 1 and 2; Personal, Social and Health Education at Key Stages 3 and 4*, London: Department for Education and Employment and Qualifications and Curriculum Authority.

DfEE (2000) *Developing a Global Dimension in the School Curriculum*, London: Department for Education and Employment in collaboration with Department for International Development, Qualifications and Curriculum Authority, Development Education Association and the Central Bureau.

Downey, M. and Kelly, A. V. (1978) *Moral Education: Theory and Practice*, London: Harper & Row.

Edwards, S. (1999) 'RE and Emancipation: A Critical Approach to Cultural Development in the Comprehensive School', unpublished M.A. dissertation, Coventry: Institute of Education, University of Warwick.

Felderhof, M. (2000) 'Religious education and human rights', in N. Holm (ed.) *Islam and Christianity in School Religious Education*, Åbo (Finland): Åbo Akademi University, 21–39.

Fitzgerald, T. (1990) 'Hinduism and the "world religion" fallacy', *Religion*, 20, 101–18.

Gay, J. (2001) 'The future of religious education', letter in *The Church Times*, 16 February.

Gearon, L. (2002) 'Religious education and human rights: some postcolonial perspectives', *British Journal of Religious Education*, 24 (2), 140–51.

Geaves, R. (1998) 'The borders between religions: a challenge to the world religions approach to religious education', *British Journal of Religious Education*, 21 (1), 20–31.

Grimmitt, M. H. (1987) *Religious Education and Human Development: The Relationship between Studying Religions and Personal, Social and Moral Education*, Great Wakering: McCrimmon.

—— (2000) 'Constructivist pedagogies of religious education project: re-thinking knowledge, teaching and learning in religious education', in M. H. Grimmitt (ed.) *Pedagogies of Religious Education: Case Studies in the Research and Development of Good Pedagogic Practice in RE*, Great Wakering: McCrimmon, 207–27.

Hackett, R. (ed.) (2000) *Book of Abstracts: Eighteenth Quinquennial World Congress of the International Association for the History of Religions*, Durban: IAHR.

Hargreaves, D. H. (1986) 'Curriculum for the future', in G. Leonard and J. Yates (eds) *Faith for the Future*, London: National Society and Church House Publishing, 53–60.

—— (1994) *The Mosaic of Learning: Schools and Teachers for the Next Century*, Demos Paper 8, London: Demos.

Hawke, R. A. (1982) 'Moral education in a multi-religious society', in R. Jackson (ed.) *Approaching World Religions*, London: John Murray, 163–73.

Heater, D. (1990) *Citizenship: The Civic Ideal in World History, Politics and Education*, London: Longman.

Hirst, P. (1974) *Moral Education in a Secular Society*, London: Hodder & Stoughton.

Hookway, S. (2002) 'Mirrors, windows, conversation: RE for the millennial generation', *British Journal of Religious Education*, 24 (2), 99–110.

Hull, J. M. (1991) *Mish Mash: Religious Education in Multi-cultural Britain: A Study in Metaphor*, Birmingham Papers in Religious Education, Derby: Christian Education Movement.

—— (1996) 'A gift to the child: a new pedagogy for teaching religion to young children', *Religious Education*, 91 (2), 172–88.

Humanist Philosophers' Group (2001) *Religious Schools: The Case Against*, London: British Humanist Association.

ICCS (2001) *Intereuropean Commission on Church and School Newsletter* 24, Münster: ICCS, 2–3.

ICE (1954) *Religious Education in Schools:The Report of an Inquiry made by the Research Committee of the Institute of Christian Education into the working of the 1944 Education Act*, London: National Society and SPCK.

Ipgrave, J. (1999) 'Issues in the delivery of religious education to Muslim pupils: perspectives from the classroom', *British Journal of Religious Education*, 21 (3), 147–58.

—— (2001) *Pupil-to-pupil Dialogue in the Classroom as a Tool for Religious Education*, Warwick Religions and Education Research Unit, Working Paper 2, Coventry: Institute of Education, University of Warwick.

Jackson, Robert (1987) 'Changing conceptions of Hinduism in timetabled religion', in R. Burghart (ed.) *Hinduism in Great Britain: Religion in an Alien Cultural Milieu*, London: Tavistock, 201–23.

—— (1992) 'The misrepresentation of religious education', in M. Leicester and M. Taylor (eds) *Ethics, Ethnicity and Education*, London: Kogan Page, 100–13.

—— (1996) 'The construction of "Hinduism" and its impact on religious education in England and Wales', *Panorama: International Journal of Comparative Religious Education and Values*, 8 (1), 86–104.

—— (1997) *Religious Education: An Interpretive Approach*, London: Hodder & Stoughton.

—— (2000a) 'Law, politics and religious education in England and Wales: some history, some stories and some observations', in M. Leicester, C. Modgil and S. Modgil (eds) *Spiritual and Religious Education*, London: Routledge. (*Education, Culture and Values* 5, 86–99.)

—— (2000b) 'The Warwick Religious Education Project: the interpretive approach to religious education', in M. H. Grimmitt (ed.) *Pedagogies of Religious Education: Case Studies in the Research and Development of Good Pedagogic Practice in RE*, Great Wakering: McCrimmon, 130–52.

—— (2001a) 'Reflections on research in religious education', in T. Dodd (ed.) *Aspects of Education: Developments in Religious Education*, Hull: Studies in Education Ltd, University of Hull, 76–103.

—— (2001b) 'Creative pedagoy in religious education: case studies in interpretation', in H-G. Heimbrock, P. Schreiner and C. Sheilke (eds) *Towards Religious Competence: Diversity as a Challenge for Education in Europe*, Hamburg: Lit Verlag, 34–52.

Jackson, R. and Nesbitt, E. M. (1993) *Hindu Children in Britain*, Stoke on Trent: Trentham.

Jacobson, J. (1998) *Islam in Transition: Religion and Identity among British Pakistani Youth*, London: Routledge.

Kassam, N. (ed.) (1997) *Telling it like it is: Young Asian Women Talk*, London: Livewire.

King, R. (1999) *Orientalism and Religion: Postcolonial Theory, India and 'the Mystic East'*, London: Routledge.

Kymlicka, W. (1999) 'Education for citizenship', in J. M. Halstead and T. H. McLaughlin (eds) *Education in Morality*, London: Routledge.

Lister, R. (1997) 'Citizenship: towards a feminist synthesis', *Feminist Review*, 57, 28–48.

Loukes, H. (1973) *Teenage Morality*, London: SCM Press.

McPhail, P., Ungoed-Thomas, J. and Chapman, H. (1972) *Moral Education in the Secondary School*, London: Methuen.

Marshall, P. J. (ed.) (1970) *The British Discovery of Hinduism in the Eighteenth Century*, Cambridge: Cambridge University Press.

Marshall, T. H. (1950) *Citizenship and Social Class*, Cambridge: Cambridge University Press.

Mukta, P. (1997) '"New Hinduism": teaching intolerance, practising aggression', *Resource*, 20 (1), 9–14.

NCC (1990) *Education for Citizenship*, Curriculum Guidance 8, York: National Curriculum Council.

Nesbitt, E. M. (1990a) 'Pitfalls in religious taxonomy: Hindus, Sikhs, Ravidasis and Valmikis', *Religion Today*, 6 (1), 9–12.

—— (1990b) 'Religion and identity: the Valmiki community in Coventry', *New Community*, 16 (2), 261–74.

—— (1998a) 'British, Asian and Hindu identity: self-narration and the ethnographic interview', *Journal of Beliefs and Values*, 19 (2), 189–200.

—— (1998b) 'Bridging the gap between young people's experience of their religious traditions at home and school', *British Journal of Religious Education*, 20 (2), 102–12.

—— (2000) *The Religious Lives of Sikh Children: A Coventry Based Study*, Monograph Series, Leeds: University of Leeds, Community Religions Project.

Oberoi, H. (1994) *The Construction of Religious Boundaries: Culture, Identity and Diversity in the Sikh Tradition*, Delhi: Oxford University Press.

Ouseley, H. (ed.) (2001) *Community Pride not Prejudice: Making Diversity Work in Bradford*, Bradford: Bradford Vision.

Oxfam (no date) *Curriculum for Global Citizenship*, Oxford: Oxfam.

Pocock, Catherine (2000) *An Investigation into the Contribution of RE to Citizenship and Preparation for Adult Life*, Oxford, Farmington Institute. Online. Available HTTP: <http://www.farmington.ac.uk/> (accessed 5 July 2001).

Prinja, N. K. (1996) *Explaining Hindu Dharma: A Guide For Teachers*, Norwich: Religious and Moral Education Press.

Prinja, N. K., Tatwawadi, S. R., Satyanarayana, M. C. and Dhanda, D. V. (1998) 'New Hinduism as seen by British Hindus', *Resource*, 20 (3), 11–14.

QCA (1998) *Education for Citizenship and the Teaching of Democracy in Schools*, Final Report of the Advisory Group on Citizenship, London: Qualifications and Curriculum Authority.

Runnymede (2000) *The Report of The Commission on the Future of Multi-ethnic Britain*, London: Runnymede Trust.

Said, E. (1978) *Orientalism*, London: Routledge.

SCAA (1994) *Model Syllabuses for Religious Education: Faith Communities' Working Group Reports*, London: School Curriculum and Assessment Authority.

Schools Council (1971) *Religious Education in Secondary Schools*, Schools Council Working Paper 36, London: Evans and Methuen.

Skeie, G. (1995) 'Plurality and pluralism: a challenge for religious education', *British Journal of Religious Education*, 17 (2), 84–91.

Smart, N. (1967) 'A new look at religious studies: the Lancaster idea', *Learning for Living*, 7 (1), 27–9.

—— (1968) *Secular Education and the Logic of Religion*, London: Faber.

Smith, B. K. (1996) 'Re-envisioning Hinduism and evaluating the Hindutva Movement', *Religion*, 26, 119–28.

Smith, W. C. (1978) *The Meaning and End of Religion*, London: SPCK.

Tames, R. (1982) 'Islam and political education', in R. Jackson (ed.) *Approaching World Religions*, London: John Murray, 174–81.

Tomlinson, S. and Craft, M. (eds) (1995) *Ethnic Relations and Schooling: Policy and Practice in the 1990s*, London: Athlone Press.

Troyna, B. (1983) 'Multiracial education: just another brick in the wall?' *New Community*, 10, 424–8.

Wilson, J., Williams, N. and Sugarman, B. (1967) *Introduction to Moral Education*, Harmondsworth: Penguin.

Wright, A. (1993) *Religious Education in the Secondary School: Prospects for Religious Literacy*, London: David Fulton.

—— (1998) *Spiritual Pedagogy: A Survey, Critique and Reconstruction of Contemporary Spiritual Education in England and Wales*, Abingdon: Culham College Institute.

—— (2001) 'Religious literacy and democratic citizenship', in L. J. Francis, J. Astley and M. Robbins (eds) *The Fourth R for the Third Millennium: Education in Religion and Values for a Global Future*, Dublin: Lindisfarne 201–19.

Østberg, Sissel (1999) 'Pakistani Children in Oslo: Islamic Nurture in a Secular Setting', unpublished Ph.D. thesis, Coventry: Institute of Education, University of Warwick..

—— (2000a) 'Punjabi, Pakistani, Muslim and Norwegian? Self-perceptions and social boundaries among Pakistani children in Oslo', *International Journal of Punjab Studies*, 7 (1), 133–59.

—— (2000b) 'Islamic nurture and identity management', *British Journal of Religious Education*, 22 (2), 91–103.

Chapter 5

Cultural diversity and common citizenship

Reflections on ethnicity, religion, nationhood and citizenship among Pakistani young people in Europe

Sissel Østberg

Synopsis   This chapter discusses how Muslim children's and young people's reflections on issues such as ethnicity, religion and nationhood can contribute to a sound and grounded discussion of citizenship education. The empirical data are drawn from research among Pakistani Muslim children and young people in Norway and Britain. Based on the findings from two research projects, the chapter argues for a 'transcultural' approach to citizenship which combines local belonging, cultural diversity and global visions. Norwegian or British citizenship does not imply a unitary culture or a multiculturalism formed by unitary and closed cultural 'systems'. The concept of transcultural citizenship expresses the combination of cosmopolitanism and localism found among young Muslims in Europe today. The chapter also touches upon how the terror attacks in New York and Washington DC on 11 September 2001 and the following war against terrorism may influence the lives of young Muslims in Europe in a direction away from transculturalism. At the end of the chapter the concept of transcultural citizenship is linked with the idea of intercultural learning. Some examples will show how religious education and citizenship education may contribute to developing unity based on a positive stance towards diversity.

In European societies generally and in the educational sector specifically there seems to be increased interest in the concept of citizenship.[1] The Warwick symposium (3–5 September 2001) was an expression of the same interest, with a special focus on religious education and citizenship. Before we go deeper into a specific religious education discussion, there is a need to consider the following questions. Why has this discourse on citizenship emerged at the beginning of the twenty-first century? What are the possible political agendas behind this focus? How can empirical data on children's and young people's reflections on these issues inform us and contribute to a sound and grounded discussion?

This chapter will discuss these questions with reference to empirical data from research among Pakistani Muslim children and young people in Norway and Britain. The emphasis of the chapter will be on the last question above, but as an introduction – and as a framework for the discussion – some reflections on possible political agendas will also be introduced.

The chapter was originally written before the terror attacks in New York and Washington on 11 September. These tragic events and the following reactions, discussions and warfare have made the topic of the chapter more relevant than originally wished for. Ways in which terrorism and the war against terrorism might influence the lives of young Muslims in Europe and effect the idea of transcultural citizenship will be discussed under the heading 'Processes of stereotyping, exclusion and animosity'.

Recent discourse on citizenship may have emerged as a response to a perceived cultural fragmentation resulting from pluralism and lack of shared values in society. In the Norwegian context it is possible to analyse the primary school curriculum reform of 1997 as an effort to establish a common cultural framework for all Norwegian pupils regardless of cultural background (cf. Skeie above, Chapter 3). Within this discourse, the emphasis on a common cultural heritage and common citizenship is supposed to transcend cultural diversity. This conceptualization of citizenship links it up with national citizenship. 'We are all Norwegians.' 'We are all British.' This understanding is often based on two assumptions: first that citizenship means formal citizenship, and secondly that common formal citizenship implies common cultural values, i.e. a culturally homogeneous nation. In this respect, Norway is more in line with Britain and Germany, but contrasts with France, in the way of conceptualizing citizenship or civic identity. As Jessica Jacobson states: 'throughout modern British history the notion of civic identity has not acted as a profoundly significant ideal in the way that it has, most obviously, in France' (Jacobson 1996: 11).

An on-going Norwegian debate precipitated by a proposed new law on dual citizenship is also relevant in this context (NOU 2000: 32).[2] In contrast to many countries (which practise territorial citizenship),[3] Norwegian citizenship is given to children whose mother or father is a Norwegian citizen. Dual citizenship has until now not been accepted. The majority of the members of the committee argue for a change in this rule, with only one member arguing for a continuation of the present system (NOU 2000: 32). The argument from the majority of the members is that practical problems (especially linked with such issues as military service and diplomatic assistance abroad) can be overcome. The main argument both from majority and minority members of the committee hinges on the question of loyalty. The minority position argues that it is not possible to be loyal to two national states at the same time. Citizenship, in other words, is interpreted as an expression of national identity. The majority position argues that loyalty is not so much informed by formal citizenship as by informal factors such as settlement, job situation, social and cultural attachments. This argument is in accordance with the empirical data presented in this chapter.[4]

Another political factor behind the present focus on citizenship may be a renewed emphasis on human rights in the political debate. Citizenship is, in this context, linked with globalization and universal values encompassing the diversity of local cultural practices. Liberal values and cosmopolitanism are at the centre of this interpretation of citizenship. 'The world belongs to us.' Both approaches to citizenship – the nationally oriented and the liberal cosmopolitan – are normative; that is, they are expressions of political and/or educational values. Before linking the question of citizenship up with normative values, anti-racism, etc., however, there is a need to reflect on whether the discourse of citizenship includes ethnic and cultural diversity.

This chapter will argue for an approach to citizenship which combines local (including national) belonging (attachment to places), cultural diversity and global visions (of a political and/or religious character). This will be termed *transcultural citizenship* (cf. Welsch in Featherstone and Lash 1999: 194–213). This term is, of course, linked with other similar terms like multi-culturalism and interculturalism. The prefix 'trans-' is chosen to underline the transitional movements between different cultural entities and to avoid the notion of citizenship values composed of distinct and closed 'cultures'. This discussion will be taken up at the end of the chapter.

The Norwegian research shows that the reflections and experiences of Pakistani children and young people in Norway represent transcultural citizenship. The findings are supported by Jacobson's research among young British Pakistanis. Although this chapter is based on research among minority groups, the findings may be representative of the attitudes and lifestyles of broader groups of young people in Europe today. Trans-culturality is an experience shared by both majority and minority young people in most of Europe. More research is needed, however, within this field, especially following the events of 11 September 2001. At the end of the chapter the idea of transcultural citizenship will be linked with the concept of 'intercultural learning' as used by Hans-Georg Ziebertz (Ziebertz 2001) and also with other related educational concepts.

The following discussion is based on two studies from Norway and one from Britain. The studies from Norway include fieldwork among Pakistani children and their families in 1994–95 (Østberg 1999) and a follow-up study of the same children and young people in 1999–2001. The second study is funded by the Norwegian Research Council and will be completed in July 2002. Both periods of fieldwork were conducted in Oslo, but a field visit was also undertaken in Pakistan. The core group studied consists of fourteen children and young people in five different families. In 1999–2000 they were all in the age group 14–22, five years older than during the first study. Through visits to their homes, schools, mosques, leisure activities and families in Pakistan, a much larger number of Pakistanis have been observed and interviewed throughout these years (Østberg 1999, 2000a, b).

The British study was conducted by Jessica Jacobson as a qualitative field-work study within a Pakistani community in London (Waltham Forest) at the beginning of the 1990s (Jacobson 1998). Her core group of interviewees was made up of thirty-three second-generation British Pakistanis aged 17–27. Comparisons between the studies will be undertaken where relevant. Some references will also be made to a Norwegian study of Muslim young women in France which focuses on their 'return to Islam' (Jacobsen 1999). The studies are not concerned with citizenship specifically, but issues such as nationhood, national identity and citizenship are part of the analysis of ethnic and religious identities. As ethnographic research, the studies contribute to a deeper understanding of social boundaries and allegiances as experienced and expressed by the young people themselves. The structure of the chapter aims at representing the mode of reflection among the children and young people by starting with the most concrete and experience-near approach to the topic, that is, their affiliation to local places and personal networks. The chapter then goes on to discuss religious space and boundaries and the question of citizenship.

Local places

The Norwegian-Pakistani[5] children were strongly attached to their local communities, whether they were parts of central Oslo or the suburbs. Many of them preferred to live in rather small flats, having to share rooms with brothers or sisters rather then moving to new locations. If they moved, it was mostly within the same area, and family members or friends frequently lived in the neighbourhood. The settlement pattern from the earliest years of immigration (the early 1970s) to the 1990s was a socially upward move from the central part of town ('little Pakistan') to a suburb. When I returned to the families after five years, some of them had moved even farther. They had bought their own detached or semi-detached houses some miles out of town. The young people did not move out of their parental home, and with maybe four young people above the age of 18 there was a need for more space. The young people themselves complained, however. They missed their childhood place, their old friends and the intensity of life in the city.

In 1995 Rashid (then 14), in explaining why he managed so well in contrast to other boys who had got involved with gangs said:

> But me – I have lived here in this flat. I know what kind of friends to have, not to participate in gangs and that sort of thing. We have friends from before . . . that's the point. We are born here . . . I speak Norwegian and have friends from childhood. I don't need to join a gang to get friends. That's for those coming from abroad.

Five years later Rashid (now 19 and living out of town) says:

> Earlier, having friends meant you could play football in the open fields in the neighbourhood. Now I don't have the same friends because we no longer play football in the open fields. Miss it terribly, though! All the boys agree we miss it. The friends now are more like school friends.

Jamshed (aged 15), who had moved out of town, said: 'Living in the town, every day some friends popped in. Here it is very quiet.'

'Home' for Norwegian-Pakistani young people was not Norway or Oslo but Furuseth, Tøyen or Lambertseter, that is, specific parts of Oslo. In this respect they are probably not very different from most children or young people.[6] They differed, however, from some of their friends in the way that they also felt an affiliation to local places in Pakistan. Their attachment to Pakistan was not to the country as such, but to villages in Kharian or to areas of Rawalpindi, Lahore or Karachi. They talked about 'our village' or 'the village where my parents grew up'. At least after some weeks of holiday they felt at home there. Among Norwegian-Pakistanis it is also common to have invested in a house or property in their 'home village'.

The distinction between an urban and a rural background was empha-sized, especially for those who felt Karachi or Lahore to be their Pakistani locality. This attachment to local places is, of course, connected with attach-ment to people and social classes. The ones with an urban background distanced themselves from the rural Punjabi majority among Pakistanis in Norway. In a discussion on a televisioin programme focusing on arranged marriages and female oppression in rural Pakistan, Yasmin (19), whose family had an urban background, said:

> It seems as if nobody is happy in Pakistan, you know! OK, in Pakistan there are Punjab and Gujrat [rural districts], but there are Karachi, Islamabad and Lahore too. In all the big cities there is really too much freedom, I think. Parents don't choose for them any more, they choose for themselves. That's the guy I want to marry. OK, that's fine.

The distinction between urban and rural background was also very promi-nent for the British Pakistanis in Jacobson's study, even more important than the region of origin. One of her interviewees said:

> You have two types of Pakistanis. There's one which are from the town area, and there's one from the villages. . . . And I'm from the town area, and I try to mix with the town people. Because when it comes to mixing with the villagers – I suppose I don't mind, but I try not to.
>
> (Jacobson 1999: 86)

The local place is a social more than a geographic place.

Childhood, youth and national identity

As the Norwegian anthropologist Marianne Gullestad writes, national identity is linked with childhood experiences, that is, to the nooks and crannies of childhood localities (Gullestad 1999). The paragraph above on local places confirms this. When comparing Norway and Pakistan, the children and young people all regard Norway as 'their country'. They were born here and they do not know of any other homeland. Pakistan is the homeland of their parents, and an ideal country for holidays. For Rashid (19) a move to Pakistan was not an alternative.

'You are going to stay on in Norway?'

'By all means!'

He has no intention of settling in Pakistan because things would be so difficult. 'All these small things, you know, like you are not supposed to ask for the price if you want to buy something . . .'

This is very much in accordance with the findings from London. Jacobson writes: 'About half of the respondents, when asked if they would like to live in Pakistan, said that they would miss the way of life and general social environment which they know in Britain, and/or that they would feel somewhat alien among Pakistanis in Pakistan (Jacobson 1998: 69). One of her female respondents expressed it this way: 'When I go to Pakistan – I'm lost. I don't fit in. I can enjoy it for a while, but I am different from them at the end of the day. I'm a lot different from them.'

As both children and young people the Norwegian-Pakistanis' attitude to Pakistan was characterized by ambivalence. On the one hand, it was the homeland of their parents and their extended family, a source of their cultural and religious identity and a place where they enjoyed their relative richness and high status as European relatives. On the other, it was for them a country of corruption, dirt, poverty and, for some, deviation from *shari'a*. This was mostly true of the strict, normative Muslims who support the opposition party Jamaat-i-Islami in Pakistan and who regard Saudi Arabia as an ideal society.

However, as a medical student in Poland, Yasmin (19) has acquired a new national identity by representing Norway abroad. The Norwegian students in Poland are different from her classmates at home. They all share an interest in reading and studying. 'They are like me,' she says. 'In Poland all of us are Norwegian students.' However, in Poland she shares a flat with three Indian students, two Muslims and one Hindu and, as an example of the new companionship with her fellow Norwegian friends, she told of how they all dressed up in Pakistani dress at a celebration in Poland! A discussion of citizenship in a European context has to take this type of cultural diversity and transculturality into consideration. As expressed by Liisa Malkki, 'To plot only "places of birth" and degrees of nativeness is to blind oneself to the multiplicity of attachments that people form to places through living in, remembering, and imagining them' (Malkki 1992: 38). This point will be considered further in connection with the discussion of intercultural learning at the end of the chapter.

Local places and personal global networks

Pakistani young people in Norway and Britain live in a trans-territorial world, built up by local and global personal networks of family relations, ethnicity and religions. Their feeling of belonging to Norway or to Britain is not primarily to the respective countries as national states or territories, but to the places where they were born and the localities where they grew up. As discussed above, there is not necessarily a contradiction here. As Marianne Gullestad says, national identity has to do with childhood experiences (Gullestad 1999).

In a similar way, the Norwegian-Pakistani children and young people have no strong affinity to Pakistan as a state, only to the local community where their family lives, either in an urban or a rural region (cf. Jacobson 1998). Their extended family, however, may also be spread around the world: in the Middle East, England or the United States. In addition to this border-crossing personal network, they all belong to a global Islamic *ummah*, transcending time and national borders (see below). Their ethnic and religious identities should not be analysed within a transnational paradigm (Norway–Pakistan), but within a paradigm combining local belonging, being in a minority position and being part of global networks. This understanding has implications for an understanding of citizenship as well – and for religious education – and this will be discussed in the final section.

Religious space and boundaries

Growing up as a Muslim in Norway or in Britain links children and young people with holy places in the Islamic world, first of all with Mecca through daily prayers and through *umrah* or *Hajj* (pilgrimages). Saima, aged 14, wears the *hijab* ('scarf') because she feels this is to take religion seriously. Her great experience was a visit to Mecca (*umrah*). She enjoyed the 'smell', the people, the good feeling of being one of them. 'You feel you are not the only one. Everyone is like you, they are all with you. Now I know it is not only a fantasy. Thinking about it makes me happy!' Religiosity for Saima is linked with Mecca (and Saudi Arabia), not with Pakistan.

Prayer itself creates a religious space in the everyday world. Through washing (*wudu'*), the prayer carpet, the direction of the Kab'ah (*qibla*) in Mecca and the bodily movements (*rak'at*) a space is established, connecting the individual with all other Muslims in the world today and backwards in time to holy events and places. Whether Pakistani young people in Norway or Britain pray regularly or not, this religious space is there as part of their orientation in the world. By crossing the border from childhood to adolescence, being a Muslim is increasingly experienced as a boundary in their lives. In a discussion with Rashid (aged 19) about his relationship with Norwegian girls and Pakistani girls, he says that he finds it easy to talk to Norwegian girls, or to 'Pakistani girls who have turned Norwegian', but rather problematic to talk to Pakistani girls. When talking to them, he is afraid of saying something wrong, using wrong or 'bad' words in Urdu, or inappropriate slang expressions. When I asked him if he doesn't find Norwegian girls too free, he answered: 'Not really. The only thing distinguishing me from them, from the point of view of the Norwegian girls, the only thing is when we come to religion.'

The conclusion of Jacobson's study is that religious boundaries are clear-cut and pervasive, whereas ethnic boundaries are more permeable (Jacobson 1999: 127).

In this perspective, Islam may be regarded as both a religious and a social boundary. As a social boundary it seems to gain importance the older the children get. All the Norwegian-Pakistani young people in my study said they had more Norwegian friends as small children. To have friends as children meant to play football in the open fields in the neighbourhood. Nasir (aged 18) said:

> Five years back I had more Norwegian friends. They are still my friends. Those who live in the neighbourhood play in the same football club or are in the same class and that sort of thing. Those I associate with, however, those I spend my leisure time with, they are new friends . . . Pakistanis.

Like most young Pakistanis, Nasir does not join his Norwegian friends in the evening or at the weekends because they drink alcohol and stay out very late.

In lower secondary school Bushra had many Norwegian girlfriends. Her best friend at that time was Norwegian. At the age of 17, she says, 'Now we haven't the same interests and that sort of thing . . . They go to parties and so on.' Now Bushra meets her Norwegian friends at school and her new Pakistani girlfriends in their homes. Especially in the holidays they meet for girl parties, *mehndi* parties (before weddings) or birthdays. She spends most evenings at home watching Pakistani television dramas (soaps) with her mother and other family members.

Islam as a religious boundary should not be regarded only as a boundary putting restrictions on young Muslims in Europe, but is by many 'chosen' as a new strategy in their identity formation. As one of Christine Jacobsen's French Muslim girls of Arabic origin says, 'The difference between our parents and ourselves is that they have "inherited" Islam, whereas we have returned to Islam through a spiritual process' (*démarche*; Jacobsen 1999: 81, my translation from Norwegian). According to Jacobsen's study, the Islamization[7] among second-generation women of Maghrebian origin in France may be understood as 'a statement about identity' (Jacobsen 1999: 7). This 'return to Islam' is, however, just one among many 'statements about identity'.

A deliberate 'return to Islam' was also noticeable among some of my informants. When asked what was the biggest change in her life from when she was 9 till she was 14, Saima said, 'Now I wear *hijab* and dig techno.' Moreover, she insists that wearing *hijab* is voluntary.

> You may choose for yourself. Either you follow the religion fully or you do it just a little bit. It is different from one girl to another how she thinks about Islam, whether it is important or just something at the side.

For all girls, whether they were wearing *hijab* or not, Islam as a religious and social boundary was linked with gender identity. This topic cannot be fully developed here, but should be kept in mind as an important element in the identity formation of young Muslims in Europe, both male and female.

Transcultural citizenship

All respondents in Jessica Jacobson's study were British citizens. In answering questions about their own Britishness, most of them referred to the fact that they had British citizenship or 'nationality' (Jacobson 1998: 67). Jacobson concludes by stating: 'In most of the cases, however, the young people spoke in such a way as to suggest that they believe citizenship to entail a kind of belonging to British society that is official but not truly meaningful' (Jacobson 1998: 67). As one of them said:

> It just – doesn't ring true, when, you know, nationality – I am British because I'm born here, but it just doesn't mean anything, to say I'm British – it doesn't conjure up an image, it doesn't hit me *here* [she puts her hand to her heart] or anywhere.

Of the Norwegian-Pakistani young people in my study, most of them are Norwegian citizens because their parents have become Norwegian citizens. Those who are not (because their parents are still Pakistani citizens) proclaimed that they would become Norwegian citizens as soon as they reached the age of 18. 'After all, we were born here. This is our country,' was a common statement. Even more common was the pragmatic argument that to be a Norwegian citizen makes it easy to travel in Europe. 'You don't need a visa.'

However, the concept of citizenship was not an experience-near concept to Norwegian-Pakistani young people (and certainly not to children). When I asked Khalid (aged 18) what citizenship he had, he first said: 'Don't know.' Then he added: 'I possess a Norwegian passport, so I guess I am a Norwegian citizen . . . I am definitely not a Pakistani citizen!' Their Norwegian citizenship was partly a formality that had to do with passports, partly it was something they took for granted, like citizenship as the formality necessary for the right to vote in parliamentary elections (*Stortingsvalg*). It seemed to be a formal boundary, easy to refer to but not really meaningful.

There was a marked contrast between the enthusiasm they showed in talking about their local places, their friends and families and their Islamic belief and the way they talked about citizenship. Even for young people, citizenship seemed to be an abstract concept, not relevant to their daily life. Interestingly enough, one of the few fathers who insisted on keeping his Pakistani citizenship (against all gentle advice from Pakistani friends and his own children), argued that for him it was a matter of identity. 'I have not chosen to be a Pakistani. I am born one.' Culturally he characterized himself as 'increasingly Norwegian' and his lifestyle confirmed that. He said that if the new law permitting dual citizenship went through Parliament, he would be the first to apply!

The lack of content of and enthusiasm for the concept of citizenship among young Pakistanis in Europe may be a worrying signal – a sign of a lack of recognition of the cultural values and identities represented by these young people. If they feel that the concept of citizenship does not contain their values and identities, they will, of course, feel detached from that concept. However, they cannot be characterized as 'homeless' in the sense of being without attachment to people and places and without feelings of loyalties. The next section will introduce and discuss the vulnerability of transcultural citizenship. What social processes may represent a contradiction with the present experiences of young Muslim people? In what ways might Pakistani young people and other Muslims in Europe change their current attachments and loyalties? Is the concept of transcultural citizenship a utopian idea and should more emphasis be put on perceptions of exclusion as part of the identity process?

Processes of stereotyping, exclusion and animosity

The discussion above has underlined the plural, situated identities of Pakistani young people in Norway and in Britain, their move between and across a diverse set of cultural contexts, territories and global networks. However, this emphasis on flexibility and fluidity should not mislead us into assuming that their lives are easy and without edges or boundaries. Some of these can be traced back to social processes within Pakistani Muslim communities in Europe, and some are imposed upon young Muslims by external structures or events – by the majority discourse. As mentioned above, the Pakistani families in my study from Oslo were strongly influenced by television programmes, for example. Yasmin and others felt they had to respond to the biased pictures of arranged marriages presented in the media (see above). Their willingness to participate in the research project was often based on a wish to contribute to a more varied picture of Islam and Pakistani culture than the stereotypes presented in the media and sometimes also in school. Not many incidents of direct racism were reported, but the fight against stereotyping (particularly concerning Islam and gender issues) was part of their everyday life.

Animosity towards Islam has for a long time been a dominant majority discourse in the Western world (Eriksen 1995). Against this background it is not difficult to understand the tendency among Muslims to establish a common front when such stereotyping intensifies and expresses itself publicly, for instance in connection with the Rushdie affair or antagonism to the establishment of a private Muslim school in Norway.

This process of stereotyping imposed upon Muslims from 'the outside' is a type of exclusion process that contributes to the identity formation of young people. An 'us' identity as Pakistanis in contrast to 'them' (majority Norwegians) is strengthened. In a moderate sense, this aspect of the identity process does not imply a threat to common citizenship values in the sense of transcultural citizenship. However, in a time of increased tension it may turn into the dominant discourse among Muslims. In such situations internal diversities will be under-communicated and the strongest voices among the Muslims may take the lead. The post-11 September 2001 situation has taken us to this point. The spontaneous joint reaction against terrorism united people across religious and ethnic boundaries. It was a good soil for the nurturing of citizenship values. Whether it will remain so depends on the ability of the majority cultures in the Western world to accept the multi-voicedness of its citizens – in other words, accepting transculturalism as part of the concept of citizenship. The war against terrorism in the form of bombing Afghanistan or stigmatizing innocent Muslims may, however, have the opposite effect. The animosity towards America and the rest of the West may increase as an answer to Western animosity towards Islam.

Of the Pakistani Muslim young people in my study, only a few have expressed anti-American or anti-Western attitudes. On the contrary, most of them identified with the West, with a multi-ethnic and multicultural West. Since 11 September 2001 I have been in touch with only some of my informants. They are all suffering from what they experience as increased scepticism towards Muslims, but their everyday life goes on as usual, that is, they are mostly concerned about such matters as schooling, marriage and their relationship to their parents. For the rest of the chapter I will continue the discussion based on the findings from the studies in Norway and Britain in the 1990s.

Transcultural citizenship, intercultural learning and religious education

Pakistani young people as presented in these studies may partly be characterized as cosmopolitan, partly as locals. They are locals in the sense that they are not 'footloose'. They feel at home in a local community (or in more local communities) and they feel 'at home' in an Islamic world. They may, however, be termed cosmopolitan in the sense that their everyday life is a mixture of cultural elements, of personal global networks and a flow of meanings. Today's cosmopolitanism does not necessarily imply that there is one world culture – or if there is, 'It [the world culture] is marked by an organization of diversity rather than by a replication of uniformity' (Hannerz 1994: 237). The 'test' of today's global world, being in Muslim, Hindu or secular societies, is whether we will manage to preserve and develop such cultural diversity.

Likewise, citizenship today should be marked by an organization of diversity. Norwegian or British citizenship does not imply a unitary culture or a multiculturalism formed by unitary and closed cultural 'systems'. On the contrary, as is evident in the attitudes of Pakistani young people in Norway and Britain, 'today's cosmopolitans and locals have a common interest in the survival of cultural diversity' (Hannerz 1994: 249). The young people want to be Norwegian *and* Pakistani, Asian *and* British, Muslims *and* cosmopolitan. The concept of transcultural citizenship may express these shared interests of cosmopolitans and locals.

Another matter is whether these identities – and the switching between them – are understood and recognized by the majority populations in Europe. In the introduction to this chapter the Norwegian discourse was characterized by a combination of monocultural nationalism (we are all Norwegians) and universalist cosmopolitanism (we all share the same ideas of freedom, individualism, etc.). The political and social consequence of both discourses is a tendency to inclusion in the form of assimilation. Equality seems in a Norwegian dominant discourse to imply 'sameness'. 'If you are different, we will make you like us.' A counter-strategy to this assimilation policy (open or hidden) may be an increased marking of boundaries from the side of the minorities. As was discussed in the previous section, the Western reaction to the terror attacks on the United States may have such an effect. If the rhetoric emphasizing unity against terrorism does not manage to include cultural and religious diversity within it, the result may the opposite of what is intended. If this chapter has promoted the concept of transculturalism to describe the identity formation of young Muslims in Europe, we have also been reminded of how central perceptions of exclusion are to identity formation. The identity formation of young Muslims in Europe is marked not only by a cultural flow of diversity but by a discovery of boundaries sometimes externally imposed and sometimes 'chosen'.

I will now move from a descriptive and analytical approach in order to introduce a normative position by indicating some values implicit in the discourse of transcultural citizenship. Transcultural citizenship is characterized by a positive stance towards diversity itself and 'a willingness to engage with the Other' (cf. Hannerz's statement on today's cosmopolitanism).

Transcultural citizenship in this sense transcends the question of formal citizenship by focusing on the rights and obligations of all citizens living in a common and specific community. Citizenship presupposes some sort of unity, and this unity is not given but has to be developed and nurtured. Unity is not achieved by simply living together nor does it necessarily imply the sharing of all cultural and religious values. An explicit recognition of diversity is a condition for the development of shared citizenship values in a multicultural society. Such recognition is an acknowledgement of the individual and, in some cases, of the group to which the individual feels attached (Taylor 1994). The development of citizenship and the ability to act upon such values presupposes a feeling much stronger than acceptance; it presupposes a feeling of belonging. Engagement with the Other presupposes a feeling of being someone and belonging somewhere. This being someone and belonging somewhere should, however, include the idea of plural identities and transculturalism and should not be limited to monocultural ideas of identity.

This understanding of transculturalism fits well with the arguments put forward by Ziebertz in his work on intercultural learning (Ziebertz 2001). Intercultural learning is presented as an alternative to both the monocultural and the multicultural approaches which are both found to be grounded in a static conception of cultures as unified and reified entities. The former is in danger of ending up in fundamentalism whereas the weakness of the latter is relativism: 'anything goes'. Neither approach is adequate as a pedagogical principle. Although not all educationists would agree with Ziebertz' particular representation of multiculturalism (cf. the discussion of this concept in Jackson 1997 and Chapter 4 above), his work (like Jackson's) reflects increasing awareness that today's pluralism is without clear-cut borders between closed traditions, cultures or religions. The use of specific terminology is not the main point, but the reflections informed by conceptual discussions. Borders exist, and play a role in identity processes and social interaction, but they are less predictable and more permeable and fuzzy-edged than before. Children and young people are combining cultural and religious elements, they are moving in and out of different contexts, and they feel it is their right as individuals to decide what to adapt and what to reject from traditions and values. The concept of transcultural citizenship, as advanced in this chapter, is aimed at expressing this form of modern pluralism related to citizenship (Skeie 1995).

The challenge for religious education is to establish a pedagogy that is appropriate and meaningful to all children and young people in the class-room, regardless of their family background, their 'nativeness' or 'the birth-place of their parents' (Malkki 1992: 38). The majority of pupils in European classrooms may not even know what tradition they represent or 'where' they belong. What unites the pupils in a plural, multicultural society should be the awareness of belonging to the same society despite all diversity. To put it another way, cultural diversity and plurality are characteristics of our society. Religious education can be a tool for achieving this type of diverse and reflective unity. As Ziebertz says: 'in a pluralist, multicultural society, unity is not something given but something to be worked for. Unity must be found in diversity' (Ziebertz 2001: 231). This may appear similar to, but actually is the opposite of, creating a common cultural framework for all pupils (cf. the Norwegian national curriculum of 1997). Intercultural learn-ing, including inter-religious learning, is not only an acceptance of plurality but a celebration of diversity and a recognition of the Other as comple-mentary to one's own position. According to Ziebertz, 'The chief task of Inter-cultural Learning will have to be the preparation of students for life in diversity by addressing such diversity, and by helping them to develop appropriate strategies to look critically at diversity' (Ziebertz 2001: 232). How can this be achieved through religious education?

Two examples of pedagogical thinking relevant to citizenship training will be given. The Warwick Religious Education Project aims at presenting reli-gions through individuals, the groups these individuals belong to and the wider religious traditions (Jackson 1997). The variety within each religion is made explicit through the issue of representation. Jackson calls this an interpretive approach to religious education. Religions can never be pre-sented in a neutral, objective way. Presentations in research, textbooks and teaching will always be interpretations. To make this a focal point of the teaching and learning process is to make diversity and plurality explicit. In this way an interpretive approach will contribute to reflexivity and encourage pupils to draw upon their own experiences.

Whereas the Warwick Religious Education Project has an anthropological basis and orientation, Michael Grimmitt's concept of 'learning from religion' has a more psychological or existential character. He says:

> When I speak of pupils *learning from* religion I am referring to what pupils learn from their studies in religion about themselves – about discerning ultimate questions and 'signals of transcendence' in their own experience and considering how they might respond to them, about discerning *Core Values* and learning to interpret them . . .'
>
> (Grimmitt 1987: 225)

Grimmitt (1994) discusses what he means by core values, common to secular and religious worldviews. An 'ideological exploration' of such core values (for example, the value of order, purpose and meaning and the value of human spirituality) will provide pupils with more than a multi-faith approach to religious education. A true 'inter-faith religious education' may be achieved. Grimmitt says: 'What is particularly lacking in contemporary pluralism is any sense of commonality based on the recognition of the interdependence and interrelatedness of cultural groups' (Grimmitt 1994: 139).

Common to both approaches, and especially relevant in our context, is the emphasis on interpretations, individual choices and autonomy. The focus is not so much on the diversity of religious traditions and cultures as on what is going on between, across and within the diversity of traditions present in local communities and as part of individual lives. In this way the two approaches are excellent tools for training in citizenship.

Through inter-religious learning students would also learn that diverse traditions or individual viewpoints are not derivations from a pure core of content but are the way religions and worldviews are expressed. Diversity is normal and your own interpretation is appreciated. This 'learning from' would have as its starting point a recognition of diversity and plurality and a recognition of the Other. The normative foundation would be a responsibility to and for others and the world, 'by positioning myself in my relations with others and by taking my place in the world' (Melucci 1997: 65). Citizenship nurtured in this soil might even be a citizenship meaningful to young Pakistanis in Europe.

Notes

1 As an example the University of Tromsø, Norway, in November 2001 arranged a large conference on diversity in development. Discourses of Citizenship was one of the main topics.

2 Norges Offentlige Utredninger (Norwegian Public Statements) prepared by a department, presented to Parliament for debate and decision. NOU 2000: 32 is prepared by the Ministry of Local Government and Regional Development.

3 The United Kingdom, the republic of Ireland, Canada, Australia and the United States. These countries also accept dual citizenship.

4 The majority of the committee has also rejected a proposal to make language competence a condition of acquiring Norwegian citizenship. The new law proposals have not yet (November 2001) been passed by Parliament (the Stortinget).

5 Norwegian-Pakistani is used as equivalent to the term Pakistani. The latter term was the term applied by the children and young people themselves. They ascribed themselves as Norwegian *and* Pakistani.

6 It was interesting to notice that an Asian young man interviewed on television in connection with the riots in Bradford, in summer 2001 underlined that the trouble-makers came from another town. 'Why should we destroy our own area?'

7 Her informants do not call themselves integrists, Islamists or political activists, just Muslims (Jacobsen 1999: 18).

References

Eriksen, T. H. (1995) *Det nye fiendebildet*, Oslo: Cappelens Forlag.

Featherstone, M. and Lash, S. (eds) (1999) *Spaces of Culture: City, Nation, World*, London: Sage.

Grimmitt, M. (1987) *Religious Education and Human Development: The Relationship between Studying Religions and Personal, Social and Moral Education*, Great Wakering: McCrimmon.

—— (1994) 'Religious education and the ideology of pluralism', *British Journal of Religious Education*, 16 (3), 133–47.

Gullestad, M. (1999) 'Barndom og nasjonal identitet', *Nytt Norsk Tidsskrift*, 2, 122–8.

Hannerz, U. (1994) 'Cosmopolitans and locals in world culture', in Mike Featherstone (ed.) *Global Culture: Nationalism, Globalization and Modernity*, London: Sage.

Jackson, R. (1997) *Religious Education: An Interpretive Approach*, London: Hodder & Stoughton.

Jacobsen, C. (1999) *Å vende tilbake til islam. Islamisering, kjønn og identitet i en fransk kontekst*, Report 21/99, Bergen: Imer Norge.

Jacobson, J. (1996) 'Perceptions of Britishness', paper presented at a conference on 'Multi-cultural Competence' at Bergen College of Higher Education, Bergen, Norway, 28–30 August.

—— (1998) *Islam in Transition: Religion and Identity among British Pakistani Youth*, London: Routledge.

Malkki, L. (1992) 'National geographic: the rooting of peoples and the territorialization of national identity among scholars and refugees', *Cultural Anthropology*, 7 (1), 22–44.

Melucci, A. (1997) 'Identity and difference in a globalized world', in P. Werbner and T. Modood (eds) *Debating Cultural Hybridity: Multi-cultural Identities and the Politics of Anti-racism*, London: Zed Books.

Skeie, G. (1995) 'Plurality and pluralism: a challenge for religious education', *British Journal of Religious Education*, 17 (2), 84–91.

Taylor, C. (1994) 'The politics of recognition', in Amy Gutmann (ed.) *Multi-culturalism: Examining the Politics of Recognition*, Princeton NJ: Princeton University Press.

Welsch, W. (1999) 'Transculturality: the puzzling form of culture today', in M. Featherstone and S. Lash (eds) *Spaces of Culture: City, Nation, World*, London: Sage.

Ziebertz, H.-G. (2001) 'Inter-cultural learning in a new millennium:between fundamentalism and relativism', in L. J. Francis, J. Astley and M. Robbins (eds) *The Fourth R for the Third Millenium: Education in Religion and Values for the Global Future*, Dublin: Lindisfarne Books.

Østberg, S. (1999) 'Pakistani children in Oslo: Islamic nurture in a secular context', thesis submitted to the Institute of Education, University of Warwick, for the degree of Doctor of Philosophy (to be published in the monograph series of the Community Religions Project, University of Leeds).

—— (2000a) 'Punjabi, Pakistani, Muslim and Norwegian? Self-perceptions and social boundaries among Pakistani children In Oslo', *International Punjab Studies*, 7 (1), 133–59.

—— (2000b) 'Islamic nurture and identity management', *British Journal of Religious Education*, 22 (2), 91–103.

Chapter 6

The good South African citizen: then and now

H. Christina Steyn

Synopsis This chapter explores the history of religious education and citizenship education in the South African context and contrasts it with the proposed new policies in this regard. Although the Christian National Education system has now been superseded, the legacy of those years is still alive in many of the lives of the country's citizens. The new proposals with regard to citizenship education have received virtually no opposition, which indicates that the democratic ideals of the constitution are widely accepted in the country. The proposals with regard to multi-religion education have, however, received serious opposition from religious leaders and members of the general public. To a great extent, it seems that it is the privileged position of Christianity in the previous system that has accustomed many people to the idea of religious instruction as an integral part of the task of the school. The various types of objections to multi-religion education are analysed and considered in the light of the constitution and the values it represents.

Religious education and citizenship education have for a long time been intertwined in South Africa's Christian National Education system, and the manipulation of the children of South Africa through the education system must count as an important factor in explaining why democracy did not come to South Africa sooner. Without understanding some of the factors that have shaped the minds of the people of South Africa over the last forty years one cannot understand the reactions to the proposed new approaches in education.

In this chapter I will review the history of religious education and citizen education in South Africa and compare it with the proposed strategies for dealing with them in future. Although the policy has not yet been implemented, it is already incorporated into the Revised Draft Curriculum Statement for South African schools.[1] At the time of writing there have been public hearings on the curriculum, and the element of religion education has sparked public demonstrations against the proposed policy. It is clear that the radical departure from the previous dispensation is causing much anxiety in religious circles.

Christian national education in South Africa

Religious education

Religion has long been an important pillar of education in virtually all the various education systems in South Africa. One of the few exceptions was after the Second Anglo-Boer War in 1902, when Lord Milner changed the structure of the education system in the newly acquired territories of the Transvaal and the Orange Free State. Church participation was discontinued and the language of instruction was changed from Afrikaans to English. This led to immediate resistance and the establishment of a movement for Free Christian National Education (Vrye Christelike Nasionale Onderwys).[2] Most of these CNE schools were eventually closed after 1907 as the people heeded Prime Minister Smuts's plea to bury the differences between Boer and Briton. There was, however, continued reaction from some Afrikaner circles where a conservative religious and an exclusive and separatist Afrikaner culture was propagated.

In 1939 a Church conference was held in Bloemfontein where education was the main topic of discussion. A committee was appointed to study the matter and after many years' deliberations a policy statement, called the *Christelike Nasionale Onderwys Beleid* (the Christian National Education policy), appeared in 1948, just in time to give guidance to the newly elected National Party government.[3] The Christian National Education policy (see Rose and Tunmer 1975: 120 ff.) consisted of fifteen articles which dealt with fundamental principles, different levels of education and the education of the non-white people of South Africa. Although the first article of the document specified that the document was directed at the Afrikaner child, in time it became the basis of the education of all racial groups in South Africa.

Article 2 stated that religious instruction should be the key subject which determined the 'spirit and direction' of all education. Article 6, on the content of education, stated that the child should learn about 'the entire creation of God' but that everything should be taught in 'the light of the Word of God'. The most important element of education was religious teaching, which would be 'Bible history and instruction in Christian dogma'. The document further stated that, with regard to the content of education, there might be no 'anti-Christian or un-Christian or anti-National or un-National propaganda' in any subject. Article 8 included the following statement: 'We believe that the church must keep a watch over the spirit and direction of education [and] that it must exercise the necessary vigilance and discipline over the life and doctrine of the teachers as members of the church' (Rose and Tunmer 1975: 124). Furthermore, the teacher should be 'a man [sic] of Christian life and world view'.

These excerpts from the CNE policy document adequately show the integration of religion across all fields of education, and, although the policy was formally implemented only in 1967 in all state schools in all provinces, this was very much how children were raised in South Africa for a long time before 1967. The primacy of religious instruction was also the basis on which the 1953 Bantu Education Act (see below) was formulated.

In order to accomplish the ideals set out in CNE policy, a regulation was promulgated by the Minister[4] which made 'religious instruction, founded in Scripture', a compulsory subject for all teachers in training. Although provision was made for students to be granted exemption from studying this subject on the grounds of religious beliefs, one can only imagine how few students had the courage to decline to do this subject if one reads what one Biblical Instruction lecturer at the University of South Africa wrote in a study guide as late as 1990:

> There seems to be no real reason for conscientious objections to the study of Biblical Instruction. It would be valid only in the case of a teacher expected to teach Biblical Instruction while convinced that the Christian faith rests on false assumptions: for example, someone who is convinced that Christ did not rise from the dead. In terms of the Education Act of 1967, however, such a student may well be asked to find other work.[5]
>
> (Unisa 1990: 34)

The same author described the aim of Biblical Instruction as follows:

> Thus effective Biblical Instruction is not simply the transmission of knowledge, nor is it simply a matter of acquiring good habits and behaviour. Children must personally accept, and trust for their personal salvation, the triune God introduced to them in the Bible . . .
>
> (Unisa 1990: 30)

On the subject of tolerance the author wrote: 'In all this a public school must show tolerance and respect for differing doctrinal convictions, as long as there is no denial of Jesus Christ as the Messiah . . .' (Unisa 1990: 19).

In another widely used prescribed book (aimed particularly at black teacher education colleges) on religious education and biblical studies, which saw its fifteenth impression in 1995, the following reasons for the inclusion of religious instruction in schools are put forward and the inclusion of the subject is justified on 'cultural, spiritual and moral grounds':

> This is a Christian country and it is only right that our children should be taught the Christian faith – also in our schools . . . A child who

follows the Christian faith is more likely to behave in a moral way than a non-Christian or an un-religious child.

(Kitshoff and Van Wyk 1983: 4)

This type of religious indoctrination was therefore not only what learners were exposed to during school years, but also what teachers in training were taught to be necessary for learners if they were to grow up to be stable and steadfast citizens. However, Christianity alone was not enough to produce the exemplary citizen, and citizen education was added to ensure development in the desired direction.

Citizen education

Citizen education in pre-democratic South Africa was differentiated and must be understood against the background of the assumptions about nations and peoples that were prominent at the time. The CNE document stated, 'We believe that God has willed separate nations and peoples, and has given each separate nation and people its particular vocation and tasks and gifts.' The people of South Africa were viewed as belonging to separate nations and citizen education differed vastly for the different groups. The CNE document prescribed that a subject called Civics must be taught and added that 'every pupil must be formed into a Christian and national citizen of our country'. Every citizen had his or her own 'rights, responsibilities and duties towards home, church, society and state'. Geography was an important subject that should be taught in such a way that pupils will 'love our soil, also in comparison and contrast with other countries'. The subject of History should be taught in the 'light of revelation' and this subject was the means of 'cultivating love of one's own' (Rose and Tunmer 1975: 122).

Despite the official lip service to national unity and racial co-operation (see Transvaal Education Ordinance 1953, article 3) the Afrikaner youth of South Africa were indoctrinated to put their Afrikaner consciousness before their South African citizenship. Afrikaner children were taught that the Afrikaners were chosen by God to fulfil a divine destiny at 'the southern tip of Africa' and that they had a sacred obligation to christianize the black people of the country. This ethnic nationalism was committed to the idea of inherent superiority and was extremely authoritarian. It was also prescriptive, and it was, for instance, common practice to exhort Afrikaner children not to marry outside their ethnic group (that is, not to marry an English partner – marriage to other racial groups was never contemplated) and so betray their identity and their nation.

The last article (No. 15) of the CNE document dealt with 'African (Bantu) Teaching and Education'. It stated that 'the calling and task of white South Africa with regard to the native [was] to Christianize him and help him on culturally', and that this was to be done on the 'principles of trusteeship, no equality, and segregation'. Teaching and education of the black people were to be 'grounded in the life and worldview of the whites, most especially those of the Boer nation as the senior white trustee of the native'. It also added that, 'on the grounds of the cultural infancy of the native', it was the 'right and task of the state in collaboration with the Christian Protestant churches', to control education until this task could be taken over by 'the native himself, but under the control and guidance of the state'. All this was to be done with the important proviso that 'the financing of native education must be placed on such a basis that it does not occur at the cost of white education' (Rose and Tunmer 1975: 128).

A few years after the National Party took control of the country, the Bantu Education Act (1953) was passed. It was designed around the recommendations of a report of the Native Education Commission (1949–51), also referred to as the 'Eiselen Report' after the chairman of the commission. One of the specific aims was to develop the character and intellect of black children and to equip them for their 'future work and surroundings'. In other words, the education system was designed specifically to make the African child fit into a social role prescribed for him or her by the government.

Another recommendation was that provision should be made for teaching 'social patterns and values' which would 'make a man a good member of his community, a good parent and a useful member of society'. The important values to be instilled were listed as 'punctuality, initiative, self-confidence, a sense of duty, persistence, sociability, mannerliness, neatness, reliability, the power to concentrate' (Rose and Tunmer 1975: 252). These are particularly revealing virtues. The intention of the education provided is clear from what was included in the list of virtues and, more especially, from what was omitted. The aim of citizen education was to create citizens who would serve the purpose of the state; considerations of basic principles of justice, truth, freedom, and critical thought were actively discouraged.

It should be noted that in time the idea of trusteeship made way for the notion of separate development in which black people were given a small portion of the land as 'homelands' of which they were to become citizens and where they were to find fulfilment as citizens, and white South Africa could continue the pretence of being a democratic state. This change of policy, however, did not change the education black people were to receive. It is clear that religious instruction, together with citizen training, was to be the agent which would produce the type of citizen that the government valued. Critical thinking was discouraged and passive acceptance and adaptation to the world were promoted. One cannot escape the impression that teaching black children to be Christians encouraged them to be passive and obedient, not to humans but to God, and they were encouraged to endure the injustices of their lives with fortitude in the hope of reaping a just reward in the life to come.

Education in post-apartheid South Africa

Much has changed in South Africa since the demise of apartheid. With the adoption of the new constitution in 1996 the country became a secular state with a democratic constitution and a Bill of Rights which safeguards the rights of all its people. A democratically elected government rules the country, and the Dutch Reformed Church (which provided theological justification for the country's racial policies) has rejected apartheid and confessed that apartheid is indeed a sin. The education system has been radically overhauled and a new outcomes-based education system has been adopted.

A National Education Department, which is responsible for developing the policy and legislative framework on which all education and training rest, has been established. Although each province has its own education department, these are all under the broader supervision of the National Department. Theoretically, all schools are open to learners of all races, but in practice, depending on geographical location and language, many schools are still homogeneous in student composition. Many urban schools are completely integrated with regard to both learners and teaching staff, but there are still many Afrikaans-medium schools which are entirely composed of white students, since black students prefer their education in the medium of English. In many rural areas the schools are often composed of only black students who live in surrounding areas.

Proposed policy for religion in education

Although education for citizenship in a democracy has been incorporated into the learning material from the earliest versions of the new education prescriptions, the role of religion has only recently become clear. At the time of writing (December 2001) the new policy on religion in education has still not been officially announced. However, two documents published by the Department of Education, have incorporated the aims of the proposed policy. In the first document, the *Manifesto on Values, Education, and Democracy* (August 2001),[6] it is stated that religion education will be integrated into the life orientation and social science learning areas[7] (from grade R [pre-primary] to 9) and that religious studies will be introduced as an optional examinable subject for matriculation purposes (grades 10–12) (Department of Education 2001a: 44).

In contrast to the past, with its religious indoctrination, religion education will aim at exposing learners to different belief systems in order to foster respect for adherents of these religious traditions. Religion education will be introduced into schools in order to provide learners with the opportunity to explore 'the diversity of religions that impel and inspire society, and the morality and values that underpin them'. This is said to 'affirm the values of diversity, tolerance, respect, justice, compassion, and commitment' in young learners (Department of Education 2001a: 78). However, tucked away inside the *Manifesto* is a statement that has taken many by surprise. With regard to school assemblies it states that 'under no circumstances are they to be used as occasions for religious observance' and adds that they are not occasions for imposing religious uniformity, but rather forums 'where diversity is celebrated, along with the values of our Constitution' (Department of Education 2001a: 45).

Another document, the *Draft Revised National Curriculum Statement*, states that exposure to a range of belief systems will contribute to the development of positive attitudes, before prejudices set in (Department of Education 2001b: 19). Concerning religion and citizen education, the specific outcome in the learning area Life Orientation reads as follows: 'The learner is able to demonstrate an active commitment to constitutional rights and social responsibilities, and show sensitivity to diverse cultures and belief systems.' For assessment purposes, the learner in each of the grades should be able to demonstrate prescribed knowledge and skills. For instance, in the pre-primary year (grade R) learners should be able to identify at least three symbols linked with the belief systems of their families, and in grade 1 learners are required to be able to discuss similarities and differences in at least three belief systems on issues such as diet, clothing, sacred places and decorations. Thereafter there are different requirements for each of the following grades around which lessons in religion should be developed.

These documents show clearly that although the Minister has yet to make any formal announcement about religion in education it is intended that multi-religion education will be an element in the education of all the learners in the country.

Proposals for citizen education

The *Manifesto on Values, Education and Democracy* outlines sixteen strategies to instil democratic values in young South Africans. It remarks that it is not the intention of the Education Department to impose the values, but rather to generate discussion and debate. These values are inspired by the constitution and express South Africans' shared aspirations, also setting the moral and ethical direction for the future. The values are: democracy, social justice and equity, equality, non-racism and non-sexism, *Ubuntu* (human dignity), an open society, accountability, rule of law, respect and reconciliation.

Two of the educational strategies to promote these values have particular relevance to citizen education: first, the nurturing of the 'New Patriotism' and the affirmation of our common citizenship, and secondly the re-introduction of History into the curriculum. The first strategy concerns the promotion of a common identity through a shared sense of pride in commonly held values. This New Patriotism will be forged through alle-giance with the sixteen constitutional values mentioned above. It is sug-gested that the New Patriotism be taught in such a manner that it does not increase already high levels of xenophobia among the people. It 'should be less about being South African and more about understanding what South Africa stands for' (Department of Education 2001a: 78). The *Manifesto* also suggests that a verbal affirmation of citizenship be adopted (although the initial recommendation of the Working Committee on Values in Education has not been followed that it should be introduced in schools as a pledge of allegiance for use at weekly school assemblies).[8] The second strategy of interest is the reintroduction of history as a means of nurturing critical enquiry and the promotion of an historical conscious-ness. It is aimed at promoting an informed awareness of the past and thus 'preventing amnesia, checking triumphalism, opposing a manipulative use of the past, and providing a buffer against the "dumbing down" of the citizenry' (Department of Education 2001a: vi).

The authors of the *Draft Revised National Curriculum Statement* declare that two of the key principles which guided the development of the National Curriculum Statements (NCS) were the issues of human rights and social and environmental justice. Although there will not be a separate subject to deal with these issues, they are considered so important that it is envisaged that all learning areas will include information and discussion on the issues of human rights, social and environmental justice, race, gender, age, disability and sexual orientation.

In order to demonstrate attainment of the specific outcomes for active commitment to constitutional rights and social responsibility, the grade R learner should be able to identify four basic rights and responsibilities, iden-tify the South African flag and its colours, identify at least three symbols linked with the belief systems of their families and listen and tell stories with a moral value from his or her culture. In each of the following nine years there are specific assessment standards against which this learning outcome can be measured. In grade 8, for instance, learners should be assessed on their participation in legal or official structures through letter writing, lobbying, petitioning, and using the law to protect rights. On analysis, it is clear that the major components of citizenship as described by various scholars in the field (Ichilov 1998; Marshall 1950; McLaughlin 1992; Newmann 1977) receive attention.

With the adoption of this learning outcome the scene has been set for both citizen education and religion education to be incorporated in the ten-year compulsory education of all South African children. However, the indication that religious observances will no longer be part of the official school structure in the future has led to controversy.

'A fierce debate'

In June 2001 the Minister of Education announced in Parliament that a new policy on religion was being devised and that it would involve multi-religion education. The reaction in the media was immediate. The *Interkerklike Komitee vir Opvoeding en Onderwys* (Inter-Church Committee on Education) of the three Afrikaans Reformed Churches announced that they would take a strong standpoint against an inter-faith approach to religion education (*Beeld*, 7 June 2001). A spokesperson for the *Gereformeerde Kerke* (Reformed Churches) urged parents to protest against the unbiblical views which their children were being brought into contact with at school and added that parents should be obedient to God rather than to the Government (*Beeld* 14 June 2001). Other negative reactions were heard from the South African Association for Biblical Studies and Religious Studies and a number of Afrikaans cultural organizations (e.g. *Vryheidsfront-jeug* (Freedom Front Youth); *Afrikaner Eenheidsbeweging* (Afrikaner Unity Movement)).

With the publication of the *Manifesto on Values, Education and Democracy* and the *Draft Revised National Curriculum Statement*, the outline of the proposed policy has become apparent and the reactions in the media have intensified. On 13 November 2001 public hearings on the new draft curriculum were held in Parliament and fifteen organizations made representations. Six of these bodies mentioned religion education, of which two were vitriolic in their opposition to the proposals. Supporters of these groups demonstrated (with television cameras rolling) in front of Parliament that day. However, not all the responses were negative. A presentation from the South African Democratic Teachers' Union[9] wanted it made clear that teachers should not be responsible for religious instruction and that religion education should aim at the promotion of tolerance between people of different cultures (SADTU 2001: 1). The submission from the South African Teachers' Union[10] was also mainly positive, although it raised the question of the wisdom of introducing learners to religions other than their own at too early an age (SAOU 2001).

The reactions to the Minister's June announcement and the two documents are of three types. Some object to the suspension of religious instruction and nurturing in one's own religion, and this view usually includes an objection to the ban on religious observances during school hours. Others object to the manner in which religion education will be taught at school. Finally there are those who object to the teaching of content from religions other than their own.

The organizations (e.g. the Dutch Reformed Church, the Apostolic Faith Mission of South Africa, the Church of the Province of Southern Africa, United Christian Action) which object to the elimination of religious instruction and religious observances at school often do so on constitutional grounds. They argue that parents and pupils have a constitutional right to receive instruction in their own religion, and almost all have given notice that they are prepared to take the matter to the Constitutional Court to ensure this right. This call on the constitutional rights of parents is explained in an unpublished paper by a Dr Vic Brink (2001), written in response to a discussion forum at the University of Pretoria on religion in education (August 2000). Brink's paper warns that it is possible that the final formulation of the policy will lead to a 'fierce debate'. According to Brink, Article 15 (2) of the constitution specifically protects religious practices in schools. He writes:

> These provisions mean that there may be full religious practice in schools, as in the past. These include: collective Bible reading, prayer and singing, a religious message by an educator, minister of the church, or any other person, and any other form of religious practice or campaign where God is worshipped or the gospel is proclaimed.

The author further states that 'Religious education from a Christian perspective can also not be prohibited. Children should be taught about other religions, but the presenters . . . may make sure that the Truth concerning Jesus Christ be presented very clearly in the process' (Brink 2001: 6).

There seem to be different ways of interpreting Article 15 of the constitution, and for the sake of clarity it is quoted in full:

(1) Everyone has the right to freedom of conscience, religion, thought, belief and opinion.
(2) Religious observances may be conducted at state or state-aided institutions, provided that:
   (a) those observances follow rules made by the appropriate public authorities;
   (b) they are conducted on an equitable basis; and
   (c) attendance at them is free and voluntary.

The *Manifesto* sheds some light on this matter when it states that 'according to the constitution, schools may be made available for religious observances "as long as it is outside of school hours", that attendance is not mandatory and facilities are made available on an equitable basis' (Department of Education 2001a: 44). It would seem that the 'relevant authority' is interpreted by the Department of Education as being itself, while the Schools Act of 1996 still allows school governing bodies to decide on religious observances in school when it states:

> Subject to the Constitution and any applicable provincial law, religious observances may be conducted at a public school under rules issued by the governing body if such observances are conducted on an equitable

basis and attendance of them by learners and members of staff are free and voluntary.

This is a matter that will have to receive urgent attention if the issue of religion in schools is going to be settled any time soon.

In the light of this argument, it is interesting that the first testing of Article 15 (Article 14 in the interim constitution) in the Constitutional Court in 1997 in the State *v.* Lawrence, Justice Albie Sachs gave a summary of what he considered the intention of the article to be. He wrote:

> To my mind . . . section 14 was intended at least to uphold the following principles and values: South Africa is an open and democratic society with a non-sectarian State that guarantees freedom of worship; is respectful of and accommodatory towards, rather than hostile to or walled-off from, religion; acknowledges the multi-faith and multi-belief nature of the country; does not favour one religious creed or doctrinal truth above another; accepts the intensely personal nature of individual conscience and affirms the intrinsically voluntary and non-coerced character of belief; respects the rights of non-believers; does not impose orthodoxies of thought or require conformity of con-duct in terms of any particular world view. The Constitution, then, is very much about the acknowledgement by the State of different belief systems and their accommodation within a non-hierarchical framework of equality and non-discrimination. It follows that the State does not take sides on questions of religion. It does not impose beliefs, grant privileges to or impose disadvantages on adherents of any particular belief, require conformity in matters simply of belief, involve itself in purely religious controversies or marginalise people who have different beliefs.
>
> (Sachs 1997)

He goes on to show how in the pre-constitutional period the state clearly sided with Christianity, but adds:

> Any echo today of the superior status in public law once enjoyed by Christianity must therefore be understood as a reminder of the sub-ordinate position to which followers of other faiths were formerly sub-jected . . . Thus, any endorsement by the State today of Christianity as a privileged religion not only disturbs the general principle of impartiality in relation to matters of belief and opinion, but also serves to activate memories of painful past discriminations and disadvantages based on religious affiliation.
>
> (Sachs 1997)

He adds that the object of section 15 is 'to keep the State away from favouring or disfavouring any particular worldview', and that the state is required to act evenhandedly in matters of religion. To my mind, this shows clearly why the state cannot allow the majority (of the population or the school governing body) to prescribe religious practices for schools. This, however, does not prohibit a school from arranging religious activities for learners outside school structures, provided that attendance (for both learners and staff) is voluntary and provision is made on an equitable basis for all groups who apply. Once this is clarified in the public mind, there will probably be less resentment against the new policy.

The issue of teaching about religion is not the only one which is drawing heated reaction. Some Christian groups (e.g. the Catholic Institute of Education) object to the type of religion studies that will be presented. They claim that the department is aiming for a 'neutral' and 'value-free' presentation of religion and that this will be a cold and factual presentation which will rip the heart out of religion. This, of course, demonstrates a misunderstanding of the model, since a study of religions other than one's own can never be 'neutral'. The mere fact that one is learning about 'other' religions teaches one more about one's own tradition, and these reflections are to be encouraged. However, it is not the aim of religion education to facilitate religious experiences or to influence learners to make religious choices. The spiritual privacy of learners should be respected and educators should not be expected to take on the duties of parents or religious leaders. This approach to religion education is not value-free, either, but is aimed at democratic values of respect, equality, peace and social harmony. The aim of religion education is to help learners grow into responsible citizens with an understanding of universal human aspirations and needs and so to develop empathy and respect – which will hopefully result in a more peaceful country and world. This in no way diminishes the value of personal spirituality.

A few minor organizations such as the Pestalozzi Trust (a group which assists home schooling) and United Christian Action object to all religious and religion education. Their submissions to the public hearings clearly show that they misunderstand the intention of the new policy. However, even if they did understand it correctly they would not support it, since they are strident in their opposition to the new curriculum, which they see as 'state controlled propaganda and social engineering' (McCafferty 2001: 1).

The road ahead

The strategy the Minister of Education has been following is one of consultation with religious leaders, and by December 2001 he had held meetings with leaders of most religious groupings. Despite initial negativity, many of these leaders have now indicated that they would support the new policy.

It seems that the knee-jerk reaction of many people can be overcome if they understand that religious observance will be allowed outside school hours (on a voluntary basis) and that learning about religions other than one's own does not involve participation or imply agreement. There even seems to be a genuine understanding among many leaders of the need to learn about one another in the country and in the world, although the deeply felt resentment of many others must not be underestimated. However, it seems clear that the proposed policy will soon become a reality. When that day comes it will not be the end of the road, only the beginning. The implementation of the policy will have problems all of its own.

The next hurdle to be overcome is the in-service training of teachers who will be responsible for religion education. Considering the training that teachers received during the apartheid years, this will require a complete shift in perception and will surely prove to be a mammoth task. Some research has been done on how to include teachers and get them to participate in the introduction of the policy and on ways to encourage dialogue and openness in classrooms so that the aims of the policy can be realized. In a research project Cornelia Roux and her co-researchers have devised a series of workshops for teachers in different parts of the country in order to introduce them to religion education – its aims, its value and its potential for personal growth (Roux 1998, 2001). In these workshops, teachers are encouraged to investigate their own attitudes and beliefs in order to prepare themselves to act as facilitators for religion education. The researchers were able to allay the teachers' fears and to help them overcome their first negative impulses towards the model. The teachers eventually took ownership of the programme and have made major strides in acquiring new knowledge, developing new skills and changing attitudes.

Other significant research which will prove invaluable is on appropriate teaching strategies in religion education. The controversial content of the subject requires careful study of methodologies which will ensure that the aims are reached and learners experience the subject as enriching rather than regarding it with apprehension. René Ferguson (1999, 2001) points out that co-operative learning increases the level of participation, improves the quality of learning and encourages learners to work towards positive learning outcomes. Other research on pedagogy (e.g. Grimmitt 2000, Jackson 1997) and on dialogue in the classroom can make a positive contribution to future practice (see Chapters 8–10 in this volume).

Another serious obstacle in the way of successful implementation is the lack of suitable resources. Although there are a few South African publications available they are not nearly sufficient. This matter will have to receive serious consideration and a concerted effort will have to go into producing appropriate material. It is hoped that the Institute for Comparative Religion in Southern Africa will receive the necessary funding in order to expand its efforts in this regard. Without the necessary resource material for both teachers and learners the new venture will not succeed.

Conclusion

My concern is that the influence of the many years of indoctrination and the privileged position that Christians have become accustomed to over the years will lead to strong resistance to the introduction of multi-religion education in South African schools. However, in a democratic country with a liberal constitution there can be no favouritism shown by the state, and citizens have an obligation to respect the equal rights of fellow citizens, whatever their faith. Although the state cannot prescribe how citizens should lead their lives, and they are free to practise and even to condemn others in their private lives, in the public arena citizens are guided by democratic rights and everyone has to put aside their privately held religious convictions in order to coexist in peace with fellow citizens. One can only hope that, in the discussions and public debate which have now started, all will be able to bear in mind the common fate and purpose that bind people together in their new democracy while still appreciating the particular significance, to each of the participants, of the beliefs that divide their thinking.

Notes

1 A new curriculum was proposed for South African schools in 1996 called *Curriculum 2005* – a reference to the year in which the curriculum would be fully implemented in all schools and grades. It was, however, such a cumbersome document that it was decided to revise and simplify it. The process eventually led to the publication of the *Revised Draft Curriculum Statement* in August 2001, which is the document relevant to this chapter.
2 Historically, Christian National Education is a seventeenth-century ideology that originated in the Netherlands in the wake of the religious wars with Spain. The state, the Church and the school were so closely identified that it was said that 'all schooling was Church schooling' and all functions of the modern school were carried out by the Church. This ideology was firmly based in the theology of John Calvin.
3 The South African version of Christian National Education was strongly influenced by the thought of Abram Kuyper (1837-1920, founder of the Free University in Amsterdam), to form a new unique type of Calvinism which could accommodate the racial policies of the new government.
4 R.1192 – SA-R, *Government Gazette*, 20 June 1975.
5 This course was discontinued in 2001 when the old curriculum for the Higher Education Diploma was phased out.
6 The *Manifesto* brings together, among other sources, the findings of a Ministerial Working Group on Values in Education, and an unpublished report on religion education.
7 Instead of subjects, the curriculum is divided into learning areas. In the Foundational Phase (grades 1–3) there are three areas: Literacy, Numeracy and Life Skills. In the Intermediary Phase (grades 4–7) there are five: Languages, Mathematics,

Arts and Culture, Science and Technology, Life skills and Economy and Society. In the Senior Phase (grades 8–9) there are eight: Languages, Mathematics, Natural Sciences, Technology, Social Sciences, Arts and Culture, Life Orientation, and Economic and Management Sciences. Learning programmes in these areas aim to promote integrated learning via different themes (called programme organizers).

8 The pledge reads: 'I promise to do my best to promote the welfare and well-being of all my fellow South African citizens. I promise to show self-respect in all that I do and to respect all of my fellow citizens, our various traditions, and our Constitution. Let us work for peace, friendship and reconciliation and heal the scars left by past conflict and let us build a common destiny together.'

9 The union represents about 140,000 mainly black teachers.

10 *Suid-Afrikaanse Onderwysersunie.* Membership of the union is mainly white and Afrikaans.

References

Brink, V. (2001) 'The new religious education policy', unpublished article, University of Pretoria.

Department of Education (2001a) *Manifesto on Values, Education and Democracy*, Pretoria.

—— (2001b) *Draft Revised National Curriculum Statement.* Pretoria.

Ferguson, R. (1999) 'Strategies for teaching religion in colleges of education', unpublished dissertation, University of Stellenbosch.

—— (2001) 'Networks and circles: a constructivist approach towards the empowerment of student teachers for religion, values and citizenship education', paper presented at the fourth meeting of the International Network for Inter-religious and Inter-cultural Education, 3–5 September, University of Warwick.

Grimmitt, M. H. (ed.) (2000) *Pedagogies of Religious Education: Case Studies in the Research and Development of Good Pedagogic Practice in RE*, Great Wakering: McCrimmons.

Ichilov, O. (ed.) (1998) *Citizenship and Citizenship Education in a Changing World*, London: Woburn Press.

Jackson, R. (1997) *Religious Education: An Interpretive Approach*, London: Hodder & Stoughton.

Kitshoff, M. C. and Van Wyk, W. B. (1983) *Method of Religious Education and Biblical Studies*, Cape Town: Maskew Miller Longman.

Marshall, T. H. (1950) *Citizenship and Social Class*, Cambridge: Cambridge University Press.

McCafferty, R. (2001) Submission on behalf of the United Christian Action, public hearing on the Revised National Curriculum Statement, unpublished statement.

McLaughlin, T. H. (1992) 'Citizenship, diversity and education: a philosophical perspective', *Journal of Moral Education*, 21 (3), 235–47.

Newmann, F. M. (1977) 'Building a rationale for civic education', in J. P. Shaver (ed.) *Building Rationales for Citizenship Education*, Arlington VA: National Council for the Social Studies.

Rose, B. and Tunmer, R. (eds) (1975) *Documents in South African Education*, Johannesburg: Ad Donker.

Roux, C. D. (1998) 'The need for a paradigm shift in teaching religion in multicultural schools in South Africa', *South African Journal for Education,* 18 (2), 84–9.

—— (2001) 'Religion in education and democratic values: a South African perspective', paper presented at the fourth meeting of the International Network for Inter-religious and Inter-cultural Education, 3–5 September, University of Warwick.

Sachs, A (1997) Constitutional Court of South Africa Cases CCT 38/96, CC39/96, CC40/96 www.concourt.gov.za/cases/1997/lawsum/shtml (accessed 19 December 2001).

SADTU (South African Democratic Teachers Union) (2001) 'SADTU Submission, public hearing on the Revised National Curriculum Statement', unpublished statement.

SAOU (Suid-Afrikaanse Onderwysersunie) (2001) SAOU Submission, public hearing on the Revised National Curriculum Statement, unpublished statement.

Turner, B. S. (1990) 'Outline of a theory of citizenship', *Sociology,* 24 (2), 189–217.

Unisa (1990) *Biblical Instruction (HED) Only study guide for BIBHOD-H, BIBHOT-3,* Department of Didactics, Pretoria: Unisa.

Chapter 7

Learning the difference

Religion education, citizenship and gendered subjectivity

Judy Tobler

Synopsis Any thinking about the aspiration to be fully human – a theme that appears to be common to the study of religion and citizenship theory – must surely include attention to gendered subjectivity and difference. However, feminist critical theorists have uncovered a glaring gender-blindness in modern citizenship theory that serves only to reinforce patriarchy and to privilege the male citizen as the norm. This chapter aims to engage with three main areas of feminist scholarship. First, a review of feminist citizenship theory examines strategies to accommodate gender difference in citizenship theory and to reform the gendered structure of the public–private dichotomy. Secondly, an analysis of the politics of motherhood points to the pivotal significance of the equality–difference debate for women's citizenship. Thirdly, the insights of the feminist philosopher and psychoanalyst Luce Irigaray are used to argue that discourses of citizenship and religion are inextricably linked in the production of gendered subjectivity and intersubjectivity, civil identity as a citizen among other citizens, and justice for women and men as different citizens of equal worth. In conclusion, it is suggested that religion education and citizenship education can fruitfully contribute to one another. Examples are offered in support of using the creative dimensions of religious myths and symbols as resources in the classroom for understanding difference and diversity, for creating and re-creating gendered subjectivity, for encouraging self-esteem and active citizenship for women and men, all of which can be engendered by a desire and respect for 'learning the difference'.

In reflecting on 'the journey to full possession of our humanity – which is surely the oldest and most compelling story of all' Sarah Benton concludes: 'A politics of citizenship founded on liberty, equality and above all *fraternity*, offers little of value to members of the sorority' (1991: 163). Iris Young similarly reflects: 'Feminists in particular have analyzed how the discourse that links the civic public with fraternity is not merely metaphorical' (1989: 253). In the spirit of exploring what it means to be fully human, the underlying intention of this chapter is to explore links between citizenship discourse and religious discourse, and whether those links point to a fruitful reciprocal relationship between the fields of citizenship education and religion education. However, in the quest to be fully human, which may well include the aspiration to be a full citizen of a particular community, I suggest that the experience of citizenship is not the same for women as for men. My core aim, therefore, is also to engage the spirit of feminist critique of citizenship theory in order to focus on problematizing issues of equality, difference and particularity in relation to gendered subjectivity. If the intention of teachers in citizenship education and religion education is to educate learners in the rights and duties involved in being 'good citizens', I would argue that the term 'citizenship' itself has to be unpacked and critically examined by educators in those fields. I am convinced that this should include rigorous critical reflection on the significance of gendered subjectivities for the ways we think about, define and shape citizenship status and practice.

Citizenship, then, is a term denoting both status and practice, in other words, as rights conferred on an individual as well as an individual's participation as a full member of a community. The former is derived from the rights discourse of liberal political tradition and the latter from the obligations discourse of civic republican tradition (see Lister 1997a, b; Voet 1998: 132–4). The ground-breaking social theory of the British sociologist T. H. Marshall, in the 1950s, advanced citizenship theory towards a social liberalism that not only embraced civil and political rights and obligations but also perceived citizenship as a social and relational category, including 'a set of social relationships between individuals and the state and between individual citizens' (Lister 1997b: 29). Some feminist theorists add emphasis to the importance of ethical and moral dimensions of citizenship (see Prokhovnik 1998: 85) and, even further, advocate awareness of its affective meanings for subjects, according to their differing life circumstances. Clearly, citizenship is multi-dimensional in concerning itself not only with the physical, political and economic conditions of life but also with the psychological, emotional – even the religious and spiritual – dimensions of being human (see James 1992). The ideal of the 'good citizen', for instance, may have profound symbolic significance for an individual's feelings about his or her identity, both as an independent human being and as an active participant, with others, in shaping the collective identity of a community. Citizenship, it could be said, is intimately bound up with human identity, subjectivity and agency – in short, as Hannah Arendt suggested, with being fully human (cited in Prokhovnik 1998: 90).

Any thinking about the aspiration to be fully human – including any classroom situation where students are encouraged to reflect on their own identities as well as their assumptions about others who are 'different' (see Chapter 1 above) – must surely include attention to gendered subjectivity and difference. Feminists appear to be united in recognizing that a glaring gender-blindness pervades modern citizenship theory, a blindness which could, at first glance, be assumed to signify gender-neutrality or equality between the sexes; in reality, though, it is a blindness that overlooks gender difference and ignores any significance it might have for *unequal* citizenship status and practice. Feminist theorists assert that this lack of gender-sensitive analysis of citizenship serves only to reinforce patriarchy and to privilege the male citizen as the norm. Even so, many corrective feminist strategies still tend to leave the division between the public and private realms of society intact (see Prokhovnik 1998: 89). Since the public–private opposition, among many other dualist notions, is undeniably gendered and hierarchical, it constitutes one of the strongest foundations of patriarchy. But it remains to be seen whether feminist citizenship theory, so far, offers enough to disrupt that foundation which privileges the public domain, and traditionally male-dominated political activity within it, so that a more 'woman-friendly citizenship' can be generated (see Voet 1998: 140–1).

In this chapter I intend to engage with three main areas of feminist scholarship. First, in a review of some important feminist literature on citizenship, a variety of critical approaches to accommodating gender difference in citizenship theory and to reforming the gendered significance of the public–private dichotomy will be examined. Secondly, I intend to focus on analysis of the politics of motherhood that seems pivotal to the equality–difference debate around gendered subjectivity and women's citizenship. And finally, drawing mainly on the insights of the feminist philosopher and psychoanalyst Luce Irigaray, I aim to show that discourses of citizenship and religion are inextricably linked in the production of gendered subjectivity and intersubjectivity, civil identity as a citizen among other citizens, and justice for women and men as *different* citizens of equal worth.

Citizenship and feminism

Feminist responses to citizenship theory are numerous and diverse but the very fact that there is a substantial body of feminist critique implies that a problem does exist for women in this area. Iris Young points out that modern political theory's assumption of 'a universality of citizenship in the sense that citizenship status transcends particularity and difference' implies a conception of equality as sameness and blindness to individual and group differences; in reality, however, some groups are privileged and others are oppressed or disadvantaged as 'second-class citizens'. Young therefore advocates differentiated group representation, with provision for 'special rights that attend to group differences', to ensure a form of active citizenship and public decision making that is inclusive of everyone (Young 1989: 250–1). Women, needless to say, are one of the main categories of citizens identified as disadvantaged in the modern state, with 'its public realm of citizenship paraded as universal values and norms which were derived from specifically masculine experience' (Young 1989: 253).

Young's transformative approach to reforming citizenship theory opens up avenues for other feminist theorists to develop new theory that is sensitive to difference and inclusive of disadvantaged groups. South Africa is a prominent example of an ethnically, culturally and religiously plural society in which individual and group identities are being reconceived and reconstructed within a nation-state that now grants political and civil citizenship to all South Africans. The contested issues of socio-economic as well as racial and gender disparities continue to be worked out, not without conflict and widespread violence. Although South Africa could also be defined as a state based on a 'multicultural' model of citizenship, the problem that could be overlooked in granting special rights to particular cultural groups (whether minority cultures or previously colonized and oppressed indigenous cultures) 'is the risk of treating cultural groups as homogeneous', thus opening the way for such groups 'to impose restrictions on their own members in the name of traditional authorities and practices' (Lister 1997b: 37). It is vital to remember that, even in states where religious freedom and the expression of cultural diversity are ensured, freedom *in* religion, for women and girls, is often constrained or even non-existent.

Clearly, different interests *within* groups also have to be problematized by citizenship theory, especially gendered differences and the oppression of women within cultural and religious groupings. A study conducted in the Zulu-speaking community of KwaZulu-Natal in South Africa, by the anthropologist Suzanne Leclerc-Madlala, is an important case in point (*Mail and Guardian*, 10–16 December 1999: 38). Leclerc-Madlala challenges claims to 'cultural rights' and 'sacred rights', based on the revival of 'lost African traditions', in relation to the practice of virginity testing carried out on young Zulu girls. Today, she reports, 'self-proclaimed [male] guardians of tradition' insist that the recent resurgence of virginity testing on young girls is a reinterpretation of traditional agricultural rituals, now utilized in a 'culturally appropriate way to combat things like teenage pregnancy and the spread of sexually transmitted diseases and HIV/Aids'. In South Africa, she points out, the first sexual experience for the majority of young women is coerced, and yet many female pupils are expelled from school for pregnancy. In the reality of a South Africa where teenage pregnancies and HIV infection rates soar, it seems that it is women's bodies that are singularly expected to carry the burden of re-creating and maintaining purity. Leclerc-Madlala therefore interrogates practices that are abusive to women but justified on the basis of religious or cultural rights, especially given that 'cultural right' has not been applied to young men in similar ways that would apportion equal obligations to them for sexual and reproductive responsibility. I would argue that classroom discussion on the meaning of citizenship in a religiously and culturally plural nation-state is clearly a matter of urgency, calling for critical reflection on rights and responsibilities *within* any particular cultural or religious tradition students may locate themselves in.

Whether we look at majority or minority groups, cultural or religious groups, the reality of male dominance remains. Feminist theorists believe that this reality is rooted in a core problem, namely the division between public and private realms of society. An emphasis on citizenship as political activity conducted in the public realm privileges and values political institutions – usually identified with the state – that traditionally have been understood as the male domain. Consequently, everything that is traditionally understood as female has been relegated to the private sphere of home and family. Accordingly, as Susan James asserts, 'the cluster of activities, values, ways of thinking and ways of doing things which have long been associated with women are all conceived as outside the political world of citizenship and largely irrelevant to it' (1992: 48). James therefore calls for new conceptions of the political to dislodge the old, implicitly male, conceptions.

Several feminist scholars, in fact, have attempted to reformulate the public–private division in innovative ways that broaden the scope of citizenship rights and practices to include social and cultural dimensions other than the traditionally male public. Nira Yuval-Davis, for instance, calls for the identification of the private domain with the family and of the public domain with the state to be dismantled. She reconceives citizenship as a multi-tier formation comprising three domains – the state, civil society and the domain of the family – to replace the former binary opposition (1997: 13). Such a theory of citizenship would generate a process of 'transversal politics', engaging people of different gender, class, ethnicity, etc., at different times of their lives, across home, local, ethnic, national collectivities and even global agencies. For Davis, citizenship should be imagined as a dynamic *process* developing in people's lives, according to changing aspects of time and space, rather than a rigid status. Transversal politics, then, 'might offer us a way for mutual support . . . in the continuous struggle towards a less sexist, less racist and more democratic society' (1997: 22).

Ruth Lister, too, critiques the rigid division of public and private realms that universalizes a narrow ideal of citizenship based on male experience and political obligations that can be excessively demanding for women (1997a: 24). She understands the two realms as dialectically interrelated in a shifting and fluid political construction that takes shape according to context and needs (1997b: 42). Thus the political sphere cannot be separated from the rest of social life, including family life. Lister proposes activism outside formal political channels and favours community-based, local politics that would offer a more accessible and inclusive participatory citizenship. Furthermore, she is careful to point out that the civic republican expectation of citizens to fulfil their duties, for the 'common good', excludes those who are unable (for example, because of lack of economic resources, disability, age, etc.) or unwilling to participate in collective political activity. A broader definition, Lister suggests, would conceive citizenship as a right and an *opportunity* for collective action, thus generating a synthesis between liberal rights discourse and republican obligations discourse. Small-scale, informal political action would offer women, in particular, opportunities for greater self-confidence and agency, to take on roles as political actors (Lister 1997a: 29–39). This approach to citizenship, perhaps, gives space for women's collective action *within* a particular cultural group or religious tradition. As Maud Eduards (1994) argues, all human beings naturally have agency and have the capacity to initiate action and change as conscious, autonomous and purposive choice. Women no longer have to comply with the stereotypical image of themselves as passive victims, confined to the domestic domain as 'second-class citizens', an image which is, in any case, a socially and culturally constructed injustice symptomatic of a patriarchal political order (see Eduards 1994: 181–6).

Political citizenship, we might then conclude, *is* participation, *is* collective action, and is shaped by differentiated contextual factors such as group, place, time of life and so on. Even Lister (1997a), who does not divorce citizenship from the private realm, insists that for any activity to *count* as active citizenship it has to be brought into the public sphere of society. For example, at a certain stage of her life, a woman might choose to take control of her own bodily processes and demand the right to give birth to her child at home. This issue surely concerns one of the most private and intimate female bodily processes, and yet, as Kerreen Reiger (2000) shows, groups of women may organize politically to humanize childbirth and transform the hegemonic male control and medicalization of that process. Women, then, can be active citizens by engaging in political action that brings the most private of women's issues, which have historically been confined to the private domain, into the public domain (see Reiger 2000: 309–27). It is surely laudable for a woman to make her own choices about her own intimate bodily process of giving birth but this challenge to patriarchal control of women's bodily processes, kept within her own domestic space, may not be counted as active citizenship – for most feminist theorists of citizenship, only when she joins a political campaign around such issues, mounted in the public arena, would it become so (see Lister 1997a: 28).

Ann Phillips, even earlier, had pursued this line of thinking, but, with some regret or perhaps nostalgia, she marked it as a change from the old feminist adage 'the personal is political', which was born of an earlier era when feminism reshaped politics 'to cover any arena in which there are relations of dominance and power' and to dissolve the boundary between private and public (1991: 85–6). In more recent feminist citizenship theory and rights discourse, she noted, the division between public and private spheres is affirmed. Politics, Phillips had to conclude, 'is a particular kind of activity, and not to be dissolved into everything else'; consequently, being a 'good citizen' is not the same as being a good neighbour, being a good mother – or being a good feminist, for that matter (Phillips 1991: 85–6).

This concern with women's reproductive processes and the concept of 'being a good mother', as it happens, raises a key issue in feminist reconceptions of citizenship theory and the private–public divide. Women's experience of mothering within the constraints of patriarchal society has certainly been a prime subject of late twentieth-century feminist discourse, underpinned by the very insistence that the personal is political.[1] But maternity has also come under scrutiny within the parameters of certain feminist concerns about the reality, or unreality, of an essentially 'feminine' subjectivity. Lively feminist debate continues across academic disciplines between so-called essentialists on the one hand and cultural determinists (or social constructionists) on the other. An extreme essentialist standpoint focuses on sexual difference as inherent in the human species, as biological and natural, producing 'woman' as 'other', outside the parameters of cultural construction (Cooey 1994: 19). Women's experience, then, is distinctly different, founded on inherently feminine characteristics, signifying that patriarchy must be challenged through revalorizing that difference and 'positive self-evaluation for women as women' (Cooey 1994: 24). An essentialist approach to feminist citizenship theory would call for 'the distinctive characteristics and activities of women to be given special consideration' (Pateman 1992: 17).

Cultural determinist feminists, however, argue that this standpoint tends to assume a universal category, 'woman', which overlooks politically sensitive issues of difference among women across race, class, ethnicity and so on. An extreme cultural determinist viewpoint asserts 'that "woman" is, strictly speaking, entirely a social construct upon which patriarchy necessarily depends for its self-perpetuation' (Cooey 1994: 20). Gender differences that exist, in terms of women's status, role and experience, are culturally constructed according to historical and social contexts. A cultural determinist approach to feminist citizenship theory would claim that any socially constructed arrangements – including gendered systems – can be changed. Patriarchy and women's subordinate citizenship status, therefore, would be challenged through demands for equality, in the sense of identical treatment of women and men (Pateman 1992: 17).

The crux of the matter here is that sex and gender are arranged as a binary opposition that confronts women with a choice between two opposing paths, namely difference or equality. As both Cooey and Pateman insist, when sex and gender, difference and equality, are structured according to strictly dichotomous oppositions, they reinforce male domination as much as any other androcentric and hierarchically gendered binary found at the core of patriarchy. Joan Scott (1988) has succinctly described this choice as an impossible one: 'If one opts for equality, one is forced to accept the notion that difference is antithetical to it. If one opts for difference, one admits that equality is unattainable' (cited in Pateman 1992: 17). Put briefly, the demand for male citizens' rights to be extended to women renders the meaning of equality as women becoming like men; and the demand for women's 'femininity' or 'difference' to be a valued part of citizenship is doomed to failure, because that difference – imagined or real – is exactly what patriarchal citizenship, founded on male political participation in the public domain, excludes.

The politics of motherhood

The above dilemma between equality and difference signifies relations of power that mark women's subordination in the political context of citizenship. As Pateman (1992: 29) concludes, equality, in the sense of the capacity to accommodate difference as free political relations between autonomous subjects, can never accommodate difference that means subordination of one gender by another. It is the body, and most particularly the maternal body, I would argue, that is the ground on which such contested notions of sex and gender, equality and difference, essentialism and cultural determinism meet and interact. In Cooey's terms, the dichotomy of sex and gender can be collapsed into the 'socionatural process' of the body itself as potentially creator *and* creation of human ideas and agency, as both essential subject and culturally determined object (Cooey 1994: 7). The feminist political theorist Jane Flax, too, reminds us that 'embodiment is simultaneously natural and cultural' because all human experience, for both women and men, is mediated through the body (1990: 147).

These issues are clearly implicated in what Pateman calls the 'politics of motherhood', based on especially intimate, female *bodily* processes that represent women as different. 'The fact that only women have the capacity to become pregnant, give birth and suckle their infants is the mark of "difference" *par excellence*' (Pateman 1992: 18). This mark of difference *is* corporeal, *is* natural, it could be argued, and only goes to prove the essentialist point of view. But, by the same token, this mark of difference symbolizes the ways in which motherhood has been represented and interpreted – arguably by patriarchy – ways that have largely marginalized women in society, culture and religion, including exclusion from full citizenship. This, it could similarly be argued, only goes to prove the constructionist point of view. Surely, though, both 'natural' and 'socially determined' processes are involved in shaping women's citizenship, a status in itself that is not static but fluid and changing? The tension between difference and equality underlies the feminist debate on citizenship, marking a divide between those who aim to dissolve the boundary between the public and private domains and those who would reinforce it even further. The respective arguments range from a feminist, philosophical ethic of 'maternal thinking' that leans towards women's citizenship rights and duties based on difference and revalorization of the private domain to feminist 'political thinking' that leans towards advocacy of feminism as a political movement that will actively engage women in the public sphere and engender equality with men.

Sara Ruddick, one of the foremost 'maternalist feminists', unequivocally advocates that 'feminists must join in articulating a theory of justice shaped by and incorporating maternal thinking' whereby 'the personal will in fact betoken the political' (1983: 226). A mother, says Ruddick, engages in maternal *thinking* as a discipline that conceives of achievements towards which her maternal *practice* will be directed, all of which serve the interests of the child's preservation, growth and acceptability. Ruddick stresses, however, that the demands of children, and maternal interests in meeting them, are in turn shaped differently by multiple contextual factors such as culture, class, environment and historical period (Ruddick 1983: 214–15). Furthermore, the discipline of maternal thinking does not assume achievement of those ideals and their associated values.

Does maternal thinking, then, represent virtues that would create a more humane set of moral values if brought into the public realm, based on a specifically female ethic of care, responsibility, relationality and compassion, as Carol Gilligan's (1982) theory of moral development suggests? Ruddick cautions that unless maternal thinking and practice are transformed by feminist thinking and practice, aimed to eradicate women's subordination within the oppressive institution of motherhood in patriarchy, a mother's own growth may well be subordinated to the dominant social expectations of women to foster growth only in others (Ruddick 1983: 218–25). Furthermore, in terms of shaping an *acceptable* child, Ruddick highlights the vulnerability of maternal thought to generating action arising from unconscious, inauthentic obedience to the 'paternal law' that demands betrayal of a mother's care for her children, for example, in 'training her daughters for powerlessness, her sons for war, and both for crippling work in dehumanizing factories, businesses, and professions' (Ruddick 1983: 221).

In revising this chapter, after the events of 11 September 2001, I am struck by the poignant relevance, today, of Ruddick's much earlier insistence on mobilizing feminist consciousness to transform such inauthenticity, as mothers, both American and Afghan, witness their sons go to war. Ruddick's vision points to the difficult path of 'disciplined expression of conscience' that would arguably revalorize women's difference and a female ethic of care in the public realm and would be of 'general intellectual and moral benefit' in any society or culture (Ruddick 1983: 224). Moreover, one of the foremost critics of maternalist thinking, Mary Dietz, does not deny some value in maternalist feminist thinking, feeling that it does have relevance to feminist critique of the 'male liberal individualist world-view and the masculinist notion of citizenship'. Maternal thinking demands that we rehumanize the political order into 'a more humane, relational and shared community' (Dietz: 1992: 72).

For Dietz, however, the problems inherent in the maternalist perspective outweigh the benefits for feminist reconceptions of citizenship. First, since maternalist feminism is undoubtedly founded on an essentialist conception of female sexual difference, Dietz feels that maternalist thinking produces women as 'ahistorical, universalized entities' (Dietz 1992: 73). Secondly, she detects a maternalist intention to replace the 'masculinist, competitive, statist public' with the 'maternal, loving, virtuous private', which forces a choice between the two and, in either case, results in a 'one-sided view of politics' (Dietz 1992: 74).

Consequently, Dietz is unequivocal in stating that 'neither of the above will do' and in insisting that 'democratic citizenship is a practice unlike any other' requiring feminists to 'turn to virtues, relations and practices that are expressly political and, more exactly, participatory and democratic' (Dietz 1992: 74–5). Her incisive focus is on democracy, as a collective participatory politics which can be – in fact, must be – practised by any citizen, male or female, at any community level, be it 'the neighbourhood, the city, the state, the region or the nation itself' (Dietz 1992: 75). This thinking, Dietz asserts, extends beyond limited views such as liberalism's focus on the individual as bearer of rights or maternalism's wish to transfer maternal virtues into the public realm. She calls for both a political revitalization of feminism and a feminist revitalization of political activity and democratic citizenship, whereby citizenship itself is conceived of as a 'good in itself' (Dietz 1992: 77–8). Dietz's feminist reconception of citizenship is not so much about *women's* citizenship as about women participating politically in *equal* citizenship with men. Women's gendered subjectivity, or difference, particularly in the maternal context, is not of any special significance in Dietz's exclusively political theory of citizenship.

What appear to be opposing approaches to citizenship – essentialist versus cultural determinist, difference versus equality, maternal thinking versus feminist political thinking, private versus public – provide, I think, fruitful ground for informing classroom discussion on issues of citizenship, including cultural and religious diversity as well as gendered power relations *within* any cultural group or religious tradition. Again, as the United States wages war in Afghanistan and questions about Islam loom large in the Western imagination, such educational efforts to engender understanding of subjectivity and the 'other', of conflict and violence, of possibilities of a more peaceful world, gain added relevance and urgency. How, for instance, can Afghan women be full citizens, when the Taliban's oppression, violence and abuse define them as less than human? What do the women themselves think and feel about US military intervention, about alternative political groupings in their country? How much has the abuse of Afghan women had anything, if at all, to do with the teachings of Islam? Have Muslim women in Afghanistan managed to initiate any political action themselves? Certainly the clandestine and courageous activities of the underground resistance movement, the Revolutionary Association of the Women of Afghanistan, point to the permeability of the boundaries between private and public, difference and equality.[2] Feminist research in peace studies is particularly informative here. For example, Linda Rennie Forcey gives careful attention to all sides of the debate and provides a wealth of insights into women's diverse attitudes and practices relating to militarism and war (see 1994: 355–75). As she points out:

> The challenge for a feminist peace studies is to honor the special, mothering, peacemaking skills of many women (and men) while questioning impulses to universalize them. The challenge . . . is to be ever vigilant of the age-old trap of oversimplifying the notion of 'mother,' denying her differences with other mothers and other women, exaggerating her differences with men, and thereby lessening her power.
>
> (Forcey 1994: 372)

Between the two

To sum up the politics of motherhood so far, maternalist thinking, in relation to women's citizenship, accords greater value to the private domain of the family, while Dietz's plea for feminist political activity sees only the public domain as the locus for being a citizen. Both points of view, I would argue, simply reinforce the division between public and private by focusing almost entirely on one domain or the other. Raia Prokhovnik (1998) moves towards closing this gap that forces women into choosing between the two: either 'equality', favouring the traditional concept of political activity in the public domain, that is, 'more of the same with women added'; or 'difference', conceiving unrealistic expectations about the transference of maternal values from the private domain into the public sphere (Prokhovnik 1998: 94). Again, neither, on its own, will do. Citizenship, Prokhovnik insists, is 'first and foremost a moral relationship' and feminist citizenship should have 'a moral basis in that it recognizes the value of a universal grant to all members of the political community, but sees citizens as expressing their value in a range of different substantive practices' (Prokhovnik 1998: 86).

A feminist citizenship must take account of women's (and men's) gendered subjectivity and the reality that there cannot be a truly gender-neutral citizenship. The private realm, mostly the domain of women, has extended far beyond the family, including informal collectivities, voluntary work and, ironically, religion. But all these activities, traditionally perceived as 'women's work', are also traditionally given much less value than work in the public realm. Furthermore, I would add that accounting for difference among women is essential, in that women are not only differently situated from men, but also differently situated according to class, race, ethnicity and so on. Prokhovnik asserts: 'Feminists can recognize that citizenship involves whatever ethically-grounded activities, undertaken by women in the private as well as public realms, are *relevant* to *their* lives' (Prokhovnik 1998: 96). She advocates transforming conceptions of the public and private domains as different areas of creativity which do not have to merge, but should maintain interconnections in 'non-oppositional, non-rejectionist and non-hierarchical ways'. She concludes that feminist citizenship theory must take account of what people actually *do* and how they *are* citizens and that the 'fully human self' can 'be free in both public and private realms, to exercise citizenship in both realms' (Prokhovnik 1998: 98).

Prokhovnik clearly confronts the pivotal issues of citizenship as gendered and relational – especially between women and men – within and across different historical and social contexts in any political community. Luce Irigaray, the feminist philosopher and psychoanalyst, brings a particular focus to women's gendered subjectivity and citizenship in the struggle for a truly democratic civil society in which 'woman' and 'man' would relate as two autonomous, free and gendered subjects. In this final section I turn briefly to Irigaray's especially valuable insights relating to citizenship education and the interweaving of religious and citizenship discourses that inevitably link religion education and citizenship education.

In her essays on democracy in 1990s Western culture, presented in *Democracy Begins between Two* (2000), Irigaray aims to define a new kind of citizenship, giving particular attention to citizenship training and education for civil life. For Irigaray, this process requires learning to value 'being' rather than 'having', to develop respect for self and others and care for the environment: 'Training in citizenship is concerned with relationship rather than ownership' (Irigaray 2000: 10). Civil rights and a truly democratic citizenship would be based on valuing human relationships above ownership of goods, and on respect for differences of gender, generation, race, culture, tradition and religion (see Irigaray 1994: 67–87). If a theory of citizenship is to embrace these ideals, Irigaray stresses, innovative modes of communication and transmission, new language and discourses, must be found that 'do not sacrifice the singular and the particular detail to neutral, abstract and, in a sense, dead codes' (2000: 9). She thus follows feminist concerns to transform liberalism's abstract, universalized and masculinist conception of citizenship. Using her own creative and poetic language, more reminiscent of non-dualistic philosophical thought in Hindu and Buddhist religious traditions than of Western political theory, Irigaray urges us to:

> search for whatever it is that, for you, represents the place of singularity which harbours the seed of the universal. The universal cannot be reached outside the self; it is not a sum of individuals, a multiplicity

of cultures, an accumulation of possessions. The universal is not so immense that it escapes you. The universal is within you and develops out of you as a flower grows from the earth.

(Irigaray 2000: 28–9)

This claim seems to signify that only by acknowledging difference, as particularity, as the self, can an inclusive, collective civil identity be forged among subjects, as citizens.

According to Irigaray, here in agreement with modern citizenship theory, democracy belongs to everyone as an *active* right of all citizens, not as rights passively received (Irigaray 2000: 23). Each woman and each man needs to accept full political rights and duties, so that each one is entrusted with political responsibility, rather than relying on patriarchal leaders (Irigaray 2000: 174). How can such rights and participation be assured for women, in an age where violence 'directed against the body and dignity of women' is endemic throughout most of the world (Irigaray 2000: 182; see Irigaray 1992)? Or where women still tend to be seen as passive recipients of rights that constitute 'permission granted' to them, in the private domain of the patriarchal family – both in the narrow sense and in the wider sense of political or religious family (Irigaray 2000: 182, 31)? For example, it may appear that great strides have been taken towards reproductive rights for women, but in many societies, especially where conservative religion holds sway, such rights come with conditions, needing 'a masculine stamp of approval', rather than being 'the positive right to freedom of choice' (Irigaray 2000: 31).

To find solutions to these problematic questions, Irigaray clearly pursues the path of difference in the struggle for citizenship codes that recognize women as women and give them the right to a specific civil identity (Irigaray 2000: 32–6). She is, in fact, dismissive of feminist disagreements over gender as 'biological destiny' (essentialism) or as 'social conditioning' (cultural determinism). Similar to Cooey's way of thinking, I would argue, Irigaray collapses that opposition when she contends that, either way, whether 'being' or 'becoming' women, women embody a 'feminine identity', in other words a gendered subjectivity. By claiming the same rights as men – equality as sameness – or by forcing a 'deconditioning' of feminine identity, many women, she notes, have sacrificed their own identity to conform to a social, cultural and historical conditioning that 'belongs to a masculine identity'.

Irigaray is passionate about reclaiming feminine subjectivity, a passion that is woven into most of her work. She insists: 'Women's exploitation is based on sexual difference; its solution will come only through sexual difference . . . It is quite simply a matter of social justice to balance out this power of one sex over the other by giving, or giving back, cultural values to female sexuality' (1993a: 13). An autonomous feminine symbolic space or subjectivity must be created, separate from the masculine symbolic or 'paternal law' that dominates both genders, restoring female genealogies of mothers and daughters, feminine language, feminine images and symbols. This space, for Irigaray, includes *religious* symbols, since they are particularly cogent for her critique of patriarchal, monotheistic religions that tend to devalue the body, the earth and femininity, offering only a male image of the divine, only a way *up* 'to heaven, toward the father and his kingdom', a human transcendence to some world *beyond* the one we have (1993b: 15). Women, Irigaray believes, need a divine made in their own image in order to create their own subjectivity (1993b: 63). Certainly, in a multi-faith approach to religion education, female images of the divine can be found and explored in various religious myths, symbols and traditions. And perhaps at higher secondary levels of education, and most definitely in tertiary education, the critical eye of a more feminist gender-sensitive analysis can be brought to interpreting the significance of these symbols for women, as citizens, in society.

For example, Irigaray's search for a 'divine made in her own image', as part of an autonomous, feminine symbolic space, can be pursued in learning about the goddesses of Hindu tradition and to what extent different meanings of these symbols empower or disempower women's subjectivity. In this regard, the opposing characters of two particular Hindu goddesses, Sita and Kali, are informative and colourful examples (see Tobler 2002). First, Sita is widely acknowledged as the most popular epic heroine in Hindu religious tradition as the wife of the god Rama and one of the major protagonists in the great epic, the *Ramayana*. Although both Rama and Sita are worshipped as deities in Hindu devotional tradition, Sita is rarely worshipped independently of Rama – her persona, both human and divine, is almost entirely defined in relationship to her husband. The divine couple could be said to fulfil the expectations of patriarchy to perfection as well as Hindu ideals of marriage and royalty. Rama is the perfect and powerful king who dispenses his rule as a model of social integrity and justice, and Sita is his ideal wife, or *pativrata*, whose every thought revolves around her husband and who remains steadfast and loyal to Rama through thick and thin (Kinsley 1986a: 68–70).

Sita's mythic role is illustrated in several incidents throughout the narrative of the *Ramayana*, one after the other proving her self-sacrificing devotion and sexual fidelity to Rama against all odds (see Kinsley 1986a). Her character is tested through exile, abduction, ordeal by fire and banishment, all of which are marked by separation from the object of her love, but none of which dispels her loyalty to Rama. She does, however, emerge as a woman of spirit, courage and endurance, and is not beyond rebuking Rama when he is, only too often, insensitive to her situation because of his rigid adherence to his kingly duty to his subjects. Rama, in point of fact, in aspiring to be the ideal king frequently falls short of being the ideal husband but, nonetheless, Sita's identity as loyal and faithful wife to Rama remains the symbol most commonly held up as quintessential exemplar to young Hindu girls as they approach marriage. The story of Rama and Sita, I suggest, provides rich resources for classroom discussion of fairness and justice, roles and responsibilities, in relation to gender relations in patriarchy.

Kali, on the other hand, in stark contrast to Sita, is the independent and powerful 'dark' goddess of Hindu myth. In the *Devi-Mahatmya*, a sacred text devoted to the great goddess Devi, Kali often takes the form of Devi's anger, appearing on the cosmic battlefield to vanquish demons and restore cosmic order. Her ferocity, however, is often uncontrolled and bloodthirsty in ways that may even threaten the very order she aims to protect (Kinsley 1986b: 144). The most popular image of Kali, particularly in Indian iconography, is consistently hideous, horrifying and often explicitly sexual as occasional and dominant partner of the great god Shiva (see Brown 1989; Gupta 1991; Kinsley 1986b). Kali is indeed independent, powerful, ferocious and free, and in her outrageous contravention of Hindu ideals of social order and wifely virtue – ideals that Sita so readily fulfils – she undoubtedly reinforces the androcentric conception of uncontrolled, and therefore threatening and dangerous, female sexuality (see Tobler 2002). But no matter how much she may look like the 'mad mother', devotees of Kali always approach her as the protective and redeeming 'divine mother'. The deeper spiritual significance of her terrifying nature is understood as salvific, symbolizing her power to destroy ignorance and transform the deluded ego, pushing the spiritual aspirant beyond the security of social and ritual order, to the threshold of spiritual liberation (see Brown 1989; Gupta 1991).

An important question, then, raised by Rachel McDermott's critical analysis of Western appropriations of this goddess, is whether Kali can be seen as a 'genuine goddess of transformation' for women – whatever their social, cultural or religious context may be (McDermott 1996: 305). The ambivalence of Kali's nature and the paradox embedded in her symbolism – as fierce warrior and protective mother, as creator and destroyer, as goddess of life and death, as social deviant and spiritual guide – can be an empowering model for women. For instance, Kali could be understood as opening a channel for women to express long repressed anger that has, in the past, been deemed 'unfeminine'. The feminist scholar of Hinduism Lina Gupta describes this goddess as 'the personified wrath of all women in all cultures' and the expression of 'a deep, long-buried emotion' that, in the myths, is always an appropriate response to situations in which Kali finds herself. Her anger, in fact, is not arbitrary or random, nor is she 'simply malevolent' (Gupta 1991: 31). Only because the power and wrath of the warrior are conventionally understood as a male function is Kali often described as 'a masculinized female or as out of control and destructive, as if strength and valor are constructive character traits only as long as they are part of a male deity' (Gupta 1991: 32).

Kali's independence and active sexuality, too, can help redress androcentric denigration of the body and repression of female sexuality. The feminist historian of religion Rita Gross argues that Hindu images of the goddesses in general, and of Kali in particular, point to the 'reintroduction of sexuality as a significant religious metaphor . . . helping us to move beyond the lingering body–spirit dichotomy and consequent hatred of the body' (Gross 1989: 228). Kali's profound symbolic significance offers women a multi-faceted, transformative metaphor that could help them regain wholeness and heal divisions in their lives (McDermott 1996: 305). Indeed, Kali embodies a challenging, complex and vivid symbolic representation of the 'feminine' and, without doubt, she offers rich symbolic resources for lively classroom discussion around gendered subjectivity, gender stereotypes and divisive normative expectations of 'femininity' and 'masculinity' in society and religion.

Returning to Irigaray, it can be seen that her intention is to encourage women's autonomous and different subjectivity so that a civil identity, specifically appropriate to women, can free both women and men from the 'authority of the One: of man, of the father, of the leader, of the one god, of the unique truth' (Irigaray 2000: 129). At issue here is 'the reality of the two' (Irigaray 2000: 131), the imperative to cultivate the relation between *two subjects*, to create an entirely new ethic of relationship between 'woman' and 'man' that is free of dominance and promotes a moral co-existence of subjects, based on reciprocity between the sexes and a truly democratic citizenship. The androcentric split between subject and object has to be transcended, in the sense of a 'horizontal transcendence' – here, *below*, in the human world (Irigaray 2000: 47). For Irigaray, relations between citizens, within the family, for example, need to be protected by civil rights, free of the control of religion, 'leaving an individual's choice of religion free' (Irigaray 2000: 99). This does not mean, she insists, that there is no place for religion; but it does mean that we need to rethink our religious traditions in creative ways that encourage self-responsibility, ethical relations between subjects, a livable world, a culture of life that, even in the political context of civil life and citizenship, cannot exclude emotions, intimacy and love – rather than possession of goods or of each other. This kind of rethinking, I suggest, would also be progress towards freedom for women *within* religion. Full democracy, full citizenship, according to Irigaray, rests on a transformed intersubjectivity, it 'begins between two': 'A real democracy must take as its basis, today, a just relationship between man and woman' (Irigaray 2000: 118).

Conclusion

The question remains: what are the creative ways whereby such an ethically based and fully democratic citizenship might not only be theorized but also realized, since gendered subjectivity and difference continue to be played out in relations of domination, where 'the feminine is the "different" to the masculine "same"' and equality means assimilation into the male norm (see Flax 1992a: 193–5, 1992b: 112–15)? I would argue that in the development of citizenship education, religion education could play an important role in developing an appreciation of religious diversity. If attention is given by educators to gender-sensitive analysis of religious traditions, and then brought to the awareness of learners in the classroom, religion education would also play a vital part in nurturing autonomous female subjectivity within religious traditions.

In conclusion, I suggest that citizenship is created 'in between': in between the gendered subject's inner experience of subjective reality and his or her perception of objective reality; in between different, autonomous subjects, female and male – who are not the 'same' but equivalent in worth; and even in between the private and public domains. According to the object relations psychoanalyst D. W. Winnicott, this constitutes a 'transitional space', the in-between space that is the space for developing subjectivity, right from early childhood, when the infant starts to become aware of what is 'not me' (see Winnicott 1971). It is a 'third world' that is neither subjective nor objective, neither purely inner nor purely outer, the space in which people make sense of experience and are creative. In childhood, it is the growing space of relationship between the child and its mother as separate beings, the space of play. Later, it is the space out of which culture emerges, where human creativity produces 'transitional phenomena' such as the arts, philosophy, religion, all of which help to reconcile conflict between inner and outer realities, between subject and other (see Flax 1992b: 121–2). According to the feminist political theorist and psychoanalyst Jane Flax it is also the space where justice can emerge, the space where active citizenship can be a 'transitional practice' that is 'essential for creating public spaces in which justice can be nurtured and held' (1992b: 125).

Furthermore, I would add that active citizenship begins with the development of subjectivity and self-esteem. As Susan James argues, if an individual's subjectivity is to become an independent voice and agent in the world, moving fluidly between the private and public domains, self-esteem and belief in one's 'own voice' are essential (James 1992: 61–3). Self-esteem, in turn, depends on and is the result of growing up in an environment of 'secure, loving relations', especially in the family, and is thus the bridge between dependence and independence, the private and public spheres. If self-esteem is considered essential for active citizenship, then any citizenship theory must address gendered subjectivity, must give space for women's autonomous, feminine subjectivity: 'Self-esteem can only be created and maintained in practices that are sensitive to and respectful of difference' (James 1992: 63).

Women and men can *be* citizens and *act* as citizens in both the private and the public realms of human relations and society. Citizenship theory, I would argue, needs to be consciously inclusive of all aspects of what it means to be fully human, including physical, intellectual, emotional and spiritual dimensions of subjectivity. Being fully human, in ways that reconcile tension and conflict in intersubjective relations, emerges from human creativity in that transitional space between self and other, a creativity that is imagined, articulated and practised differently, in ways that are *gendered*. If citizenship and religion are both located and creatively practised in that in-between space, surely they can and must contribute to one another. The creative dimensions of religion – myth, symbol, ritual – offer myriad resources for understanding difference and diversity, for creating and re-creating gendered subjectivity, for encouraging self-esteem and active citizenship for women and men, all of which can be engendered by a desire and respect for 'learning the difference'.

Notes

1 For example, see Nancy Chodorow (1978), Dorothy Dinnerstein (1976) and Adrienne Rich (1986).
2 See Janelle Brown, 'The Taliban's bravest opponents', on http://www.salon.com/mwt/feature/2001/10/02/fatima/ for information on RAWA and an interview with an active member of the organization.

References

Benton, Sarah (1991) 'Gender, sexuality and citizenship', in G. Andrews (ed.) *Citizenship*, London: Lawrence & Wishart, 151–63.
Brown, C. Mackenzie (1989) 'Kali the mad mother', in C. Olson (ed.) *The Book of the Goddess Past and Present: An Introduction to Her Religion*, New York: Crossroad, 110–23.
Chodorow, Nancy (1978) *The Reproduction of Mothering: Psychoanalysis and the Sociology of Gender*, Berkeley CA: University of California Press.
Cooey, Paula (1994) *Religious Imagination and the Body: A Feminist Analysis*, New York and Oxford: Oxford University Press.
Dietz, Mary (1992) 'Context is all: feminism and theories of citizenship', in C. Mouffe (ed.) *Dimensions of Radical Democracy: Pluralism, Citizenship, Community*, London and New York: Verso, 63–85.
Dinnerstein, Dorothy (1976) *The Mermaid and the Minotaur: Sexual Arrangements and Human Malaise*, New York: Harper & Row.
Eduards, Maud L. (1994) 'Women's agency and collective action', *Women's Studies International Forum*, 17 (2/3), 181–6.

Flax, Jane (1990) *Thinking Fragments: Psychoanalysis, Feminism, and Postmodernism in the Comtemporary West*, Berkeley CA: University of California Press.

—— (1992a) 'Beyond equality: gender, justice and difference', in G. Bock and S. James (eds) *Beyond Equality and Difference: Citizenship, Feminist Politics and Female Subjectivity*, London and New York: Routledge, 193–210.

—— (1992b) 'The play of justice', in *Disputed Subjects: Essays on Psychoanalysis, Politics and Philosophy*, New York and London: Routledge, 111–28.

Forcey, Linda Rennie (1994) 'Feminist perspectives on mothering and peace', in Evelyn Nakano Glenn, Grace Chang and Linda Rennie Forcey (eds) *Mothering: Ideology, Experience, and Agency*, London and New York: Routledge, 355–75.

Gilligan, Carol (1982) *In a Different Voice: Psychological Theory and Women's Development*, Cambridge MA: Harvard University Press.

Gross, Rita (1989) 'Hindu female deities as a resource for contemporary rediscovery of the Goddess', in C. Olson (ed.) *The Book of the Goddess Past and Present: An Introduction to Her Religion*, New York: Crossroad, 217–30.

Gupta, Lina (1991) 'Kali the savior', in P. M. Cooey, W. R. Eakin and J. B. McDaniel (eds) *After Patriarchy: Feminist Transformations of World Religions*, New York: Orbis Books, 15–38.

Irigaray, Luce (1992) *Elemental Passions*, trans. Joanne Collie and Judith Sill, London: Athlone Press.

—— (1993a) *je, tu, nous: Toward a Culture of Difference*, trans. Alison Martin, New York and London: Routledge.

—— (1993b) *Sexes and Genealogies*, trans. Gillian C. Gill, New York: Columbia University Press.

—— (1994) 'Civil rights and responsibilities for the two sexes', *Thinking the Difference: For a Peaceful Revolution*, trans. Karin Montin, New York: Routledge, 67–87.

—— (2000) *Democracy Begins between Two*, trans. Kirsten Anderson, London: Athlone Press.

James, Susan (1992) 'The good-enough citizen: female citizenship and independence', in G. Bock and S. James (eds) *Beyond Equality and Difference: Citizenship, Feminist Politics and Female Subjectivity*, London and New York: Routledge, 48–65.

Kinsley, David (1986a) *Hindu Goddesses: Visions of the Divine Feminine in the Hindu Tradition*, Berkeley CA: University of California Press.

—— (1986b) 'Blood and death out of place: reflections on the goddess Kali', in J. S. Hawley and D. M. Wulff (eds) *The Divine Consort: Radha and the Goddesses of India*, Boston MA: Beacon Press, 144–52.

Lister, Ruth (1997a) *Citizenship: Feminist Perspectives*, London: Macmillan.

—— (1997b) 'Citizenship: towards a feminist synthesis', *Feminist Review*, 57, 28–48.

McDermott, Rachel Fell (1996) 'The Western Kali', in J. S. Hawley and D. M. Wulff (eds) *Devi: Goddesses of India*, Berkeley CA: University of California Press, 281–313.

Pateman, Carole (1992) 'Equality, difference, subordination: the politics of motherhood and women's citizenship', in G. Bock and S. James (eds) *Beyond Equality and Difference: Citizenship, Feminist Politics and Female Subjectivity*, London and New York: Routledge, 17–31.

Phillips, Anne (1991) 'Citizenship and feminist theory', in G. Andrews (ed.) *Citizenship*, London: Lawrence & Wishart, 76–88.

Prokhovnik, Raia (1998) 'Public and private citizenship: from gender invisibility to feminist inclusiveness', *Feminist Review*, 60, 84–104.

Reiger, Kerreen (2000) 'Reconceiving citizenship: the challenge of mothers as political activists', *Feminist Theory*, 1 (3), 309–27.

Rich, Adrienne (1986) *Of Woman Born*, 2nd edn, New York: Norton (orig. edn 1976).

Ruddick, Sara (1983) 'Maternal thinking', in Joyce Trebilcot (ed.) *Mothering: Essays in Feminist Theory*, Lanham MD: Rowman & Littlefield, 213–30.

Scott, Joan W. (1988) *Gender and the Politics of History*, New York: Columbia University Press.

Tobler, Judy (forthcoming) 'Goddesses and women's spirituality: transformative symbols of the feminine in Hindu religion', in Azila Reisenberger (ed.) *Women's Spirituality in the Transformation of South Africa*, New York: Waxmann, 51–72.

Voet, Rian (1998) *Feminism and Citizenship*, London: Sage.

Winnicott, D. W. (1971) *Playing and Reality*, London: Tavistock Publications.

Young, Iris Marion (1989) 'Polity and group difference: a critique of the ideal of universal citizenship', *Ethics*, 99, 250–74.

Yuval-Davis, Nira (1997) 'Women, citizenship and difference', *Feminist Review*, 57, 4–27.

Part II
Dialogue and communication

Chapter 8

Dialogue, citizenship and religious education

Julia Ipgrave

Synopsis　This chapter uses illustrations from a research project into children's religious thought, and examples from their discussions, to set out a threefold understanding of dialogue as context, ideal and activity. The model of dialogue is related to the local, national and global background to the lives of children in our society, and to the political and educational drive for the promotion of citizenship. The knowledge and skills to be acquired and developed through citizenship studies are seen to have much in common with the learning objectives of a dialogical religious education. A vital role is recognized for religious education in the preparation of young people for a plural and democratic society. Examples of intercommunal, inter-religious tension in the United Kingdom and the world have demonstrated alike that religion is not just a private, but a public concern; that it will benefit children and society if pupils at school are conversant in its language. The chapter moves on from the exigencies of the present social, political and religious climate to argue that the very nature of religious thought – its engagement with 'big questions' and the multiple answers it presents – makes the religious education class an ideal forum for the development of the skills of dialogue and negotiation, and of the intellectual and moral awareness that constitute the citizenship ideal.

Background

Dialogical RE

This chapter arises from work on children's religious understanding that I have been carrying out with Warwick Religions and Education Research Unit. This work has involved both analysis of instances of children's dialogue and the development of approaches and exercises for the promotion of pupil-to-pupil dialogue in primary schools. In the former area of activity the examples of dialogue were drawn from a series of group discussions set up in a junior school in Leicester with minority non-Muslim children (who identified as Christian or Hindu) in a predominantly Muslim school community. In small, religiously mixed groups the children were free to explore and share their own ideas around a number of words supplied to them to stimulate discussion, and in response to questions, formulated by some of their own number. Words and questions raised issues of religious identity, practice and belief. Analysing the children's conversation involved relating their understanding and meaning to their immediate and their wider contexts of social encounter.

This research has shown how these children are led by their experience of religious plurality to seek new joint understandings with their peers, exploring the very nature of religion and of God. In this, the potential for developing children's interest and skills in a dialogical RE for the primary school classroom has become clear. Working in several Leicester schools, I have been trialling dialogue activities (definition, categorization, prioritization exercises, problem solving from case studies, debates around key questions) through which children were able to bring together their various experiences and opinions in a collaborative development of ideas (Ipgrave 2001). The scope of these dialogue activities has been expanded through the use of e-mail links between pupils of different schools, initially between 10 year olds in an inner-city, predominantly Muslim school and a suburban Roman Catholic school, both in Leicester, and latterly between other ethnically diverse Leicester schools and the predominantly 'white' schools of more rural East Sussex.

Citizenship

While I have been engaged in this project, 'citizenship' has come to the fore as a focus of government attention and political debate. Aims of this government drive for citizenship are the creation of a sense of national unity (that also values internal diversity) and the education of members of the population for active citizenship. Both aims are stated in government publications. In a Home Office report, *Race Equality in Public Services* (Home Office 2000: 1), the New Labour government set out its vision of 'One Nation', a country where 'every colour is a good colour . . . every member of every part of society is able to fulfil their potential . . . racism is unacceptable and counteracted . . . everyone is treated according to their needs and rights . . . everyone recognizes their responsibilities . . . racial diversity is celebrated.' The Crick Report (QCA 1998) produced by the Advisory Group on Citizenship spoke of its desire 'for people to see themselves as active citizens, willing, able and equipped to have an influence in public life'.

Added impetus to this movement has come from events that have given cause for critical self-examination among those exercising political and legal authority at national and local level. These events include the publication of the Stephen Lawrence inquiry report with its accusations of institutional racism; the demands and criticism of government handling of the influx of asylum seekers into the United Kingdom; public order disturbances among young people in towns and cities in the north of England in 2001;

and the terrorist attacks in New York and Washington DC of 11 September 2001 which brought to prominence relations between Muslim and other communities in the United Kingdom, and the challenge of multiple loyalties faced by many of the population.

The government expressed confidence in the ability of education to effect changes necessary for the creation of a responsible citizenship and harmonious state. Citizenship, as a curriculum subject, has been prescribed for secondary school pupils of Key Stage 3 (11–14 year olds) and Key Stage 4 (14–16 year olds) from August 2002, in the revised national curriculum. The aim of the programme of study is 'the development of pupils into citizens' (QCA 1998). In the interests of continuity and progression between key stages, the implications of this new educational initiative for primary education have also been considered. To support teachers of the younger Key Stage 1 and 2 pupils with whom I am working, non-statutory guidelines for citizenship have been produced. In this chapter, I reflect on the relation between this current interest in citizenship and the work of my project, bringing together official statements and examples of children's dialogue to illustrate my argument. I trace the links in skills, background and purposes between 'citizenship' and the classroom interchanges of my project, and emphasize the distinctive contribution religious education can make in developing these skills and achieving these purposes. A unifying theme is that dialogical relationship of individual to wider society which supplies the context of our actions, thoughts and words; the relationship between the forces of diversification and those of community cohesion.

Dialogue

Dialogue as activity

The kind of dialogical religious education that I have been promoting shares several of the aims of citizenship set out in the curriculum guides. Obvious links between citizenship and the dialogical activities I have been using can be found in the citizenship programme of study for secondary pupils set out by the Qualifications and Curriculum Authority (QCA). Here pupils are being supported in the acquisition of the skills needed for the exercise of democracy. Under the heading 'Developing skills of enquiry and communication' is statement 2c, that 'pupils should be taught to contribute to group and exploratory class discussions, and take part in debates', and also the note to 2b, that 'pupils could use e-mail to exchange views'. The citizens who emerge from the process are expected to be able to 'justify' their personal opinions and 'to think about, express and explain views that are not their own' (QCA 1999b: 184). All these skills are required by and developed through pupil-to-pupil dialogue.

One example of such dialogue is the following extract from a classroom debate with 9 year olds around the question 'Is human life more precious than animal life?' The debate followed a programme of study on religious attitudes to creation and the natural world, with a particular focus on the rare Bengali tiger and an article on the death of an Indian village boy ('Mr Kumar's grandson') killed by one of these powerful creatures.

T.A. We're the same, though, because God made us and God made tigers and we're animals too, really.

M.Z. We're the same because God made people to look after animals and he made animals to help people.

F.A. Tigers are more precious because lots of people – there are lots of people but tigers are in danger of becoming extinct.

S.N. But people can die before they should, in accidents, or they could be ill. People are in danger too.

M.Z. But there are lots of humans – tigers might die out.

S.N. But perhaps Mr Kumar is worried that it's his only grandson – that then there might be no one in his family – *they* might die out.

M.Z. But not the whole species!

Here the children show developed dialogue skills as they bring together knowledge they have gained from their study, their own views and those of Mr Kumar, as they find problems with different arguments brought forward and counter them with their own. They are weighing up the respective claims of God's purposes and the conflicting interests of different groups (tigers and people).

The dialogue that links citizenship studies and this approach to religious education, however, goes deeper than the development of skills common and valuable to both.

Dialogue as context

The concept of 'citizen' sets up a dialogical relationship between the individual and something wider and bigger than the self: the collective to which the citizen belongs. In the QCA national curriculum document that collective is generally understood to be the United Kingdom, though there is also mention of the smaller units of school and neighbourhood, and the wider unit of the world; the 'school, local, national and global level' (QCA 1999b: 184). The relationship is a reciprocal one involving expectations and response on both sides (present in the QCA document in the language of rights and duties, p. 184). Citizenship also involves a relationship between the individual self and other members (or citizens) of the same collective, who retain degrees of individuality and difference even when included in the whole. This is evident in the importance given in the citizenship programme to 'the diversity of national, regional and ethnic identities in the United Kingdom' (p. 184). To employ terms from M. M. Bakhtin's theories of dialogism, we have here at play the 'centrifugal' forces of diversity and the 'centripetal' force of collective identity (Bakhtin 1981). Understanding of who we are and what we say develops through the tension between these forces.

The societal context that feeds the thought of the children with whom I have been working is one of diversity in religion, culture, colour and ethnicity. These different discourses that constitute the background of much of their discussion supply them with a wealth and variety of potential meanings that they can employ in their conversation. As they meet together in classroom and playground they bring to that shared meeting point a wealth and variety of experiences and understandings. An illustration of the interanimation of meanings that results from recognition of diversity and a search for common ground is found in the following contribution to a group discussion from an 11 year old African Caribbean boy:

J.H.   Quite a lot of my friends only believe . . . I say to them, 'Do you believe in Jesus?' They go, 'No' . . . But when they ask me, I say, 'Yes, I believe there's only one God.' And they ask me, 'What colour do you think he is?' And most people my colour will say he's black, but I think he's all mixed colours – black, white, Asian – blue, pink. I think he's every single colour in the world. I don't just think he's one particular colour.

Because, even though you have one God . . . God must be like everyone's colour because to me I think he's everyone's God, because in my religion I think there's only one God and he's everyone's God, so he's got to be everyone's different colour. He can't just be black and be everyone's God.

J.H.'s words reflect the dialogism of his context, the differences in the wider community in which he moves, and a sense of the unity of all people. His social circumstances may be particular to him, but any gathering of people represents both a diversity of views, loyalties and identities and common membership of the group. Tension between the diversity of individual experience and the shared experience of membership of a community is present in microcosm in every class unit or grouping of children within which discussion is taking place. Dialogue is there already in the composition of the group, not just in the activity the teacher sets. Earlier, citizenship was described as a dialogical relationship between the individual and a collective whole. To be engaged in dialogue within a group is to be, as it were, a citizen of that group.

Dialogue as ideal

Dialogue, then, can be viewed as both activity and context. It has a third meaning, too, as an ideal to be strived for. Here again dialogue has particular significance for concepts of citizenship. In the recent promotion of citizenship, two motivating interests can be identified. The Crick Report, that signalled the arrival of citizenship as a national curriculum subject, looked for both 'the development of pupils into citizens' and 'a change in the political culture of this country' (QCA 1998); citizenship education is concerned with the preparation of young individuals for adult life, and the reform of society. There is a joint focus on what is and what could be. The former is observable in the curriculum programme's concern for an increase in pupils' 'knowledge and understanding about becoming informed citizens' (QCA 1999b: 184). Under this heading pupils are taught, for example, about 'the key characteristics of parliamentary and other forms of government', 'the legal and human rights and responsibilities underpinning society', 'the diversity of national, regional, religious and ethnic identities in the United Kingdom' (p. 184). The second focus is implicit in the vocabulary used by prominent public figures cited in support of the programme: citizenship studies will 'enhance democratic life for us all . . . beginning in school and radiating out' (Professor Bernard Crick), 'create a society where people matter more than things' (Archbishop Desmond Tutu). The quotation from Doreen Lawrence (p. 183), whose 17 year old son was brutally murdered in a racist attack, is a reminder that improvement is urgently needed. The young people we are teaching are not just to slot into existing structures of society but are to be agents for its reform.

This sense of the significance of young people's role in society is clear in the following discussion with an 8 year old boy who was participating in my research:

C.S. But, you know, if more of us would be able to get along better it would boost the chance of even more people getting along better, and if the kids do it then the grown-ups might try and do it too, so it's like we're sort of teaching the grown-ups.

J.I. So do you think that's your role as young people?

C.S. Yes, to teach other generations.

C.S. reveals the methods he favours for the construction of a community with 'more people getting along better' when he proposes a negotiated solution to inter-religious tension:

C.S. religious people get together and find different languages and everything and actually find a language that actually says a word that's appropriate for being a religion and then people can get along and I think it'll be much more – there won't be so much trouble in the future.

The reformed community to which C.S. and participants of the citizenship programme aspire bears the hallmarks of the liberal democratic ideal: pupils are to develop 'skills of participation'; pluralism is respected in an approach where pupils take account of 'other people's experiences' and 'views that are not their own'; individual freedom is there in the pupils' right to hold and express 'personal opinions about . . . issues, problems or events'; and underlying the whole programme is confidence in the pupils' powers of reason, as they are encouraged to 'think', 'analyse', 'justify', 'reflect' and 'debate' (QCA 1999b: 184). These hallmarks of democracy have much in common with the 'procedural values' that all people in Britain can be expected to share, according to the Parekh Report, *The Future of Multi-ethnic Britain* (Runnymede 2000):

> Procedural values are those that maintain the preconditions for democratic dialogue. They include people's willingness to give reasons for their views, readiness to be influenced by better arguments than their own, tolerance, mutual respect, aspiration to peaceful resolution of differences, and willingness to abide by collectively binding decisions that have been reached by the agreed procedures.
>
> (Runnymede 2000: para. 4.30, 53)

These are not virtues to be imposed as a set list of rights and wrongs for members to learn; rather they are virtues to be exercised, and constitute an approach to issues and problems that involves critical judgement, evaluation and negotiation between different points of view. This democratic ideal is also a dialogical ideal sought by teachers who promote a class ethos of collaboration, of questioning and reasoning, of openness to the ideas of others and to the possibility of learning from them, of confidence in the communication of one's own point of view.

It should also be acknowledged that the democratic ideal is not entirely coterminous with dialogue. There are, in addition to values agreed through processes of dialogue, a few non-negotiable 'substantive' values 'that underpin any defensible conception of the good life' (Runnymede 2000: para. 4.30, 53): fundamental human rights and duties recognizing the equal worth and dignity of all, on which an open liberal democracy is founded (Home Office 2001a: para. 3.12, 20). The relationship between these and the dialogical process described above is set out in the Home Office ministerial report of December 2001, *Building Cohesive Communities*: 'The public realm is founded on negotiation and debate between competing viewpoints, at the same time as it upholds inviolable rights and duties' (Home Office 2001a: para.

3.12, 20). Alongside the dictates of reason, these substantive values form a foundation for the evaluation of views put forward in religious and ethical debate.

Threefold dialogue

Understandings of dialogue as something that is practised, experienced and sought are incorporated into the threefold definition of the term that has been central to my project (Ipgrave 2001: 19). *Primary* dialogue is the context of diversity, *secondary* dialogue is a positive, open response to that context, and *tertiary* dialogue encompasses the forms and structures of communication that give scope to dialogical activity. A teaching approach to dialogue can be organized around these three principles when it:

- recognizes the context of diversity, valuing the varied experiences pupils bring to class and preparing them for future encounters with difference;
- encourages an ethos of openness to that diversity and to the possibility of change in outlook and understanding;
- sets up learning strategies, activities and exercises that facilitate dialogue.

Citizenship and religious education

The close relationship between these three aspects of dialogue and citizenship has been described. Supporters of a dialogical RE can view the new drive for citizenship in a positive light. The introduction of citizenship into the curriculum encourages new reflection on the purposes and approaches of RE teaching, and the requirements of the new programme give added impetus to the provision of dialogue opportunities and development of dialogue skills. The inter-faith e-mail project between schools in Leicester and East Sussex, for example, has been set up explicitly to address RE and citizenship needs. The closeness of some of the subject matter of religious education, citizenship and personal, social and health education (PSHE) has also aroused interest. Some responses have embraced the similarities positively, and teaching resources are coming on to the market to guide teachers in an integrated delivery of the three subject areas, for example the Professional Council for Religious Education's booklet *PSHE and Citizenship: Positive Partnerships*, providing 'a range of ideas and approaches to teaching RE which complement, link to and extend PSHE and Citizenship' (Draycott 2002).

Detailed examination of recent national guidelines shows possibilities for a mutually beneficial cross-fertilization between religious education and citizenship. In the QCA's non-statutory guidelines for RE, children are to be involved in such community awareness programmes as those which require them to 'find out about the different faith communities represented in their local community' (Key Stage 1); 'find out about and present information about religious affiliation in the United Kingdom' (Key Stage 2, 4f); 'find out about various different charitable organizations' (Key Stage 2, 2h); 'explore what happens when someone experiences any sort of prejudice' (Key Stage 2, 4e). Within the citizenship programme (as set out in the national curriculum handbooks for primary and secondary pupils) are elements that mirror aspects of religious education. Primary age children are to 'learn to understand and respect our common humanity, diversity and differences' (QCA 1999a: 136), secondary pupils are to be taught about the 'diversity of religious identities in the United Kingdom and the need for mutual respect and understanding' (QCA 1999b: 183). They are also encouraged to think about and research topical 'spiritual' and 'moral issues' (pp. 183–4).

In the flurry of interest that followed the arrival of citizenship as a curriculum subject, some less confident voices were heard in the world of religious education. As a statutory curriculum subject, yet with aims, content and approaches determined at a local rather than national level, religious education has a unique status. As a result it is often deemed to be particularly vulnerable to marginalization (see Jackson's discussion of David Hargreaves' views on the position of religious education at pp. 70–77 above). Against views such as those of Hargreaves, that see religion as a private affair, or a 'second language' of home and community, justifications of religious education's inclusion in the curriculum for all schools have emphasized the public utility of the subject in a plural society, as well as its personal value. Aims ascribed to religious education in state schools have included preparing children for the diversity of the society in which they live, developing awareness of the influence of belief, values and traditions on individuals, communities, societies and cultures; promoting a positive attitude to other people, teaching principles of tolerance and respect for difference; encouraging reasoned, informed judgements on moral issues, and providing pupils with opportunities to reflect on personal beliefs, values and experiences (SCAA 1994). All these aspects of learning are also covered by the combination of citizenship and PSHE – an overlap that some feel may make a separate religious education redundant. For Michael Grimmitt it is evidence of a government lack of faith in RE and constitutes a threat to its position:

> The fact that the Labour government from August 2002 intends to introduce into all secondary schools compulsory lessons (equivalent to 5 per cent of curriculum time) in *Citizenship Education* and a new curriculum in *Personal, Social* and *Health Education*, further undermines the educational contribution that RE is making and suggests that this government, like the previous one, has little belief in RE's personal and

community value other than as a means of appeasing the faith communities and maintaining the concordat between state and church which
has been reflected in all educational legislation since 1870.

(Grimmitt 2000: 11)

Where RE is about moral teaching, the viewpoints of the religious traditions
are just some of the many to be taken into account during ethics debates
in citizenship lessons; where RE is about raising awareness of diverse traditions, religious diversity is but one of the different diversities with which
citizenship deals. Few would deny that religious perspectives have a place
in Britain today, but the question is whether those perspectives are significant enough in the public arena, or distinctive enough, to merit a curriculum
slot of their own. My answer to this question is that they are, and in what
follows I intend to demonstrate the ability of a dialogical religious education
to 'complement, link to and extend' citizenship, the importance of a distinctly religious perspective for the understanding of our society, and the
particular contribution religious debate can make to the development of
the active citizen.

Religion as a public concern

Religious pluralism and communal tension

The inclusion of religious diversity among the other diversities listed in the
QCA national curriculum document (QCA 1999b: 184) is not just an attempt
to produce a catch-all statement covering as many examples of diversity as
possible. Difference of religious identity has become a major force in community relations in the United Kingdom; as such it is of public interest.
The inclusion of religious education in the curriculum has been seen as a
way of inculcating respect for the pluralism in society and for the right of
people to differ in their deepest beliefs and faith practices (both principles
of liberal democracy). In the QCA guidance on religious education, it is
clearly stated that an aim of the subject is to prepare young people for
'life as citizens in a plural society' (QCA 2000: 2). Set alongside this positive
approach to diversification is real concern that difference of religious identity
may be a cause of fragmentation in British society. There is an urgent need to
combat inter-religious ignorance and prejudice.

This concern has been boldly expressed by commentators on the riots of
2001, involving youths in areas of the towns and cities of Oldham, Burnley,
Leeds and Bradford inhabited predominantly by Pakistani and Bangladeshi
communities. The causes of the unrest are complex; social deprivation in the
neighbourhoods involved is likely to have been a factor. Another may be the
trouble-making activity of the British National Party, whose attention has

been directed towards the Muslim community (McRoy, 'BNP's anti-Muslim crusade', *Q News: The Muslim Magazine*, 2001: 18–19). Where extreme right groups have previously couched their hostility in racial terms, religious distinctions are becoming more prominent; the British National Party leader interviewed on BBC Newsnight (summer 2001), stated that 'it is not an Asian problem but a Muslim problem'. Parekh quotes another example of the inclusion of religious categories in extremist literature: a piece of propaganda which called on the government to use the army to remove all mosques, temples and synagogues from 'this Christian land' (Runnymede 2000: para. 17.3, 237). Where racism targets religious groups, or uses religious justification, anti-racism, the Parekh report argues, has to adopt different strategies. The distinctive power and influence of religious identity and argument need to be recognized.

The press has also pointed to the segregation of communities and schools as a root cause of trouble, making alarming comparisons with the religiously segregated schools of Northern Ireland. Lord Ouseley's report on Bradford, a response to rioting in 1995 which, coincidentally, came out at the same time as the riots of 2001, spoke of a city 'fragmenting along racial, cultural and faith lines', and of the 'virtual apartheid' of education. Concern that government initiatives to increase the number of faith schools might aggravate this trend were expressed in the press after the events of the summer (for example, in the *Sunday Times*, 15 July 2001) and addressed in the two subsequent reports on 'community cohesion' produced for the Home Office (2001a, b). The need for differences to meet was the conclusion drawn by several analysts and the line taken in the report of the Ministerial Group on Public Order and Community Cohesion: *Building Cohesive Communities* (Home Office 2001a). Lack of dialogue was seen as a contributory factor to the unrest:

> Disturbances occurred in areas which had become fractured on racial, generational, cultural and religious lines and where there was little dialogue, or much contact, between the various groups across those social divides.
>
> (2001a: para. 1.6, 8)

> Geographical segregation is likely to contribute to a lack of opportunity for different communities to meet, to have a dialogue and work together.
>
> (2001a: para. 2.16, 13)

More dialogue was recommended as part of the solution. As an educational response to the problem, the independent review team into Community Cohesion chaired by Ted Cantle suggested programmes of cross-cultural contact (Home Office 2001b: para. 5.8.18, 36). The children of my project also recognized the importance of encounter with those of different religious backgrounds for promoting harmony. One 11 year old described the benefits of education at a school with a religious mix as follows: 'I can learn from all of them, so I know that when I grow up I know about everyone and their gods – who they are, and I won't be racist.'

Classroom talk is vitally important as a context where differences can meet, but dialogue needs extending further if it is to address the problem of segregated schools. The team advocated dialogue not only within schools but also between schools (2001b: para. 5.8.12, 35). The inter-faith e-mail links being developed with Leicester and East Sussex schools provide examples of such school partnerships. The independent team welcomed the expansion of citizenship education within schools as a way of promoting greater social harmony, though religious education was not specifically mentioned in its report. Where religious differences, and ignorance and prejudices about other faith groups, are such a source of tension in the community, religious education well taught (particularly a dialogical approach encouraging engagement with, and not just awareness of, views other than one's own) has a vital role to play in expanding and enriching pupils' experience of other faith communities and in the breaking down of barriers. It is a very public-minded, community-oriented role.

Exploring democratic solutions

The children with whom I have been working similarly introduce the language of religion into that of communal relations. They also bring knowledge of political procedures into their considerations of religion. Part of the context of many of our children's religious thinking is (either through direct experience or through media coverage) that of tension between faith groups. That this tension is seen as a problem, by children as well as adults, is clear in the responses of some of the participants in my project. Those with whom I was working were well aware of trends towards 'segregation' and the 'ghettoization' of the area in which they lived as members of the non-Muslim minority. Relevant to this theme of citizenship are the children's reflections on the power relations between different groups in the community, and their recourse to the language of democracy in an attempt to resolve the tensions. Thus, talking about the school situation, 9 year old A.Y. says:

> It's how big the group is really. If the Muslims are bigger than the Christians and Hindus, the Muslims will take the mick out of all of us. If we have the same groups [numerically] we don't argue, so you can't take the mick out of people because we've got the same people in each group.

Discussing the local community, a group of three 10 year olds (a Christian, a Hindu and a Rastafarian) come across the same issue of the power of the majority:

R.A. It's because there's lots of Muslim people that can start – they can sort of like – not *rule*, but . . . they can start deciding where they want to put mosques. If they want other buildings down they feel they can decide for themselves without having a meeting and invite everyone in the community except for just one religion.

R.A. sees the power of decision making as the issue. In her thinking, decisions should be made at 'meetings', where 'everyone . . . as a community' can have a say. Her dialogue partner, J.H., picks up the language of political democracy:

J.H. Yeah, have a vote. Tony Blair should stand up and say, 'I order a vote. If you want the mosque you vote and if you don't want a mosque, you want something else, you vote.'

But here the language of democracy comes up against the problem of numbers:

R.A. But actually there's more Muslims and they would vote.

The children's argument starting from the numerical dominance of Muslims has come full circle, and they meet the age-old problem of how to ensure minority voices are heard in a democracy. Not finding an answer in a vote, they resort to criticism of the minority groups for not taking an active enough role in local politics – 'I think they're lazy' (J.K.) – and to the language of pressure groups – 'They should be fighting for the right to have more churches' (R.A.). The children are decrying the apathy of their elders and echo the Crick Report (QCA 1998) in their calls for a change in the political culture of their locality.

Links between religious issues and citizenship are very clear in this exchange, and the question of mosque building in their area of the city has led the children to develop the use of political discourse as well as to question and explore the limitations of the existing political structures. A more optimistic recourse to democratic models for the resolution of conflict between religious factions is the model of negotiation provided by 8 year old C.S. and his suggestion that a new, unifying religion should be established. In these examples the children are both engaged in dialogue themselves and calling for dialogue as a solution. Their concerns stem from the experience of difference where it has created tension. The aim is to smooth out tension and achieve unity. They are tackling key issues of religious identity in society today, showing awareness of problems and a desire for justice and harmony.

Religion as a public language

Awareness

So far issues of religious identity have been presented in the social language of community and diversity, and the political language of democracy and representation; these are discourses of citizenship of general application outside the field of religion. They could, for example, be applied to issues of race and ethnicity equally well. However, I wish to argue that religion is not only another category of diversity to be discussed in the 'public language' of citizenship (see Jackson's discussion of Hargreaves, Chapter 4, above) but is itself a public language, a 'first language' in its own right, and therefore a proper subject of study in our schools.

One of the most significant events in raising public awareness of the significance of religion in national life and community relations was the Salman Rushdie affair, involving demonstrations of protest and the burning of copies of *The Satanic Verses* by British Muslims and Ayatollah Khomeini's *fatwa*, in February 1989, against the (British) author for slandering the Prophet and his wives. The affair gave prominence to the power of religious feeling. While relations between communities in Britain had tended to be understood in terms of race or ethnicity, the *Satanic Verses* protest highlighted religious sensitivities. The Bradford Community Relations Council noted that recent events had:

> increased the awareness of all of us about the significance of religious demands in meeting the specific needs of ethnic minority communities. Perhaps we have been too ready to fit all issues into an equal opportunities framework at the expense of those needs which are of specifically religious nature.
>
> (Cited in Lewis 1994: 160)

The inadequacy of race equality-speak to encompass religious issues is also recognized in the Parekh Report, where it is observed that most race equality organizations, being broadly secular rather than religious, are frequently found to be insensitive to forms of racism that target aspects of religious identity (Runnymede 2000: para. 17.3, 237). There is also the danger that ignorance of specifically religious needs may result in unwitting offence to religious sensibilities. An example of the difference between ignorance and awareness of the religious practice and thinking of others at the classroom level was a discussion between participants in my research study where non-Muslim children were expressing their indignation at a teacher's demand that a Muslim classmate should remove her headscarf. Commitment to respect for religious diversity alone is not enough; there needs to be some public knowledge of religious issues in order to avoid unnecessary upset. There is an obvious role for religious education here.

Accountability

There is another sense in which religious language is a public language – one which has become increasingly evident in recent months. A new imperative towards knowledge of religious beliefs and differences since 11 September is acknowledged in the independent report *Community Cohesion:*

> The events of Sept 11th have led directly to a much more serious interest in testing possibilities of co-operation between Islam and the West. Understanding Islam, and differences within Islam, has become an imperative for political negotiators and community mediators alike.
> (Home Office 2001b: appendix B 1.8, 62)

The public nature of religious language has been demonstrated by the press; the Islamic term *jihad*, for example, became a common ingredient of newspaper headlines and articles (Farrell and Zahid 2001; Taher 2001) and the influence religious belief in paradise and heavenly reward may have had on the motivation of terrorists was debated in their columns (Watson 2001). It became public knowledge that the Prime Minister was reading the Qur'an to guide his pronouncements in the immediate aftermath of the terrorist attacks, and High Street bookshops reported a significant increase in sales of the Qur'an, indicating popular interest in religion as a guide to interpreting world events. The increased interest in religion was not just recognition of its power and influence on public affairs, but also an understanding that religious belief should be publicly accountable: that people's religious stand should be judged against the common human values of 'all people of conscience' (Muslim Council of Britain, 12 September) and against the standards of Islam itself. Muslims and non-Muslims alike were quick to distance the actions of the terrorists, and the particular understanding of religion they embody, from 'true' Islam. On 13 September *The Sun* had a double-page spread under the heading 'Islam is not an evil religion', and the *Evening Standard* on the same day published an article by the Muslim writer Ziauddin Sardar, which contrasted the atrocities with what he knows of Islam: 'What I know are the clear, unequivocal values, moral premises and ethical restraints of Islam. They make the sanctity of human life a paramount obligation, and care for the innocent, the suffering, the bereaved, a sacred duty' (Sardar 2001).

The significance of these events and reactions for religious education is considerable. They call into question the adequacy of a view of religion as something privately defined by individual believers. Such a view would mean that the understanding of Islam outlined above, and that which allows the mass slaughter of thousands of innocent people, are equally valid interpretations of the tradition. Instead a dialogical axis is set up between each person's viewpoint and the central core of the tradition to which they belong. This dialogue mirrors the 'relationship between the individual and something wider and bigger than self' that is citizenship; it also opens up statements of religious opinion and belief to the critical evaluation and moral judgement of the democratic process. As is stated in the Parekh Report, 'Dispute and disagreement are integral to democracy. When believers use religion to justify practices that others judge to be unethical, immoral or illegal, it is right that they should be challenged' (Runnymede 2000: para. 17.18, 245).

The children with whom I work were prepared to exercise their critical judgement in their evaluation of religious practice and to measure actions taken in the name of religion against moral criteria and against their own understanding of the teachings of the religions to which the actors belonged. Below are two examples of practices, at the local and international level, being challenged in this way:

R.A. They [Muslim friends] taught me some things about religion – what they do. Sometimes they say if we do something wrong in the mosque the headmaster will hit you.

J.H. And I don't think they should do that because that's wrong. That's wrong – that's wrong to hit.

H.M. You know those people in Algeria, those Muslims who are cutting their throats, I think that they're not being proper Muslims, they're not following their religion, I don't think.

On the same principle I have myself used arguments based on certain ethical norms (substantive values) to challenge some of my pupils' unqualified support of Osama Bin Laden as champion of their Islamic faith.

Debate

Between sympathetic awareness and critical calling to account there is another level of public engagement with religion that is closest to the heart of the dialogical religious education I advocate. It is one that recognizes that there is room for disagreement without judgement; which acknowledges that partners in the discussion may 'belong to a variety of moral traditions and subscribe to and live by a range of values' and does not 'rule out legitimate moral differences' (Runnymede 2000: para. 4.29, 53). It is the level of *secondary* dialogue where participants are prepared to risk their own ideas and be open to changing their minds in the light of their encounter with other points of view.

The independent *Community Cohesion* report recognized the temptation to 'play safe' by avoiding areas of disagreement, but was insistent that in the interests of community cohesion the differences should be aired in the public arena. The team recommended a bold approach to controversial issues; a harmonious society requires being open with one another about differences of belief, tradition and culture:

> In our anxiety to eliminate the forms of insulting behaviour and lan-
> guage, we have created a situation in which most people are now
> unwilling to open any subject which might possibly lead to differences
> of opinion. In this lies a big danger. If neighbours are unable to discuss
> differences, they have no hope of understanding them. Those who wish
> to cause trouble have a fruitful field in which to operate. The recommen-
> dations of our report seek to create conditions in which all of us can
> engage in open debate on issues which affect us all and when, as is
> inevitable, disagreements become plain there will then be a real
> chance that they can be accepted with mutual respect.
>
> (Home Office 2001b: para. 5.1.16, 20)

As in communal relations, so in the religious education classroom, there is a temptation to shy away from areas of disagreement between religious tradi-tions, groups and individuals and emphasize a shared core of common values or to take refuge in a purely descriptive approach to the other, using external phenomena (such as dress and customs) as indicators of difference. Andrew Wright calls these approaches into question when he advocates a critical religious education that recognizes the ambiguous and controversial (Wright 2000: 177) and that gives pupils the tools of 'religious literacy' to deal with them. Only in this way can we prepare children for encounter with the religious influences in society. Wright's arguments can be linked with the government interest in the development of 'active citizens' when he writes that the aim of critical religious education is: 'the empowerment of children to learn to be responsible and wise as they encounter the vitally important, though extremely dangerous, horizon of religion' (p. 186).

The ability of young people to deal with the dangerous and controversial was well demonstrated in one of the most successful RE lessons I have observed. In the RE session, a low-ability class of mainly Muslim teenagers debated at length different interpretations of *jihad*; giving space (within the security of the classroom) to a wide variety of Muslim and non-Muslim understandings; applying the term to different situations, backing up their very different views with reference to the scriptures or to ethical norms. The lesson pre-dated the attacks of 11 September but many of the arguments used by the young people were mirrored in the discussions which followed, through which community leaders, the media and the public sought to gain an understanding of the events.

Hargreaves uses the lack of consensus about morality in our secular, religiously diverse society as a reason for the removal of religious education from all but 'faith schools' (see Chapter 4). By contrast, I would draw on the arguments of the *Community Cohesion* report and of Wright, and on my experience of classroom dialogue, to propose that it is the very existence of difference that makes public debate on religious questions and the development of children's religious literacy so important both in the interests of communal harmony and for the preparation of young people for 'life as citizens in a plural society'.

Religion and the preparation of the citizen

Religious identity and ideas

Earlier in the chapter, two motivating interests were identified in the drive for citizenship in schools: the reform of society and the preparation of the individual for life as an adult citizen of that society. The two are clearly linked, as the reform of society is dependent on the contributions made by the individual citizens. While the emphasis of the previous section has been on society and the public role of religion within it, I now propose to consider briefly the contribution religious education can make to the formation of the citizen. The model of the citizen presented in the national curriculum guidelines is of someone who is informed, skilled and responsible. The role of religious education in informing citizens and increasing their knowledge of the diversity of national identities is clear, for differences of experiences, practices, beliefs and values form much of the RE curriculum content. The subject also has a particular contribution to make to the development of the citizen's skills, notably those of discussion and debate. It is the nature of religion that makes it so valuable a point of dialogical encounter, and religious education particularly useful as a training ground for citizens to acquire the necessary dialogical skills. Religion is both identity and ideas. It is woven into communal and personal history and self-understanding, yet it is also open to development and change through inter-animation with the religious viewpoints of others. The strength of the ties of loyalty, and a sense of responsibility towards the family tradition, were evident in several of the contributions made to my research project, one of them being this 8 year old boy's affirmation of his Christian identity: 'I'm proud of who I am because really it's my ancestors that started this and I'm going to carry it on for them.'

Personal commitment to a particular religious viewpoint means that dialogue participants are unlikely to put aside their own views easily when they encounter others, yet awareness of the wealth of understandings of God and the number and diversity of responses to the same key questions means there is pressure to find ways of reconciling ideas and negotiating joint understanding where they can meet. As one 10 year old said: 'I do believe in the Christian God, but the Christian God is everyone's God, so, Miss, I believe in everyone's God.'

Religion is also an area of study where the dialogical relationship between the forces of diversity and those of shared humanity is especially evident. Though there is much that is particular to different religious traditions, and individual people may have very individual beliefs, there are common questions of interest to all humankind which can be approached from as many angles as there are participants in the discussion group. 'What happens when we die?' and 'How did the world begin?' are two such which children taking part in my research raised and debated. The fact that the questions are difficult to answer means that there is always room for further thought and discussion, and anyone's contribution to the dialogue may bring new light to bear on the subject.

There are also searching new questions that arise from the fact of encounter between religious differences. Among those formulated by the children of my project are 'Do you believe in other persons' gods?' 'If you've got one God how can you believe in other gods?' 'Do you believe in religions? Which?' and 'How many gods are there?' Through discussion the children explored ideas of a God of many colours, of many names, of many lesser divinities emanating from one God, of gods with different personalities. In these exchanges they showed a capacity both to respect their own religious history and to value the views of their dialogue partners. An attempt to answer one of these questions brought about the following exchange. In it Hindu and Christian children contributed their own ideas of God's unity and plurality, acquired through their identification with particular faith traditions. They negotiated a model where the two could be reconciled and where the understanding of all participants could be developed:

A.Y. (*Christian*). I think there's one [God] and he's called all different things.
N.A. (*Hindu*). I was going to say that!
T.H. (*Hindu*). Miss, we can't actually say that because we've got so many gods.
A.Y. (*Christian*). Yeah, but they could be called – um . . .
S.H. (*Hindu*). You have to believe in all of them because all of them have got something different, like special . . .
J.N. (*Christian*). Yeah, because – look, they can all – God can . . .
A.Y. (*Christian*). Do lots of things.
J.N. (*Christian*). Change into different – like, different features. Like, he can be in you.

S.T. (*Christian*). He can come into anybody.
N.A. (*Hindu*). He can change into anything.
T.H. (*Hindu*). We've got, like, a god who you can actually see.

'Big questions' and responsible citizens

This brings me to the final point I wish to make about the particular value of religious education in the trio of citizenship, dialogue and religious education. In one of the group discussions J.H. observes, 'If I ever get to Heaven . . . there's a big question I'm going to ask God . . . How did he make the earth?' Religious education is concerned with the 'big questions'. The children who took part in my research discussions were led into considerations of the beginning of time, of the end of the world, of everlasting life, of God's character and purposes – questions on which no one, not even 7–11 year olds, can have the last word. In the dialogue activities the requirements of communication and the influence of encounter with other ideas mean that participants have to stop, think and reconsider their position in relation to these big questions.

At the beginning of this chapter, we saw citizenship as a relation between self and something wider and bigger than self. In religious education the self can be put in relation with the widest possible scheme of things. The participant in such a dialogue is enabled to see himself in a new light. Discussing with his friends the possibility of God coming down to earth to create harmony, the relationship of divine activity to human effort, 8 year old C.S. feels empowered. He is part of a new generation who can, by their example to the 'grown-ups', create a new world order. After a discussion on the beginnings of the world and the end of time, J.H. declares, 'I wish I was a little baby again – start all over again – start my life again . . . start over again at infant school and behave myself all the way through.' This statement of a desire to reform does not appear to relate to the words that immediately precede it, but it is born out of the heightened self-awareness and personal moral sense that engagement with the 'big questions' can bring. His words could be understood to denote that awakening of personal moral sense of Plato's 'living in philosophy' (Fowler 1989, *Theaetetus*: 174 a–b), a state achieved through engagement in dialogue.

In the QCA national curriculum document Terry Waite is quoted as saying, 'It is only when you know how to be a citizen of your own country that you can learn how to be a citizen of the world' (QCA 1999b: 184). I would reverse this, and recommend teachers not to start the roads to citizenship with a small field of operation, moving outwards, but to use opportunities provided by religious education to put pupils in dialogue with life's great puzzles as a way of encouraging the reflective nature and moral seriousness needed for the formation of 'thoughtful and responsible citizens' (p. 184).

Conclusion

In this chapter I have drawn attention to the close links between citizenship and a dialogical religious education. Similarities between the two curriculum areas have been found in their concern to develop skills of engagement, communication and negotiation, and their positive and reflective response to the context of plurality and diversity in which they operate. In spite of the marked overlap between RE and citizenship, I have argued that religion is too important to be relegated to a subordinate position as a branch of citizenship. Its significance in communal relations and international affairs is such that it would benefit individuals and society if young people were given the opportunities, through RE, to become conversant with and confident in the use of religious language. Moreover, the cognitive, ethical and spiritual challenges posed by the 'big questions' and multiple responses of religion make religious education a rigorous training ground for the intellectually active and morally aware citizen of the future.

References

Bakhtin, M. M. (1981) *The Dialogic Imagination*, Austin TX: University of Texas Press.

Draycott, Pamela (ed.) (2002) *Primary RE: PSHE and Citizenship Positive Partnerships*, Birmingham: Christian Education Publications.

Farrell, Stephen and Hussain, Zahid (2001) 'US attack would start a jihad, say mullahs', *Times* (London), 21 September.

Fowler, Harold North (ed.) (1989) *Plato: Theaetetus and Sophist*, London: Heinemann.

Grimmitt, Michael (2000) *Pedagogies of Religious Education*, Great Wakering: McCrimmon.

Home Office (2000) *Race Equality in Public Services*, London: Home Office.

—— (2001a) *Building Cohesive Communities: A Report of the Ministerial Group on Public Order and Community Cohesion*, London: Home Office.

—— (2001b) *Community Cohesion: A Report of the Independent Review Team chaired by Ted Cantle*, London: Home Office.

Ipgrave, J. (2001) *Pupil-to-pupil Dialogue in the Classroom as a Tool for Religious Education*, Warwick Religions and Education Research Unit, Working Paper 2, Coventry: Institute of Education, University of Warwick.

Lewis, Philip (1994) *Islamic Britain*, London: Tauris.

McRoy, Anthony (2001) 'BNP's anti-Muslim crusade', *Q News: The Muslim Magazine*, 333, 18–19.

QCA (1998) *Education for Citizenship and the Teaching of Democracy in Schools: Final Report of the Advisory Group on Citizenship*, London: QCA.

—— (1999a) *The National Curriculum: Handbook for Primary Teachers in England*, London: QCA.

—— (1999b) *The National Curriculum: Handbook for Secondary Teachers in England*, London: QCA.

—— (2000) *Religious Education: Non-statutory Guidance on RE*, London: QCA.

Runnymede Trust (2000) *The Future of Multi-ethnic Britain: The Parekh Report*, London: Profile Books.

Sardar, Ziauddin (2001) 'Don't look at your Muslim neighbours with suspicion', *Evening Standard* (London), 13 September.

SCAA (1994) *Religious Education Model Syllabuses: Model 1, Living Faiths Today*, London: School Curriculum and Assessment Authority.

Taher, Abul (2001) 'Why some Britons have joined the jihad against the West', Friday Review, *Independent* (London), 21 September.

Watson, Roland (2001) 'Terror manual for hijackers' moment of glory', *Times* (London), 29 September.

Wright, Andrew (2000) 'The Spiritual Education Project: Cultivating Spiritual and Religious Literacy through a Critical Pedagogy of Religious Education', in Michael Grimmitt (ed.) *Pedagogies of Religious Education*, Great Wakering: McCrimmon.

Chapter 9

Dialogue among young citizens in a pluralistic religious education classroom

Heid Leganger-Krogstad

Synopsis Education is supposed to prepare children and young people for life. However, schooling has often focused on future adult life and ignored the present, especially in treating children as citizens. Although schools are often considered to be protected, artificial social arenas, the school is a space where children can develop the ability to live with religious and cultural differences. Thus, how school prepares children to live in and understand a plural society is an important issue. In the light of this, I raise three key questions. First, in a national school system based on the principle of 'one school for all', what is the particular role of religious education (RE) in dialogue among pupils with different religious backgrounds, worldviews and beliefs? Secondly, what ideal pictures or concepts of this dialogue are to be found in the different positions in the discussions about RE? These can be, on the one hand, the voluntary, religiously committed, verbal dialogues among adults, or the open, experimental, on-going interaction among pupils in a given social and educational setting on the other. Thirdly, how may teaching be organized in order to facilitate a dialogical education? The chapter includes a short account of RE and citizenship in Norway. In Norway, a country with a large territory but a small and scattered population, school is used as a means of building citizenship and creating a common Norwegian identity. The chapter also aims to reveal the hidden agenda in the recent debates about dialogue in the RE classroom in Norway through a comparison of the ideas of an inter-religious Christian theologian, Oddbjørn Leirvik, with the views of a teacher educator, Tove Nicolaisen. Finally the chapter summarizes some of the work done to promote a dialogical education within a contextual approach to RE.

Religion(s): for war or for peace?

We have entered the third millennium through a gate of fire. If today, after the horror of 11 September, we see better, and we see further – we will realize that humanity is indivisible. New threats make no distinction between races, nations or regions. A new insecurity has entered every mind, regardless of wealth or status. A deeper awareness of the bonds that bind us all – in pain as in prosperity – has gripped young and old.

This statement is from the UN Secretary General, Kofi Annan's, Nobel Peace Prize lecture in Oslo, Norway. The lecture was delivered on 10 December 2001, when he accepted the Peace Prize on behalf of the United Nations and himself (Annan 2001). He claimed that, on the basis of recent history, national or state borders no longer have a protective function. From an educational perspective, it is of particular interest to see the attention his lecture gives to the role of religion and religious traditions today, either as the instigator of divisions and conflicts or as a unifying and peace-making force.[1] He said that the idea that there is only one people in possession of the truth, the answer to the world's ills, or the one solution to humanity's needs, has done untold harm throughout history, during the twentieth century in particular. However, even amidst continuing ethnic conflicts around the world, there is growing recognition of the value of cultural diversity and exchange. Moreover, by mentioning the major faith traditions, Annan made it clear that he does not consider religious diversity to be a hindrance to peace. He specifically identifies voices in each tradition which advocate 'the values of tolerance and mutual understanding'. He also gave value to religious commitment by saying that each of us has the right to take pride in a particular faith or heritage:

> the notion that what is ours is necessarily in conflict with what is theirs is both false and dangerous. It has resulted in endless enmity and conflict, leading men to commit the greatest of crimes in the name of a higher power . . . It need not be so. People of different religions and cultures live side by side in almost every part of the world, and most of us have overlapping identities which unite us with very different groups. We can love what we are, without hating what – and who – we are not. We can thrive in our own tradition, even as we learn from others, and come to respect their teachings.

With these words he values difference, both in the way that religions live side by side and in the way that difference may be integrated in one person as a set of 'overlapping identities', thus making it possible to belong to different cultures. The message seems to be that the threat to world peace does not come from the existence of different and competing world religions, but from the misuse of traditions for self-serving and power-hungry goals. Preventing abuses of religion and diversity is only possible with freedom of religion, of expression, of assembly, and basic equality under the law.

We as educationists have to reflect from this perspective on how different educational systems and ways of organizing RE can develop competence for a plural and democratic society. To illustrate this, I will use examples from a state-run school system where communality and living together are emphasized to such an extent that there is a heated debate over whether or not this clashes with parental rights and religious freedom.

One school for all: education for citizenship

Norway has an educational system of comprehensive public schools in which most children attend a school in their neighbourhood or local community. In general, pupils attend the same school and class for at least seven years,[2] often without any sort of streaming. Furthermore, 'one school for all' (*enhetsskole*) is one of the main principles of the state school system. In 2000 only 1.7 per cent of children attended private schools, for religious or pedagogical reasons.[3] Municipal schools are for all children and all children are integrated as far as possible, irrespective of physical or mental disability or learning difficulties. Even in quite small municipalities, special programmes are worked out for disabled children within the classroom setting to allow them to remain in their local community.[4] School is a common meeting place for all children within their local area. The religious family background of the pupils in a school, or a class, mirrors the culture of the local community.

This view is set forth in the principles and guidelines for compulsory education in the *National Curriculum for Compulsory School* (*Læreplanverket for den 10-årige grunnskolen*, abbreviated as L97). *Læreplanverket* 97 states:

> Compulsory school follows the same basic structure throughout the country . . . The school is . . . a place where pupils come together, learn from and live with differences, regardless of where they live, their social backgrounds, their genders, their religions, their ethnic origins, and their mental and physical abilities . . . The school thus helps to reduce social inequality and to develop a sense of community between groups. *In a multicultural society, education must promote equality between pupils with different backgrounds and counteract discriminatory attitudes.*
>
> (L97: 55; KUF 1999; my italics)

To give priority to the social interplay in the class, children of primary age have a class teacher who teaches almost all subjects. Religious education is normally among them because RE is considered a key subject for dialogue about values in the classroom. Religious studies are also a compulsory part of the study programme for teachers qualifying for general education. At the lower secondary level, subject specialists are more common. However, teams, normally of three teachers, are combined to cover all subjects in a class, to enhance social interaction in the classroom (KUF 1990: 7). Education for citizenship through social interplay in the class is considered more important than giving each pupil optimal possibilities of individual development. This national educational policy results from a long period of mainly social democratic government.

RE as a test of the principle of 'one school for all'

The 1997 school reform introduced the new syllabus for RE: Christian Knowledge and Religious and Ethical Education[5] (*Kristendomskunnskap med religions- og livssynsorientering*, abbreviated to KRL). The 1997 syllabus for RE can be seen as an application of the principle of 'one school for all'. The former practice of dividing children into two parallel classes according to their religious background (Christian or secular orientation) was looked upon as a way of undermining the Norwegian school system (Telhaug 1994: 142–50). The division of pupils in RE – the only school subject in which children were separated – was regarded as contrary to the principle of a common school for all. While RE as a school subject was supposed to promote tolerance, children were separated according to religious or secular convictions. In the face of a growing multi-religious plurality in the 1990s it became necessary either to give each religious tradition a separate education (a plural parallel model) or to devise a common subject. The latter solution was chosen, but with some limited possibilities for exemption. In addition, the legal ties between the Norwegian Church and school were severed. A consequence is that legally all teachers may teach RE regardless of their own religious affiliation.

So far we have referred only to the legal level and the ideal and formal KRL curriculum (Goodlad 1979: 60). Religious education is an important issue for many stakeholders, and there is an on-going debate about RE in school, the profile of KRL as a school subject, and the rules on exemption.[6] There is also an on-going debate about the perceived and the operational curriculum, such as the relation between the national curriculum and local adaptations, the application of the rules on exemption, and the use of differentiation in relation to children's varied religious and worldview backgrounds.[7]

RE as part of life in school

Diapractice: integrating RE and education for citizenship

Compulsory education has citizenship as its main aim, and the national school system is built to serve that purpose, but there is no special subject to ensure the goal is achieved. However, schools and classrooms are social structures where living together with difference is part of everyday life for all pupils. Human and social equality is fundamental in all activities and teaching in school, with the intention of promoting the value of equality in all pupils. Pupils live together in given social structures where the choice of classmates and working companions is limited, and the sharing of common practical experiences is of the utmost importance. In this way, social life in a class setting has relevance to religious education owing to the fact that every classroom is plural to some extent. The type of plurality may differ in various ways (Skeie 1999), but at the local level even internal plurality or differences within the same religious tradition may be demanding to live with (Leganger-Krogstad 1998). Clothing, food, attitudes to music and dance, attitudes to adults, gender questions, value preferences, sacred objects and days, sacred words and movements, holy days and rituals, and rules of decent behaviour – all these are linked with religion and life interpretation.[8] On this view of life interpretation, religious education is not limited to the school subject, but is interwoven with education for citizenship. School life is in this way dominated by *diapractice*. This means that co-operation takes place among pupils across difference in lifestyle, beliefs and values to solve practical (and simple theoretical) tasks in the school context or in the local community. In school the children play, sing, make music, dance, cook food, eat, take part in physical education and sport, enact dramas and role-play, take part in student councils, do creative arts and so on. All this might be seen as diapractice in which *verbal dialogue* is a minor part, even though, of course, verbal dialogue becomes increasingly important as children grow older and their cognitive abilities develop.

The term 'diapractice' comes from Lissi Rasmussen's thesis about dialogue between Muslims and Christians in Africa. She shows that, even with adults, it is easier to encourage groups of people from different faiths to co-operate at a practical level than to facilitate (verbal) dialogue about theology/ies and values (Rasmussen 1998). Similarly, research in Norwegian schools with a multi-religious intake shows that cross-cultural meetings happen mostly in informal settings and that teachers seldom verbalize minority perspectives in the classroom (Vedøy 2001: 92). In these informal settings the young pupils seem to lack a language to talk about religion.

Necessary dialogue and spiritual dialogue

School life is a continuous process of living together in a given plural, local social setting and therefore provides training for citizenship. Values and traditions are embedded in schooling, in the organization and the curriculum, as well as in the content and the social structures. These values have been rooted in the traditions of the more homogeneous societies of the past. In modern multicultural societies such values need to be articulated and discussed, nationally and locally. These values and principles are givens in educational procedures and in formal curricula, but will vary according to how they are interpreted and put into practice in particular schools and classrooms. Thus, through its choice of values, each school is able to create its own profile and school identity. In this process an on-going dialogue in a class is necessary to be able to create consensus over common rules of good behaviour. Oddbjørn Leirvik uses the term *necessary dialogue* about this type of verbal dialogue, because it emerges from the necessity of living together in a society (Leirvik 2001: 217–29). He distinguishes this type of dialogue from *spiritual dialogue*, dialogue where the face-to-face encounter becomes a relation of equality between I and Thou (Martin Buber), or a relation that opens the eyes to the otherness of the Other (Emmanuel Levinas) and gives spiritual growth (Buber 1923; Leirvik 1998b; Leirvik 2001: 203).

In his book *Religionsdialog på norsk* (*Inter-religious Dialogue in a Norwegian Context*, 2001) Leirvik relates mainly to interfaith dialogue in religious community settings and in political contexts. In a published lecture addressed to teachers Leirvik focuses on the distinction between necessary and spiritual dialogue, also in a school context (Leirvik 1998a). The question is whether this distinction has relevance in a school setting, and if so, to what extent? Since *diapractice* is a dominant factor in school life and RE is an integral part of it, RE cannot be confined to specific lessons. Leirvik's *necessary dialogue* corresponds to the verbal dialogue that accompanies diapractice, making common celebrations and ethical practice possible, understandable and transparent. It helps participants to discover common values, and by so doing makes it possible to live together. In this process it is important that similarities are not taken for granted. Differences in lifestyle and values need to be recognized and explained as the effects of different religions, beliefs and value systems.

In a school system like the Norwegian one, where equality is all too often confused with similarity or uniformity (Gullestad 1989: 109–22), it is essential to take differences seriously.

Dialogue in RE

Interpretation of the formal documents

In Norway pupils attend 780 lessons in RE during their ten years of compulsory education (L97: 81; KUF 1999).[9] Many of these are part of cross-curricular projects, especially in primary education. Norwegian RE is a non-confessional subject dealing with the main religious traditions, with particular emphasis on Christianity. The new syllabus combines two perspectives in the study of religions and worldviews: the perspective of insiders and that of outsiders. In Norway these perspectives have represented two different academic traditions, respectively theology (of various denominational profiles) and the comparative study of religions. With these combined perspectives, the new subject is a direct heir neither to the old confessional RE nor to its younger alternative Worldviews or Life Stances (cf. the National

Guidelines of 1974 and 1987).[10] This means that dialogue in RE is neither that of the theological, mono-religious academic tradition nor that of an academic, multi-religious study of religions.

In the *Official Norwegian Report* (NOU 1995: 9), which sets out the principles behind the new subject, the development of identity and dialogue are considered mutually interdependent entities that form a continuum. The emphasis is on identity development in the early years of education and on dialogue in the later years. 'Identity development is dependent on dialogue – as dialogue is dependent on a firm identity' (my translation) (NOU 1995: 9: 32). This is not elaborated further in the report. However, in the reader for teachers of KRL edited by the Ministry of Education (KUF 1997), dialogue is connected with the view of the pupil as a *social human being* with reference to the core curriculum. The core curriculum (the first part of the national curriculum) is designed around a seven-point description of what it means to be a human being.[11] The fifth of these, *the social aspect*, links school with society in general. Here the need for pupils to interact with each other and with adults is emphasized:

> A person's aptitude and identity develop in interaction with others; human beings are formed by their environment, just as they contribute to forming it . . .
>
> It is important to exploit the school as a community of work for the development of social skills. It must be structured in such a way that the learners' activities have consequences for others, and so that they can learn from the impact of their decisions.
>
> (L97: 40; KUF 1999)

The reader's elaboration of the dialogue concept makes co-operation and learning in community an integral part, including diapractice as well as the necessary dialogue, as explained above.

RE has as its general aim 'to promote understanding, respect and the capacity for dialogue between people with different views on questions of faith and ethical orientation of life' (L97: 94). This is elaborated as follows:

> Especially from the intermediate stage onwards, pupils will be challenged to consider different traditions and religions in relation to each other. This entails giving prominence, particularly in lower secondary school, to practical debating skills. Objective presentation, the ability to grasp and present the views of others, oral presentation and structured dialogue should all figure prominently in pupils' work with this material. In this connection, the adherence of pupils to different faiths or orientations should be seen as both a challenge and a resource.
>
> (L97: 92; KUF 1999)

'Practical dialogue skills'[12] seem to be considered as quite demanding, and their development is considered important for life outside the school as well as in it. For pupils, training for dialogue involves setting aside personal views and being able to present the views of others. *Structured dialogue*, a term mentioned in the reader, and which I understand as a dialogue in which the teacher sets the rules and determines the perspective, is supposed to be easier to cope with than a dialogue that is a genuine interpersonal encounter. Thus structured dialogue is different from spiritual dialogue as Leirvik defines it, but has spiritual dialogue as a final goal. It is possible that spiritual dialogue can take place in the classroom, but it would happen spontaneously and teachers could not plan for it. This distinction between *structured* dialogue and *spiritual* dialogue is in accordance with the interpretation in the reader:

> Skills of comparison are based on the perspective of the observer, while dialogue is based on the perspective of the participant. Dialogue is, of course, easier to practise if there are representatives of different religions and beliefs in the classroom . . . Dialogue is a direct way of communication with other persons . . . and it provides a central competence for the multicultural society . . . Dialogue promotes new understanding . . . and may change both oneself and the partner in the dialogue.
>
> (KUF 1997: 64; my translation)

Here a new distinction is drawn: between *comparison* and *dialogue*. The ability to make a comparison is seen as a prerequisite for dialogue, and is assumed to be somewhat easier to cope with than dialogue as a direct way of communication. Comparison is here understood as the initial method pupils use to work with different traditions, beliefs and religions.

So far 'dialogue' has been presented as:

- Diapractice – co-operation
- Necessary dialogue:
  - Everyday conversation to get to understand one another
  - Informal personal exchange of ideas
- Structured dialogue (in the role as pupils):
  - Empathetic work with other religions and beliefs
  - Representing other views
  - Comparison
  - Face-to-face communication
- Spiritual dialogue – personal encounter that results in change

Concepts of dialogue in the debate

Oddbjørn Leirvik

Oddbjørn Leirvik is a Christian theologian and researcher with special expertise on Christian–Muslim and Christian–Buddhist dialogue in the Norwegian context. His interest in religious minorities has led him to focus on the lack of policies for religious equality in Norway, and his ideas have become influential in public, political and academic discussions. His best known book is *Religionsdialog på norsk* (*Inter-religious Dialogue in a Norwegian Context*) (1996, revised 2001). Much of his work can also be found on his website.[13] His interest in the school as a site of dialogue derives from his interest in these wider political questions, and his view of the importance of dialogue across religious boundaries. Two chapters in *Religionsdialog på norsk* are about education. In one he discusses 'The subject of KRL as school and religious policy'. He argues, on behalf of the Muslim minority, primarily for Muslim denominational schools, but also for a combined model for RE in the common school, which includes both a separate confessional element (Christian, Worldviews and Muslim) and a dialogical common element for all pupils (Leirvik 2001: 142, 153–4, 156). With regard to this last component, he argues that it is possible to take advantage of the unique situation of the common school system to provide genuine dialogical religious education. His chapter 'Religionsdialog i klasserommet' ('Inter-religious dialogue in the classroom') discusses how far KRL can promote dialogue. Leirvik provides a detailed discussion of the official report *Identity and Dialogue*, the syllabus, and the reader. He is critical of the syllabus's lack of attention to dialogue, finding that the main focus in primary education is on the development of identity, and that dialogue is postponed until the lower secondary stage. He also notes that the attention given by the syllabus to the systematic study of religions leaves little room for dialogue. In his view, 'A dialogical approach must be one that searches for common themes . . . , developing pupils' capacity for empathetic understanding and dialogue across different religions and beliefs' (Leirvik 2001: 165). The only exception he finds is ethics, where the syllabus provides plenty of opportunity for dialogue. Leirvik wonders whether the reason for this may be that ethical dialogue is regarded by the syllabus writers as less dangerous than religious dialogue, which might be seen as leading potentially to a change in religious outlook.[14]

Leirvik's views on dialogue seem to be derived from his personal experience of inter-religious dialogue, the dialogue of religiously committed adults who are clear about their ideas and who, out of need or interest, enter into exploratory discussion. In this form of dialogue, participants represent a tradition or the viewpoints of a religious community. They can afford to enter the risky area 'between religions', but they can also choose to withdraw at any stage (cf. Leirvik 2001). Leirvik is keen for this form of dialogue, which concentrates on spirituality rather than ethics, to be promoted in schools. However, his view of dialogue is related more to the debate in the universities about the relationship between the separate academic disciplines of Theology and Religious Studies than to everyday life in schools.[15] As Leirvik remarks: 'Mutually exclusive characteristics such as tradition and criticism, normativity and neutrality, particular and universal outlooks, no longer signify the real differences between Theology and Religious Studies' (1999: 83). I agree with Leirvik's frustration with the academic field and see that integration between the separate disciplines could contribute fruitfully to teacher education in the university system.[16] Leirvik is rightly conscious of the need for further development of approaches within educational and didactical theory that transcend individual religious systems and academic disciplines (e.g. Leirvik 1999: 81–2).

There are, however, problems in bringing the experience of the shortcomings of systematic approaches from the academic field directly into a classroom where the majority of children have only a vague idea of belonging to any tradition at all.[17] Children's solidarity is mainly with the family. If young children are asked to give their views, they are likely to put forward meanings they have absorbed at home. They tend to reproduce parental views and practices, including elements of their religious background, without having the ability to explain or argue for them. In the light of this, Leirvik's ideal picture appears to remain at the level of dialogue between systems rather than a more interpersonal dialogue. Leirvik seems still to be at the level of religious systems when he argues:

> What remains, however, is the dialectic between what might be termed the 'insider' and the 'outsider' perspective. For the purpose of religious education, religions need to be approached both from the 'insider' as living sources for faith, morals and life orientation – and from the 'outsider', as objects for critical investigation.
>
> (Leirvik 1999: 83)

This differs from the view of dialogue as something that should happen from the 'bottom up', or *von unten* as Wolfram Weisse calls it (1999a: 10). In an educational setting, if pupils are not regarded as representatives of a whole religious tradition when sharing a story or investigating a ritual or a festival, the same pupils can be both insiders and outsiders according to their background, knowledge and experience. Dialogue among them is, as I see it, directed both towards an understanding of the educational material and towards an understanding of their classmates, during which a spiritual dialogue may occur. A pupil's role as mainly an insider or an outsider will change, depending on the relation between the background, the focus and the perspective of the particular lesson. By making use of structured dialogue, the teacher may help the pupils collectively to move between the perspective of the insider and that of the outsider. Appropriate teaching methods and procedures are essential for this process to work.

Tove Nicolaisen

Tove Nicolaisen is Assistant Professor of Religious Education at Oslo University College. Her special interests are dialogue between Christians and Muslims and narrative approaches to RE. I will outline her ideas and relate them to three relevant publications. The first is her Master's thesis, which analyses what she calls the 'invisible dialogue' between Christians and Muslims in Norway (Nicolaisen 1990). The second is a journal article called 'Dialogue in the KRL subject' (Nicolaisen 2001), and the third is a study incorporating an introduction to narrative theory coupled with annotated narratives from the major religions (Breidlid and Nicolaisen 2000).[18] The experience gained in researching for her thesis on dialogue between 'ordinary' Muslim and Christian women in Norway is crucial to her understanding of dialogue in KRL. Because of this dialogue's unofficial status, she calls it 'an invisible dialogue' and a 'backstage dialogue'. It was when the women got to know one another that they could put their prejudices aside and realize that 'the others' too were committed to religion. The first part of the title is a quotation from one of her respondents, a Muslim woman: 'They really are true believers.' Once the initial barriers were overcome, the women were capable of discovering things they had in common: faith in one God, religious commitment, a common heritage in the Hebrew tradition, prayer, and values such as honesty and kindness. The Christians tended to focus on differences in theology, while the Muslims emphasized ethical issues. This informal and spontaneous dialogue is the form that Nicolaisen also recognizes in classrooms.

Nicolaisen points out that the official Norwegian documents about RE project 'adult dialogue' on to children, missing the style of dialogue appropriate to children, and which children already use (Nicolaisen 2001: 73). In the detailed programme for each stage in the national curriculum the word 'dialogue' is mentioned only once, for grade 9. This is in connection with the theme 'Religious Life Today', where the intention is to introduce the students to the specific inter-faith dialogue that takes place at a global, institutional level.[19] However, dialogue is a key word in the general part of the subject syllabus. This implies an understanding of dialogue as a working method for the subject as a whole – as skills for practical dialogue.

Both Leirvik and Nicolaisen note that the authorities seem to assume there is greater space for action concerning personal change on the ethical than on the religious or worldview level. Nicolaisen sees the resistance to 'practical dialogue' in official documents in terms of reassuring anxious parents that school will not make children change their religious beliefs. She comments on this in two ways. First, she points out that the authorities cannot decide how and when the children will eventually gain new views. Secondly, she draws on her earlier research experience to confirm that parents from minority groups (especially Muslims) tend to be anxious that their children will change their ethical practice through influence from school. However, Nicolaisen and her co-writer Halldis Breidlid draw on Geir Skeie's research on identity in relation to late modern plurality (e.g. 1997, 1999), suggesting that most children will develop a transversal identity (Breidlid and Nicolaisen 2000: 55–7; Nicolaisen 2001: 76–7). This concept conveys the idea that different elements of identity can be fully integrated within the person, and is close to Østberg's idea of 'integrated plural identity' (Østberg 1997).

Nicolaisen finds Lissi Rasmussen's term 'diapractice' useful, and refers to her term *intertextual practice*, which implies meeting the other person as a text in its context and making the effort to 'read' and understand the other person. She also makes use of Leirvik's distinction between necessary dialogue and spiritual dialogue. She considers the first to be relevant to classrooms, but doubts whether the second can take place in schools. She adds: 'If it happens, it is spontaneous and impossible to pre-plan' (Nicolaisen 2001: 79). On the basis of her classroom observations, Nicolaisen confirms that system-transcending approaches within RE are part of a teacher's daily job, noting that the *practice* of education in schools and in teacher training institutions inevitably involves building bridges between theology and religious studies (p. 79).

In addition, Nicolaisen considers whether dialogue in KRL could be based on work that has been done on getting children to do philosophy (Lipman 1993).[20] The advantages of making use of philosophy are the possibilities of putting forward the simplest and most open questions – the fundamental and existential ones. The main disadvantage is that philosophy on its own is concerned only with the rationalist element in religion. Religious commitment does not necessarily conform to common sense or rationality in a classroom. Although philosophy has much to offer, it has obvious limitations if used as the basis of dialogue in religious education. Nicolaisen also reminds us that unprejudiced dialogue does not necessarily occur spontaneously in a classroom setting; it has to be established and nurtured. The teacher has to be open to spontaneous dialogue whenever an opportunity arises, and also needs to be able to facilitate dialogue in a more structured way. Furthermore, dialogue needs to start before the children possess institutionalized 'knowledge' about their own background and other pupils' background. It is a task of the educator to turn this process into an informed dialogue.

Contrary to Leirvik, Nicolaisen and Breidlid claim that dialogue does not happen only in thematic or system-transcending approaches, or 'between religions' as Leirvik puts it. For Nicolaisen and Breidlid the use of a single narrative from one of the main religious traditions has a dialogical potential in the plural classroom. This follows from their theory of three dimensions to all narratives – the human dimension, the common religious dimension and the specific religious dimension (Breidlid and Nicolaisen 1999: 152, 2000: 72). This means that all pupils, regardless of background, will have some common human and religious basis for understanding as they hear the story. At the same time, the specific religious dimension in the narrative may be a real challenge to some, yet familiar to others, in the classroom.[21] In this way the classroom can be the arena for a particularly informative dialogue. When another narrative is focused on, different pupils may contribute to the dialogue.[22]

Nicolaisen is not content with the term *inter-religious dialogue* in the classroom context. It has too many connotations of adult inter-faith dialogue, and is not inclusive of non-religious worldviews. Leirvik admits that secular humanists feel excluded by the term (Leirvik 2001: 167). To try to solve this problem, Nicolaisen coins the term 'the KRL dialogue' to emphasize its distinctness from inter-faith dialogue.

I like the way Nicolaisen looks more to educational practice than to the specific inter-religious dialogue between traditions and institutions. The focus is on pupils' needs and abilities, which is particularly crucial for RE organized as a common subject for all pupils, as it is in Norway. Nicolaisen's ideal picture of dialogue is more related to children's experience than Leirvik's, but I believe she and Breidlid underestimate the differences between the religious traditions in their theoretical work on narratives. Their view seems to be that system-transcending is something that happens mainly at the individual (cf. transversal identities) or at the interpersonal level in the dialogue. The development of the curriculum is of less concern. School, as a co-operative system, is *not* central to Nicolaisen and Breidlid's description. This means that verbal dialogue dominates the picture. As I see it, we need to keep school as a co-operative system in mind for several reasons.

Dialogical education

Aspects of the dialogue concept

One aim of this chapter is to expose the hidden agenda in the use of the term 'dialogue'. It is easy to see the difference between dialogue as a theological or political project and dialogue as an educational project. The ideal concept of dialogue in RE ought not to be the dialogue between religious traditions or between adult representatives. Instead, at school, dialogue should make use of the equal status that children have in their role as pupils, and use school as an arena for open questions, experiments, reflection, criticism and information; dialogue should be seen as an attitude and a working method. Pupils from a religious or other worldview background need to meet their tradition in a way that makes it possible to be proud of it, be informed by it, and to develop within it.

Currently the term 'dialogue' is used in a variety of ways in the context of RE. All these different meanings of the term have, in my view, a particular function and ought to be part of the concept of dialogue. Retaining this multiplicity within the concept necessitates making connections between dialogue from the practical, action side and verbal and spiritual dialogue. In the following section I will add two more distinctions to the list given above: dialogue *as an attitude and a working method* and *philosophical* dialogue. Also, in attempting to bring all these aspects of dialogue together, I will introduce the term *dialogical education*.

DIALOGICAL EDUCATION
Aspects of the dialogue concept

Action side

- Diapractice – co-operation
- Necessary dialogue
  - Everyday conversation to get to understand one another
  - Informal personal exchange of ideas
- Dialogue as an attitude and a working method in KRL
- Structured dialogue (in the role as pupil)
  - Empathic work with other religions and beliefs
  - Representing other views
  - Comparison
  - Face-to-face communication
- Philosophical dialogue
- Spiritual dialogue – the personal encounter that results in change

↓

Verbal side

The need for a dialogical education

An overview of RE in different European countries shows that most religious education takes place in separate classrooms, operated according to faith, or with children from different denominations or religions attending separate schools. There are many historical reasons for this: it is a system in which religious freedom and parental rights are valued more highly than the nation-states' need to secure unity across faiths or to promote social cohesion through education. Dialogical education in these national contexts is often expressed in terms such as *inter-religious and ecumenical*. The term

'inter-religious' is then used mainly of the need for a change in national educational policy to create new school structures, or for new models of RE to
enhance inter-religious and ecumenical education. Such developments
can be seen in Germany, Slovakia, Northern Ireland, Finland and the
Netherlands, for example (Schreiner 2000, 2001; Weisse 1999b). In some
of these contexts there is also a search for dialogical education through
changes in curriculum and didactics in RE.

In the multicultural context in northern Norway, where I carried out a field
study, children from a local minority with long historical traditions are
removed from school in RE and other subjects owing to the conflicting
values of parents and the school (Leganger-Krogstad 1998). The parents
are campaigning to set up a private faith-based school. The wish for local
adaptation of the curriculum is challenging the limits of the principle of
'one school for all'. In this community the school traditionally worked
towards a process of assimilation[23] of the Sami and Kven (Finnish) minority,
even though integration is the official policy (NOU 1995: 12). Parents would
first and foremost like their children to attend the municipal school, but only
on condition that their religious views and values are made more visible. The
local authority, on the other hand, has used 11 September 2001 in arguing
against a separate private school. More than ever, they claim, there is a
need to keep children of different faiths together in the public school.

However, even though the curricula have local adaptation as a general
aim, it is not always easy to achieve in practice. In the process of implementing a curriculum, at both the national and the local level, the majority
decide most of the content to be taught. Minorities, especially those on the
periphery, are invariably ignored or overruled. Mainstream (or central)
culture dominates the national curriculum and textbooks. Since textbooks
are a decisive factor in the teaching of RE, a homogenized mainstream
culture is spread all over Norway. Room for locally adapted RE diminishes
accordingly (Leganger-Krogstad 2000: 95).

This way of treating local cultural diversity conflicts with the school's role
in educating for life in a plural world. When the school ignores minority
cultures or local variants of the national culture, pupils are taught implicitly
that their knowledge, habits and interpretation of life are not valued as part
of Norwegian culture. In turn, this means that dialogue, both as diapractice
and as verbal dialogue, suffers, since diversity in the classroom is not recognized. Thus neither the minorities nor the majority are prepared to live
genuinely with plurality in the local community. How, then, in the long
term, can children possibly learn to understand global diversity?

In his Nobel Peace Prize lecture Annan stated that 'There is a growing
understanding that human diversity is both the reality that makes dialogue
necessary, and the very basis of the dialogue.' The local problem mentioned
above was the lack of recognition of diversity. Unless the particular form of
Christianity that the Kvens practice and the underlying Sami influence on

the local culture are both made part of the local curriculum, it will be impossible to give the children the cultural competence they need to live as young citizens in this community.

A dialogical education needs, as I see it, to be based on a contextual approach, and this approach has to make use of ethnographic methods to describe local religious life (Leganger-Krogstad 2000: 98–100, 2001: 58). An example is the approach to dialogue taken in Hamburg schools (see Chapter 10 below). This education is characterized by: a lifeworld, experience-based and thematic approach (*Lebenweltlich-erfarungsorientierte und themenbezogene Ausrichtung*), an intercultural and contextual approach (*Kontextuelle und interkulturelle Ausrichtung*) and an ecumenical and interreligious approach (*Ökumenische und interreligiöse Ausrichtung*) (Weisse 1999a: 18–24). For Weisse, dialogue in its various forms is not an aim but a key underlying principle (Weisse 1999a: 24).

Most of the principles of dialogical education in Weisse's work are similar to the contextual approach to RE as it has been developed in northern Norway (Leganger-Krogstad 2000, 2001). The first is that pupils are considered as citizens in the local society. Even if school is a protected space it is, nevertheless, a training ground for citizenship. Thus it is necessary to open school up to society. In this process the local community is studied carefully to see how religious life is part of children's background. This in turn provides a framework for education, and can be made part of RE to help children to develop the cultural competence needed to understand their own locality. Next it makes use of present manifestations (*Wirkungsgeschichte*) of religious history and everyday religion as resources for education. Thus, in this localized version of RE, children, for instance, visit each other's places of worship, and are encouraged to verbalize their own background through the adult representatives of their own faith.

Also, local customs such as the greeting of the sun at the first sunrise after the two-month-long period of darkness are included in the curriculum and given a broader context as part of the circular way of dealing with time in the Sami culture. Similarly, local views about nature and holiness are included in RE. Family structures and values in the minority cultures are made part of the curriculum and accepted as part of local diversity (Leganger-Krogstad 1998: 141). Family members are asked about the influence of particular sacred texts on their way of life, and visits to local churchyards are used as a starting point for dialogues about life and death, local history, family names, symbols, language and rituals. Likewise, ethical aspects of ecological issues are introduced through concrete and on-going local political issues where the pupils may have an influence on the outcome. Taken together, these examples show that within a contextual approach, *lived* religion includes popular religion as part of education; also religion as a lived phenomenon can often be seen to be system-transcending. A contextual approach focuses on the opportunities to investigate religious concepts through first-hand experience developed further by second-hand experience (Leganger-Krogstad 2001: 68–9).

School as a dialogic arena can be of particular importance to children. At school they have a role as pupils which may be quite different from the one they have in their family or their peer group. This is so because school is a clearly defined setting where all pupils have equal rights and obligations. Research shows, for example, that the classroom provides Muslim girls with a very important arena in which they have space and equal rights. In the classroom they are faced with the same expectations as other children and compete on equal terms with them (Valen 1999). Inside the classroom the norm is 'we' instead of the stigmatizing 'us' and 'them' which they often encounter outside the classroom, not least in the playground.

This role as a pupil is particularly important to children and youngsters in their search for an individual life interpretation. In this process the school ought to provide pupils with a risk-free zone, a zone of experimentation. Many teachers of religious education have experienced the fact that pupils need room for the expression of doubt and criticism in their lessons (Vedøy 2001: 59). Since religion is often considered a private matter, RE teachers need to respect such private or non-infringement zones (Leganger-Krogstad 2001: 65). RE teachers can provide various strategies to create such risk-free zones. These include narration methods, dramatization, role-play, discussion related to stories enabling children to discuss in the third person rather than the first, discussion from a particular standpoint, reflective writing, journal writing and private letters to the teacher with appropriate responses. These strategies can be employed as part of a structured dialogue in which the teacher is a partner, but in an asymmetrical relationship as the significant other.

Conclusion

Dialogue in the classroom should not serve primarily as dialogue between religions. That sort of system-transcending co-operation between academic traditions is a task for universities and colleges. Rather, the main task of dialogue in the classroom is to operate at an interpersonal level, building identity and empowering young people for citizenship in a plural global world.

Citizenship is not a separate subject in Norwegian education, but the whole educational system is intended as an arena for developing citizenship. RE as a subject should help pupils to achieve the cultural competence to live in a plural society through identity formation and dialogue. However, intentions in education and practical reality are often two quite different things, as seen in the example from northern Norway discussed above. Citizenship is not achieved through co-operation and dialogue if part of the pupil's religious world or worldview is excluded from the classroom agenda. A contextual approach to RE is therefore seen as a means to achieve a more dialogical education, thus providing a bridge between differences and across borders. Kofi Annan (2001) puts this in the following way:

> Today's real borders are not between nations, but between powerful and powerless, free and fettered, privileged and humiliated. Today, no walls can separate humanitarian or human rights crises in one part of the world from national security crises in another.

The insights into who are the powerful and the powerless starts in children's own lives in the treatment they receive as young citizens in their own local society. Annan began his lecture with a reference to a girl born in Afghanistan and ended it by saying: 'Remember this girl and then our larger aims'. I add: How can children be taught to take responsibility for the globe unless through school they learn how to take responsibility for their classmates by engaging in dialogue with recognition of the otherness of the other?

Notes

1 It is interesting to note that religion is also a central issue in Jürgen Habermas' speech of thanks for the *Friedenspreis des Deutschen Buchhandels 2001* (Habermas 2001). Religion is visible in the public arena in a new way and is of importance as a means of reconciliation.
2 When pupils have finished the primary level (ages 6–12) and go on to the lower secondary level (ages 13–15), 80 per cent of all pupils move to a bigger school where pupils from more than one primary school are enrolled.
3 The percentage is increasing, and the first Muslim school started up in 2001. The state gives financial support (85 per cent of costs) to these schools.
4 Thirteen national resource centres are established to provide professional help in the local school setting.
5 This is the official translation. The last word, *livssynsorientering*, can be translated in other ways, e.g.: 'worldviews', 'life stance', 'secular orientation' or 'philosophies of life'. I make use of these alternative expressions in the text.
6 It is possible to read parts of the Norwegian debate in English: see Birkedal (1994), Enger (1998), Haakedal (2001a), Leganger-Krogstad (1997), Leirvik (1999), Midttun (2000), Rasmussen (2000), Selander (1999), Skeie (1997), and Østberg (1997).
7 Three years after implementation the evaluation has been completed (St meld 32, 2000–1) and the profile of the subject adjusted in line with the findings. The subject has been renamed Education in Christianity, Religions and Ethics (*Kristendoms-, religions- og livssynskunnskap*) to retain the familiar abbreviation KRL. The new name shows it is a more pluralist subject designed to suit a more plural society. The right to partial exemption has been specified and made easier for the parents to achieve, and the syllabus has been radically reduced to half the previous size.
8 The term 'life interpretation' is used here in the way Elisabet Haakedal defines it (2001b: 166).

9 The subject in relation to religious freedom is covered in English by Tarald Rasmussen, who chaired the ministerial elected committee responsible for the first KRL draft syllabus in 1995 (Rasmussen 2000).

10 The two subjects correspond with the two perspectives of the insider and the outsider. Because of parents' choices in 1993, 94.7 per cent of compulsory school pupils took part in confessional religious education, while 4.3 per cent attended the alternative subject called Worldviews, and 0.9 per cent had no RE in school.

11 The seven aspects are: the spiritual, the creative, the working, the liberally educated, the social, the environmentally aware and the integrated human being (L97, 15–50; KUF 1999).

12 The translation uses the word 'debate' instead of 'dialogue', which would be a more accurate translation.

13 Cf. http://folk.uio.no/leirvik/.

14 Among the reasons for these questions are, as I see it, that the status of the theme of ethics within the curriculum is unclear because it is handled in three different ways. It is regarded as a common platform for RE at the first grade. Later it is closely connected with the diversity of religious traditions and secular worldviews. For older students, however, ethical principles are linked with studies in philosophy.

15 At the University of Oslo, where Leirvik is employed, degrees in Christian theology and religious studies are offered in two different faculties. Within the theological faculty efforts are being made to try to narrow the gap through inter-religious research and by setting up new study programmes such as 'Inter-religious dialogue in school and society'.

16 This is not the whole picture, however. The pluralist dialogical development originates in schools. It is also influencing teacher education in the university colleges, where interdisciplinary studies have been conducted for a long time.

17 For the sake of the Muslim minority Leirvik himself, as we have seen, would prefer a combined model for RE, with a confessional approach in groups and in shared lessons with opportunities for dialogue. This is, as I see it, what teachers try to solve early on in the ordinary classroom by differentiation due to religious and cultural background and through local adaptation of the national syllabus.

18 A theoretical discussion related to this work is available in English (Breidlid and Nicolaisen 1999).

19 Nicolaisen's message here is that a limited search for the word 'dialogue' in the syllabus will not bring forth the dialogical, educational intentions in the curriculum.

20 This tradition is developed further in a Norwegian context as 'Philosophy with children' (Schjelderup et al. 1999).

21 Nicolaisen and Breidlid have specifically looked into the parallel and conflicting narratives in Judaism, Christianity and Islam (Breidlid and Nicolaisen 1999: 144–9).

22 It seems to be taken for granted that a religious text or a narrative makes those belonging to the tradition the text comes from insiders and those from other traditions outsiders. This is erroneous, according to the narration theory presented above. As the pupils work with a text, the text makes all the pupils both insiders and outsiders. All pupils can relate to the human and the common religious message in the text. The specific religious message will be more or less difficult to relate to, depending on religious background, knowledge, experience, and degree of identification with the tradition. This is when we talk about the individual reading and interpretation of a text. In an educational setting

the pupils may collectively be trained to (simultaneously) try cognitively to take the perspective of the insider, the believer, and then change to take the perspective of the outsider, the critical partner.
23 The Samis are recognized as an indigenous people, and since 1997 have for the first time had a parallel curriculum focused on Sami identity. The Kven minority, with status as a national minority, have for centuries been at odds with the local school authorities about values in upbringing and education.

References

Annan, Kofi (2001) *The Nobel Peace Prize Lecture in Oslo*, United Nations, 10 December 2001. Online. Available HTTP: <http://www.un.org/News/Press/docs/2001/sgsm8071.doc.htm> (accessed 10 January 2002).

Birkedal, Erling (1994) 'Church and school in Norway', *Panorama: International Journal of Comparative Religions Education and Values*, 6 (2), 48–56.

Breidlid, Halldis and Nicolaisen, Tove (1999) 'Stories and storytelling in religious education in Norway', in D. Chidester, J. Stonier and J. Tobler (eds) *Diversity as Ethos: Challenges for Inter-religious and Intercultural Education*, Cape Town: University of Cape Town ICRSA, 140–54.

—— (2000) *I begynnelsen var fortellingen: fortelling i KRL (In the Beginning was the Story. Narration in KRL)*, Oslo: Universitetsforlaget.

Buber, Martin (1923) *Ich und Du*, trans. Andreas Schmidt. Online. Available HTTP: <http://www.buber.de/de/index.html> (accessed 7 March 2000).

Enger, Trond (1998) 'Religious education for all pupils – the Norwegian way', *Panorama: International Journal of Comparative Religions Education and Values*, 10 (2), 122–34.

Goodlad, John I. (1979) *Curriculum Inquiry: The Study of Curriculum Practice*, New York: McGraw-Hill.

Gullestad, Marianne (1989) *Kultur og hverdagsliv: på sporet av det moderne Norge*, Oslo: Universitetsforlaget.

Haakedal, Elisabet (2001a) 'From Lutheran catechism to world religions and Humanism: dilemmas and middle ways through the story of Norwegian religious education', *British Journal of Religious Education*, 23 (2), 88–97.

—— (2001b) 'Contextual teaching and learning in religious education', in H-G. Heimbrock, C. T. Scheilke and P. Schreiner (eds) *Towards Religious Competence: Diversity as a Challenge for Education in Europe*, Münster and London: LIT Verlag, 165–79.

Habermas, Jürgen (2001) 'Der Riss der Sprachlosigkeit', *Franfurter Rundschau*, 16 October.

KUF (1990) *Curriculum guidelines for compulsory education in Norway. M87 English edition*, Oslo: Aschehoug and Ministry of Education and Research.

—— (1996) *Kristendomskunnskap med religions- og livssynsorientering: veiledning til læreplanverket for den 10-årige grunnskolen (L97)*, Oslo: Nasjonalt læremiddelsenter.

—— (1999) *National Curriculum for Compulsory School (Læreplanverket for den 10-årige grunnskolen, 1996)*, Royal Ministry of Education, Research and Church affairs. Online. Available HTTP: <http://odin.dep.no/odinarkiv/norsk/dep/kuf/1999/eng/014005–990122/indexdok000– b-n-a.html> (accessed 15 June 2001).

Leganger-Krogstad, Heid (1997) 'Religious education in the Norwegian school system', in R. E. Kristiansen and N. M. Terebichin (eds) *Religion, Church and Education in the Barents Region*, Archangel: Pomor State University Press, 171–83.

—— (1998) 'Ethnic minority in conflict with Norwegian educational ideals', *Panorama: International Journal of Comparative Religions Education and Values*, 10 (1), 131–45.

—— (2000) 'Developing a contextual theory and practice of religious education', *Panorama: International Journal of Comparative Religions Education and Values*, 12 (1), 94–104.

—— (2001) 'Religious education in a global perspective: a contextual approach', in H-G. Heimbrock, C. T. Scheilke and P. Schreiner (eds) *Towards Religious Competence: Diversity as a Challenge for Education in Europe*, Münster and London: LIT Verlag, 53–73.

Leirvik, Oddbjørn (1998a) 'Religionsdialog i klasserommet', in D. Rian (ed.) *Religion i en verden i endring religionsvitenskapens bidrag til religionsundervisningen i skolen*, Trondheim: Tapir.

—— (1998b) 'Sjølvet og den Andre i religionsdialogen', *Norsk Tidsskrift for Misjon*, 52 (4), 217–30.

—— (1999) 'Theology, religious studies and religious education', in D. Chidester, J. Stonier and J. Tobler (eds) *Diversity as Ethos: Challenges for Inter-religious and Intercultural Education*, Cape Town: University of Cape Town ICRSA, 75–83.

—— (2001) *Religionsdialog på norsk (Inter-religious dialogue in a Norwegian Context)*, Oslo: Pax.

Lipman, Matthew (1993) *Thinking Children and Education*, Dubuque IA: Kendall Hunt.

Midttun, Ann (2000) 'Norway', in P. Schreiner (ed.) *RE in Europe: A Collection of Basic Information about RE in European Countries*, Münster: Intereuropean Commission on Church and School (ICCS) and Comenius Institute, 123–30.

Nicolaisen, Tove (1990) *De tror påordentlig: muslimer og kristne møtes i Norge: analyse av en usynlig dialog (They really do believe. Encounter between Muslims and Christians in Norway: an analysis of the invisible dialogue)*, Hovedoppgave i kristendomskunnskap, Oslo: Institutt for kristendomskunnskap, Teologiske Menighetsfakultet.

—— (2001) 'Dialog i KRL-faget' (Dialogue in the KRL subject), *Prismet*, 52 (2), 73–84.

NOU (1995) *Official Norwegian Report. Identitet og dialog: kristendomskunnskap, livssynskunnskap og religionsundervisning (Identity and dialogue: Christian knowledge and religious and ethical education)*, Oslo: KUF.

—— (1995) *Official Norwegian Report: Opplæring i et flerkulturelt Norge (Education in a multicultural Norway)*. Oslo: KUF.

Rasmussen, Lissi (1998) *Diapraksis og dialog mellom kristne og muslimer*. Online. Available HTTP <http://www.tf.uio.no/krlnett/tekster/art–diaprax–berg–nov98.htm> (accessed 13 July 2000).

Rasmussen, Tarald (2000) 'The new Norwegian "KRL" subject and religious freedom: a report', *Studia Theologica*, 54, 19–34.

Schjelderup, Ariane, Børresen, Beate and Olsholt, Øyvind (1999) *Filosofi i skolen*, Oslo: Tano Aschehoug.

Schreiner, Peter (ed.) (2000) *RE in Europe: A collection of Basic Information about RE in European Countries*, Münster: Intereuropean Commission on Church and School (ICCS) and Comenius Institute.

—— (2001) *Profile Ökumenischer Schulen. Beispiele aus Europa*, Münster and New York: Waxmann.

Selander, Sven-Åke (1999) 'State, Church and School in the Scandinavian countries – in a European perspective', in N-Å. Tidman (ed.) *Into the third Millenium: EFTRE Conference August 1998 in Copenhagen*, Malmö: Föreningen lärare i religionskunskap, 54–75.

Skeie, Geir (1997) 'Some aspects of RE in Scandinavia and Norway: an outline of a cultural approach to RE', in T. Andree, C. Bakker and P. Schreiner (eds) *Crossing Boundaries: Contributions to Inter-religious and Intercultural Education*, Münster: Comenius Institute, 155–60.

—— (1998) *En Kulturbevisst Religionspedagogikk.* Dr. art. avhandling. Trondheim: Institutt for religionsvitenskap, Det historisk-filosofiske fakultet, Norges teknisk-naturvitenskapelige universitet.

—— (1999) 'The challenge of plurality, norms and relativism in RE', in N-Å. Tidman (ed.) *Into the third Millenium: EFTRE Conference August 1998 in Copenhagen*, Malmö: Föreningen lärare i religionskunskap, 192–202.

St meld 32 (2000–1) *Evaluering av faget Kristendomskunnskap med religions- og livssynsorientering*, Oslo: Kirke-, utdannings- og forskningsdepartementet.

Telhaug, Alfred Oftedal (1994) *Utdanningspolitikken og enhetsskolen: studier i 1990–årenes utdanningspolitikk*, Oslo: Didakta.

Valen, Hildegunn (1999) Roller og verdier hos muslimsk ungdom i Oslo: en kvalitativ undersøkelse av hvordan muslimsk ungdom i Oslo forholder seg til roller og verdier i en plural kontekst. Oslo: Hovedoppgave i kristendomskunnskap, Det teologiske Menighetsfakultet.

Vedøy, Gunn (2001) KRL i flerkulturelle klasser. Oslo: Hovedfag i flerkulturell og utviklingsrettet utdanning, Avdeling for lærerutdanning, Høgskolen i Oslo.

Weisse, Wolfram (1999a) '"Dialogischer Religionsunterricht". Eine Einführung', in W. Weisse (ed.) *Vom Monolog zum Dialog. Ansätze einer dialogischen Religionspädagogik*, Münster and New York: Waxmann, 5–32.

—— (ed.) (1999b) *Vom Monolog zum Dialog. Ansätze einer dialogischen Religionspädagogik*, Münster and New York: Waxmann.

Østberg, Sissel (1997) 'Religious education in a multicultural society: the quest for identity and dialogue', in T. Andree, C. Bakker and P. Schreiner (eds) *Crossing Boundaries: Contributions to Inter-religious and Intercultural Education*, Münster: Comenius Institute.

Chapter 10

Difference without discrimination

Religious education as a field of learning for social understanding?

Wolfram Weisse

Synopsis This chapter deals with the question of whether religious education (RE) can contribute to intercultural understanding, tolerance and harmony. On the basis of a case study, it examines the way RE is organized, conceptualized and theorized in Hamburg where it is not taught in the same way as in other German provinces or regions (*Länder*). Normally pupils are divided into groups of the same denomination or religion for RE. In Hamburg they all stay together. This approach is based on theories of dialogue developed in the social sciences, philosophy, education and theology. The chapter shows how an approach 'from below' is used in the theories referred to here. Given this theoretical background, the relevance of dialogical processes at classroom level can be evaluated. The case study notes the influence of those directly involved in the debates about RE, such as educationists in universities and other institutions, Church officials and representatives of religions other than Christianity. The idea of an Academy of World Religions is presented as a new initiative to encourage dialogue between religions. Besides those who are directly involved with RE, the chapter looks at the expectations of the public and of public figures. Considering how secular a city Hamburg is, it may seem surprising that not only education officials but party politicians comment on religious education and give the dialogical approach their backing. Such support shows that dialogical RE is seen as a form of training in tolerance and intercultural understanding, a force for civic harmony.

As the mother of an eight-year-old daughter I have a strong interest in inter-religious education in primary schools. We live in the west of Hamburg, in the lower middle-class district of Iserbrook on the edge of the Osdorfer Born. You can't feel any of the cosmopolitan attitudes of a city here, and there is aggression shown towards foreigners from some homes, which the children bring to school. Since my daughter enrolled in primary school I have given up any illusion of innocent contact among children, of children who do not discriminate against others and do not judge other children by the colour of their skin or by the shape of their eyes. I would like the school to exert a corrective influence, to oppose racist tendencies and teach social awareness to children from intellectually narrow backgrounds. I disagree with the view that it is not the school's task to correct deficiencies at home and hope that the school can meet this need. School is society in miniature, where children and adolescents can learn to live together, where awareness and attitudes are created. I hope for a religious education in school which treats and teaches all religions equally. I think that a truly inter-religious education enables children to take part in an important learning process: to learn about the other world religions and to get to know and value their peers for their religion and cultural backgrounds.

This is a passage from a letter sent to the author by a Muslim mother in Hamburg (quoted in Weisse 1999: 293). It contains high expectations of education at school, especially religious education (RE). The expectations refer not only to the relevance of schooling, but also to its role in society. Religious education is considered to be a field for learning tolerance and inter-religious understanding, for learning to see differences without using them to discriminate against others, for laying the foundations of harmony and overcoming racism in society. Can such expectations be fulfilled?

I shall attempt to answer the question by using a case study which draws on experience in Hamburg and is at the same time related to the concerns about citizenship raised in Robert Jackson's opening chapter. The study focuses on the relevance of dialogue by taking advantage of the different cultural and religious backgrounds of school pupils and enabling them to gain insights from their peers. The case study concentrates on an approach to religious education which is characterized by dialogue. Therefore, this chapter is concerned with a crucial task in a multicultural society, namely to foster dialogue and communication.

However, some questions regarding terminology need to be clarified at the outset. The concept of 'religion' is here understood as a process of orientation. It encompasses Christianity and Christian denominations, but also includes other religions. It is related to the so-called world religions, but not restricted to them. The wide range of religions and religious patterns, reasoning about the origins and purposes of life, striving for justice and peace, are all incorporated into religion as defined here. I suggest the use of the term 'neighbour religion' instead of 'world religions'. The latter implies the power structure of organizations and a deliberate restriction to a set number of religions (see Chapter 2 above). The term 'neighbour religion' refers to what my neighbour in my classroom, in my village or town, and even in the global village believes. 'Neighbour' is understood here in the sense used, for example, by Immanuel Levinas: *l'autrui/le prochain* (Levinas 1993: 156) is at the centre, rather than a given belief system. Therefore the term 'neighbour religion' refers to ordinary people in the neighbourhood, not to key representatives of religious organizations. In dialogue with neighbours, the wisdom of religious traditions should be used, as they stimulate and contribute to debate, but the traditions should not be a hindrance to dealing with basic questions which are raised by every-day dialogue. Dialogue within the framework of neighbour religions does not mean dialogue from above, but dialogue from below. The latter kind of dialogue is relevant to the questions of participants, in this case pupils at school. The prerequisite for an interesting dialogue in the classroom is to make use of the different cultural and religious backgrounds of the pupils rather than separate them into homogeneous groups, an approach which is problematic (see Chapters 1 and 4 of this volume).

Religious education is part of the syllabus of all schools in Germany, including state schools. The Churches as well as the state have an influence on the principles and content of religious education in schools. Until pupils reach the age of 14, parents have the right to withhold their children from RE. Pupils above that age can choose between RE and ethics/philosophy. In addition, there is a subject called 'politics' or 'civic education', where intercultural topics may be addressed. However, the RE syllabus offers more topics and possibilities of intercultural learning than any other subject in German schools.

In Germany the education system is not centralized, but lies in the hands of the federal regions (*Länder*). Compared with the other regions, Hamburg (which counts as one such region) is an exception (see Weisse 1996). While religious education is taught separately for Catholic, Protestant and, in a very few cases, Muslim children, the practice of teaching RE in Hamburg has been different for almost half a century. Religious education is not divided according to the denomination or religion of the pupils; instead, it is taught to all pupils, regardless of their religious or cultural background. Hamburg is a multicultural city where, among a population of almost 2 million, a variety of different cultures and religions can be found: there are more than 100 languages and denominations/religions (see Grüenberg *et al.* 1994), and 8 per cent of the population are Muslims. Hamburg has always understood itself as a liberal city, where differences of belief do not count and where people from all over the world live. At the same time, however, there is a tendency to increasing xenophobia and distrust of 'fundamentalist' Muslims, a trend which has been especially noticeable since 11 September 2001. Any initiatives and forces which work towards better understanding between different groups are now both more necessary and more difficult. This is the context of our educational work.

We call our form of RE 'dialogical religious education' (Weisse 1999). Dialogue is central to our approach, in terms of both theory and practice. Dialogical RE is marked by the following elements: it is related to the experience of the pupils and to stimulus material from religious traditions; it is contextual and intercultural; it is based on the approaches of ecumenical theology and inter-religious learning.

Our approach refers to an experience-orientated understanding of dialogue, which will be explained later. In this approach, it is dialogue in

the classroom which is important – a dialogue in which pupils can participate with their different and various religious and ideological backgrounds
and during which they can form their own views and positions. Questions
about the meaning of life and death as well as ethical questions about
justice, peace and the integrity of creation are covered in such lessons.
While the spectrum of topics points to the many similarities between
religions, dialogue in RE is also designed to demonstrate the differences
between religious traditions. Individual positions are not found by mixing
different views, but by comparing and contrasting them with one another.
Religious education should make dialogue in the classroom possible by
allowing participants to refer to their different religious backgrounds,
while not requiring differences. Dialogue in the classroom fosters respect
for other religious commitments, can confirm pupils' views or help them
to make their own commitments whilst also allowing them to monitor
their commitments critically. This kind of religious education does not set
out to mirror social divisions in the population, but rather to develop
mutual understanding and respect. This is why we are opposed to separat-
ing pupils according to their religion for religious education. Given this
approach, RE in Hamburg aims to meet the expectations which the
mother expressed in the letter cited at the beginning. While this approach
to religious education has faced considerable criticism from other parts of
Germany, there has also been increasing interest. Therefore, this approach
has provoked a mixture of views (Weisse 2002). What some regard as a progressive and welcome model others consider to be a dangerous development that needs to be controlled or opposed.

In this chapter I shall describe some elements of our research in Hamburg.
We have tried to clarify the notion of 'dialogue' (Knauth 1996) and carried
out extensive empirical work such as qualitative studies of young people's
religiosity (Sandt 1996) and RE, teachers' intentions, and dialogue in the
classroom. Some of the findings are summarized below. The main part of
the chapter consists of an analysis of the discussion in Hamburg, based
on 'actor theory', which emphasizes internal (institutions and people
directly involved in religious education) and external (the positions of
politicians and representatives of public organizations) considerations, as
well as innovative plans and the relevance of religious education for social
questions.

Society, dialogue and religion

In working towards an analysis of the dominant social background we refer
to the work of the French sociologist Pierre Bourdieu (1998). He points to
the contrast between a competition-based economic logic and a social,
justice-orientated view of value. Global development detaches economic

logic from social conditions, so that the dynamics of unguided and uncontrolled development are set in motion: we see how neo-liberal utopia (that of profit maximization and boundless exploitation) turns into a kind of infernal machine, whose necessity imposes itself even upon politicians, as 'this utopia evokes powerful belief in the free trade faith' (Bourdieu 1998: 114–15).

On this view, non-formalized social groups should be enabled to participate more in social life. Despite the habit of relying on directives and wisdom 'from the top', it is now necessary to integrate greater parts of the population, including organizations at the middle level. Voices 'from below' need to be taken into account. In the wake of increasing social problems, a growing number of voices in political science and sociology warn against the uncontrolled power of elites. This necessitates a level of involvement of the population which goes beyond the current institutions of parliamentary democracy.

One such voice is the British social scientist Anthony Giddens. In his book *Beyond Left and Right* (1994) the idea of a dialogue-orientated democracy is developed as a framework within which social movements and self-help organizations are given a share in political decision making. This requires active commitment and responsibility by those who are involved, such as fringe groups, unconventional and small groups. Therefore, a democratization of democracy seems necessary. Although Giddens does not touch on the role which religious groups might play in his suggested framework, there is a hint of the tasks they could assume in the public sphere.

For some decades, religion has not been taken into consideration for the development of public institutions in Western countries, but there seems to be a new interest in this question and not just since 11 September 2001. Two publications illustrate this renewed interest: on the one hand, Samuel Huntington, a political scientist in America, recognizes the importance of religions in the public arena. In his book *The Clash of Civilizations* (1996), which has attracted a great deal of attention, he expounds the thesis that, in the not too distant future, political-ideological debates will increasingly be replaced by cultural-religious ones. Huntington starts from an understanding of culture as something rigid because, given corresponding values, he equates culture with religion. In my view, his approach is dangerous, because his analysis is based on blame, related either to culture or to religion, and takes a closed view of religions and cultures that is contradicted by empirical research in the social sciences.

The second approach is found in an extensive report by the Bertelsmann Foundation, addressed to the Club of Rome, entitled *The Limits of Social Cohesion* and edited by the Austrian-American sociologist Peter L. Berger (1997). It aims to analyse the cultural resources of society in greater detail than hitherto. Berger warns against neglecting fundamental factors of social cohesion. In contrast to Huntington, he does not suggest a 'clash' of cultures, but underlines the necessity of dialogue between cultures. He advocates a 'tolerant dialogue' which should be expressed at an intermediate level of society, and this could be within the framework of religions and religious communities.

Berger's approach gives precedence to cultural and religious aspects in order to engage in a process of mutual understanding in society. He points to the relevance of educational institutions and underlines the importance of making efforts to reach understanding in the cultural sphere in general and hence also in the area of religion. Berger makes clear that it is not competition and conflict which determine relations between cultures, but dialogue. However, he does not mean dialogue between high-ranking officials in the economy and in politics, but dialogue at the middle and lower levels, for instance dialogue between adherents of religions. Berger's framework could be used as one of the theoretical structures within which our approach to a dialogue-orientated religious education in Hamburg could be placed.

Dialogue as a principle for learning about religions: philosophy, pedagogy and theology

The following concepts take on new meaning within a dialogical approach to RE.

Philosophy and pedagogy

Dialogue is a fundamental principle in the thought of Martin Buber. Buber's work on religious philosophy and pedagogy (1962, 1986) calls for a radical change of perspective and is concerned with an understanding of religion in everyday life. The means of communicating with God is the I–Thou relationship. Genuine intersubjective interaction is a parable of the relation with God. Dialogue facilitates religious experience when individuals turn towards their fellow human beings. The realization that there is a religious dimension takes place when people actively turn towards life and perceive the singularity and uniqueness of creation. Similarly, the relationship between educator and educated is conceived as the relationship between partners in dialogue. With regard to pedagogy, Buber also postulates a change of perspective. Given his thinking in terms of dialogue, he criticizes educational methods which look exclusively upon the teacher as the representative of a culture. Such methods could be conceived only as ways to influence and ultimately to manipulate. Buber intends to create pedagogical ways of thinking which endeavour to concentrate on community and reciprocity.

The concept of dialogue has to consider the asymmetry of learning, and must not take only the teacher's point of view into account. Adults can learn a great deal from adolescents, especially in a multi-religious and multi-cultural context. Dialogue cannot start from a one-sided construction of asymmetry, but should consider and describe the dialogical–pedagogical relationship as a 'symmetry of asymmetries' (Peukert 1992: 122). If the mutual aspect of the interaction is considered, it will be possible to conduct a dialogue in which both parties realize themselves as equal partners who depend on one another. This change of perspective alters the perception of the classical problems of pedagogical action: it is not adolescents' short-comings that are important, but their abilities, including diverse knowledge, diverse perception and diverse religion. It seems to us that this radical understanding of dialogue agrees with the dialectical notion of pedagogical action which aims at individual and social transformation, an understanding which forms the basis of the reflections of the Hamburg educationist Helmut Peukert (1984, 1994). Taking Habermas's discourse on ethical concepts one radical step further, Peukert develops a pedagogical framework which has the notion of 'transformatory practice' at its centre:

> Practice . . . means to act despite the experience and endurance of system-immanent contradictions which deform one's own sphere of life and despite alienation resulting from this, to act in order to bring about changes which incline towards a way of life which does not result in alienation, a way of life in which identities can be found together so that individuals can change when conditions change.
>
> (Peukert 1984: 73)

Conversely, Habermas has recently taken up some of Peukert's ideas in focusing on the importance of religion for societal questions (Habermas 2001).

Theology

Among the theological approaches that include the inter-religious aspect we refer to Hans Kung's programme of a 'world ethos', 'ecumenical learning', and Paul Knitter's dialogical approach based on liberation theology. The main focus of our discussion will, however, be on ecumenical theology, especially on the approach of Hans Jochen Margull.

The necessity of propagating a world ethos, which would as far as possible compel the representatives of all religions to agree to work for peace and justice in a world which is threatened by hatred, war and social tensions, goes back to the German Catholic theologian Hans Kung (1990). Kung's chosen approach is one of learning 'from above', one which emphasizes the universality and the similarities of the religions instead of the differences.

A quite different understanding, that of learning from below, is incorporated in the concept of 'ecumenical learning' (Nipkow 1991; Weisse 1989). The strength of this kind of learning is that it is generated at grass-roots level and thus allows for a large number of initiatives. The advantage of this approach is the possibility of accommodating particularities and differences. Within the wide framework of the conciliar process for justice, peace and the integrity of creation, completely different priorities can be chosen with regard to concepts and the practical implementation of RE. In the same way as the ecumenical movement seeks a process of consensus, which cannot be enforced by a formally established authority, ecumenical learning is decentralized in that it does not impose thematic or didactic priorities.

Another aspect of dialogue is found in the contextual approach of Paul F. Knitter and his pluralist theology of religions. Within the framework of liberation theology, Knitter underlines the necessity of counteracting dominant structures and establishing communicative practices. In the global crisis of the world, the credibility of religion depends on how far it can contribute to the fight against transcultural structures of inequality and oppression. Knitter states that a common theological and ethical criterion for all religions is to be found here. Within its own tradition, each religion is faced with the problem of deliverance from disastrous tendencies; each religion is faced with a 'soteriological criterion', where the notion of the 'Kingdom of God' gains new relevance (see Knitter 1991, 1997). Therefore, inter-religious dialogue becomes a critical and transformative project, both challenging injustice and facing religions with a critical examination of their own practices.

Hamburg's approach to a religious education based on dialogue is closely related to the idea of ecumenical theology as developed, for example, by W. A. Visser't Hooft in his role in the World Council of Churches (WCC), and especially by Hans Jochen Margull. Margull was for long a member of the staff of the WCC as well as Professor of Ecumenical Theology at the University of Hamburg. His approach corresponds in many ways to that taken by Muslim scholars, such as Mohammed Arkoun (1992) or Abdoldjavad Falaturi (1996). So what are Margull's main concerns?

Three theological cornerstones are of central importance to Margull's approach. First, there is the understanding that all religions are incomplete and unfinished (Margull 1992; Weisse 1995). Truth in religions is historically mediated and religions are open-ended with regard to their future. Margull argues against a construction of the forms and content of religions which is determined once and for all. Secondly, he rejects the claim of religions to be absolute, and the source of indivisible truth. Margull argues that objective claims to be absolute prove to be particular claims when set against similar claims in other religions. Thirdly, Margull talks about vulnerability. The realization that Christianity, like all universal religions, forms a particular component in the overall structure of religions in dialogue leads Christians to perceive this as a fundamental 'offence to Christian consciousness'. Grief over the apparent lack of particularity of Christianity is nothing less than the grief which representatives of other religions have to endure with regard to what they perceive as the particularity of their religions. Real dialogue could consist in sharing this kind of grief: dialogue would deal with accepting history, with bearing the grief of the particularity of one's religion, with enduring together this fundamental offence, and with talking about the real wounds.

Margull's understanding of dialogue

Given the above, Margull's understanding of dialogue is characterized by the following points:

- *An encounter of people in equality.* Margull sees inter-religious dialogue as a 'confident and trusting conversation and open encounter between people of different religious backgrounds, who share equal rights' (1992: 297). Following Buber, Margull postulates for such encounters 'that nothing less than equality and respect and perhaps nothing causing offence are the preconditions for real dialogue'. Therefore he rejects the concept of a dialogue with other religions, because that concept implies the superiority or at least the dominance of one's own position. Instead, Margull calls for a dialogue between persons belonging to different religious traditions.
- *Christian identity is not monological, but dialogical.* Margull refutes the notion of an exclusive Christian identity which gradually eliminates the world and world religions, a notion to which he refers as a 'round tower of monologue'. His idea is not to understand the 'other' from our centre, but 'to understand the other as he understands himself'. In Margull's view, from the outset, people of other traditions should 'participate in our theological reflections'; they should 'become a substantial part of our reflections on faith' (1992: 323).
- In Margull's experience, the decisive starting point of dialogue is not the differences between particular religious traditions, but the common ground which people share, since all humankind is made in the image of God. For Margull, personal encounters with other believers are crucial. People should not be classified from the outside, not even by their formal adherence to a particular religion. Instead, theological reflections should aim 'to focus on the human beings who are not necessarily defined by one of the pre-defined religions'.
- *Reasons for dialogue are often rooted in social problems.* Immediate reasons for dialogue can often be found in areas of social conflict. Mutual awareness, exchange and dialogue have been and still are particularly

important in destructive and disruptive conditions, such as the genocide of the European Jewry, Western imperialism and negative views of non-Christian traditions. 'Dialogue begins to address and deal with these wounds, in order to bandage and heal them as well as to avoid further wounds' (Margull 1992: 334).

- *Inter-religious dialogue does not lead to syncretism or to a uniform global religion.* Margull's own experience led him to reject the view that syncretism and uniform global religion are the inevitable result of inter-religious dialogue. When Christians take an interest in Buddhism, for example, the explanation does not lie in the wish to achieve a syncretistic combination of religions, but often results from frustration with the Church. Further, the idea of a uniform global religion was not referred to by any party during Margull's involvement in inter-religious dialogue.

- *Dialogue and silence.* Dialogue has limits which can induce silence. There are opportune and inopportune times for dialogue; sometimes dialogue cannot go beyond the fundamental respect for the 'other'. For example, in his own inter-religious encounters Margull experienced the negative consequences of the fact that Christianity had been dominant in the past. 'Dialogue means listening for long periods of time, because we, in particular, have to overcome the stigma of being unable to listen' (1992: 287). Here Margull underlines the importance grounded in our past history of giving precedence to others and of making a point of staying in the background.

- *Theology is based on dialogue, not on the ownership of truth claims.* Encounter and dialogue are central elements of theology. Christian self-understanding needs to consider truth not as its sole possession, restricting the search for truth to its own tradition, but should regard itself as dependent on the questions and answers of people of other religious convictions. Dialogue becomes indispensable for one's own self-understanding.

This approach to religious and intercultural encounter accepts the differences between denominations as well as between religious traditions and positions. Communicative action, which is at the heart of this approach, should incorporate the existing experiences of pupils and not require religious knowledge or religious competence as a condition of dialogue. An approach emphasizing encounter should enable pupils to exchange views on religious and ideological positions, as well as helping them to develop and clarify their own positions. Dialogical RE is grounded in the philosophical, educational, and theological ideas mentioned above. Its aim is for students to learn together and to form a fundamental perception of the religious dimension within a concept of inter-religious education. Dialogical RE thus includes a multi-faith element, but goes much further than simply giving information about religions. Dialogical RE does not play down existing differences or conflicts, but underlines both the similarities and the differences between existing religions.

Attitudes to Hamburg's religious education: actors on the inside

In what follows I shall introduce the main actors who have shaped religious education in Hamburg in recent years. I will refer to influences on the development of RE, the discourse group for inter-religious education, and a plan to found a university-based 'academy of world religions'.

Two key elements have assisted in the development of a religious education shaped by diversity, tolerance and active partnership and aiming to empower pupils in relation to society. The first are the general instructions which form a preamble to all curricula for religious education. These state that RE should 'offer possibilities of giving meaning to life, encouraging pupils to act with responsibility, thereby promoting their sense of self and ability to act' (Doedens and Weisse 1997: 23). The second is the 1993 declaration regarding religious education which was drafted by teachers of RE in Hamburg and adopted by the leadership of the Protestant Church. The emphasis here is on learning tolerance, reciprocal understanding and active participation in justice. Pupils should learn to accept the plurality of society in such a way 'that a culture can develop in which people can learn to recognize, respect and understand one another, a culture where there is a creative striving and struggle for the truth, as well as reciprocal respect and tolerance of diversity' (Doedens and Weisse 1997: 19). The basis of this can be found in the biblical motif that all people are children of God and in the UN charter on the rights of children (Doedens and Weisse 1997: 13).

Moreover, the approach is supported by the established Church in Hamburg. Despite criticisms that other Churches have made of a dialogue-orientated 'religious education for all', the position of the Lutheran Bishop Maria Jepsen (2000) in Hamburg affirms the dialogical approach, especially its aim of helping young people from different cultural and religious backgrounds to live together without fear. However, it should be pointed out that most German Lutheran bishops are opposed to the introduction of the dialogical approach on a national scale.

An Inter-religious Group for a Dialogical Religious Education was formed in response to the need to design a syllabus for religious education in primary schools. The group includes representatives of Christianity, Judaism, Islam and Buddhism, complemented by academics involved in teacher training at university level. The group was established in 1995 and holds regular meetings; it is a unique venture in Germany which has built a high level of trust between the faiths. The group developed and approved the idea that all pupils should participate in religious education, regardless of their own religious and ideological backgrounds. The spirit of this venture is clearly reflected in a statement which was unanimously adopted by the group on 11 February 1997 (Doedens and Weisse 1997: 35–41). The statement calls for a 'religious education for all' which is not divided along religious or ideological lines. Multi-faith classes should enable young people

> to find their own position in a diversity of religious beliefs and communities and to find enjoyment in the common ground of diversity. Encountering and debating what is strange or even foreign as well as being open to the possibility of changing one's perspective contribute to the process of developing and discovering or rediscovering oneself and forming one's identity.
>
> (Doedens and Weisse 1997: 37)

The statement also describes religious education in school and shows how it differs from religious education in the home and in the community. Finally, the statement says that pupils should clarify their own judgement as to the meaning and claims of religions by entering into a dialogue with their fellow pupils and contributing their own opinions.

The members of the inter-religious discourse group have distanced themselves from any form of religious and political fundamentalism, as is clearly affirmed in a statement dating from November 1998 (Weisse 1999: 294–6). The statement emphasizes the socio-political relevance of religious education by referring to issues of tolerance, inter-religious communication, perceptions of difference without discrimination, alleviation of injustice and commitment to a peaceful life. Religious education thus makes a strong contribution to social cohesion.

This form of religious education needs intellectual support from institutions of higher education. The Faculty of Protestant Theology at the University of Hamburg offers courses in the 'science of religion' (*Religionswissenschaft*) and world religions but, as yet, there are no theological chairs for Muslim, Jewish or Buddhist professors. However, the establishment of an Academy of World Religions at the University of Hamburg is under consideration (Knauth and Weisse 2002). The idea started with a call for a chair of Islamic theology. So far, no such chair exists in Germany, except for a chair in Islamic Studies which does not cover Islamic theology in its entirety. The need for an academic Islamic theology, orientated to the needs of Muslims in the West, stems from the increasing socio-political participation of Muslims in Hamburg and other Western European countries. Also, given innovations in the training of teachers, it seems only right to create academic resources for Islamic theology.

From the beginning, the effort to establish academic structures for Islam was combined with the creation of such resources in Jewish and Buddhist theology, especially in the light of the increasing religious diversity of the population. The history of the Jews can be studied as an academic subject in Hamburg, but there is no possibility of studying Jewish theology.

The proposed Academy of World Religions would facilitate academic developments in Islamic, Jewish and Buddhist theology and would be designed in such a way as to relate these theologies to the Western context and to allow them to be guided by openness to dialogue. This should happen in such a way that scholars in the academy co-operate with one another, for example in programmes of joint lectures. It is equally important that students are introduced to the wider concept of the world religions. The Academy of World Religions is to be established in 2003.

Attitudes of public authorities to religious education in Hamburg: actors on the outside

Until a few years ago, religious education did not attract public attention in Hamburg. In the liberal climate of a commercial city, religion had very little meaning. When the state authorities took note of 'religious education for all' in the mid-1990s the situation changed and public interest in religious education developed rapidly. By way of illustration, it should be noted that the Secretary of State in the Ministry of School, Youth and Training in Hamburg spoke in favour of Hamburg's form of religious education:

> As a member of the government I cannot demand or stipulate such a dialogue-orientated religious education. However, I think it desirable because peace on earth is not conceivable without peace between religions. At the same time I think that such a religious education agrees with the social reality in the schools of a multi-religious society.
>
> (Lange 2000: 27)

The committee which advises the Ministry of School, Youth and Training (Landesschulbeirat) includes people from very different social groups. The committee in Hamburg discussed religious education and adopted a statement with only one abstention. The statement concludes that there are several reasons why religious education is important, pointing out especially that:

> The ability to find a new consensus is a main aim of our society, and will become even more important in the future. Religious education can help to contribute to this aim in dialogue with other religious traditions and opinions. The ability to conduct dialogue needs tolerance and empathy for the other as its basis.
>
> (Lehberger 1999: 306)

Attitudes to religious education among Hamburg's political parties have changed considerably, although responses vary from party to party. The strongest commitment is from the Green Party, which is significant, since they have been the junior partner (with the Social Democrats) in Hamburg's governing council. Religious education based on dialogue is considered to be necessary for social freedom in the city. It is important as a signal 'to foster the acceptance of multi-ethnic plurality by using religious education and schools generally. This has to happen or we are planting a social bomb' (Goetsch, cited in Neumann 2000: 121).

Voices from the Social Democratic Party have reacted positively to Hamburg's dialogical religious education. The stance of the Christian Democratic Union (CDU) in Hamburg is ambivalent. One of the MPs responsible for educational questions pleads for a 'religious education for all' and goes so far as to state that there is no place for a religious education divided along religious lines in Hamburg's schools (Beuss, cited in Neumann 2000: 119). However, other leading figures in the CDU are still in favour of religious education along denominational lines. The elections in 2001 changed the government in Hamburg: at the time of writing (March 2002) the CDU is in coalition with the small Liberal Party (FDP) and a newly formed right-wing party. The consequences for the general atmosphere in the city and for religious education remain to be seen.

Finally, another authority in Hamburg, the representative dealing with matters regarding immigrants or foreigners in the Senate (*Ausländerbeauftragte*), considers it important that greater emphasis should be laid on religion and religious education. Such a concern is closely linked with the question of equality for immigrants. The current *Ausländerbeauftragte* focuses on Islam in particular and sees the possibility of educating Muslims in theology at university level as a way to achieve equality for Muslims. She is therefore committed to establishing a chair of Islamic theology and establishing the Academy of World Religions. She favours a dialogue-orientated religious education which does not intensify social divisions, but offers a 'religious education for all' so that it can lead to mutual understanding and to the view that cultural and religious diversity can be the norm. Her view is that opportunities for dialogue should be offered to Muslims at all levels (Neumann 2001: 8).

The various views of Hamburg's public authorities, as illustrated above, have different objectives. Yet they all want to place greater emphasis on religious education; they are all opposed to RE divided along religious lines in Hamburg's schools; they all believe that religious education has great socio-political responsibility. These statements were made predominantly by people who have nothing to do with theology or RE. This is remarkable and perhaps marks a turning point in a city in which religion and religious education have so far had no public voice.

Conclusion

Religious education is important for the development of intercultural communication, tolerance and peace in the city. Peace and living together in one city can be guaranteed only if all social groups have adequate access to all political fields. These include groups which tend towards seclusion (or even fundamentalism). These are the very groups which should be integrated into political structures and processes. This is what the *Ausländerbeauftragte* means by the 'normalization of dialogue' and it is a starting point for public actors to take an interest in religious education. It must be clear that, in the field of education, the principle of participation is most important for the structure of a school and of school life. Mutual recognition of each other's existence among different groups is difficult if religious education is divided according to denominations and religions. Such a structure leads instead to a situation in which only one's own rights and one's own background are considered. If, however, pupils from different religions and ideologies work together in religious education, they can perceive that mutual understanding can be the basis of their own self-understanding. We can learn in religious education that cultural and religious differences do not have to lead to discrimination, but that mutual understanding of different backgrounds can lead to a clearer formulation of one's own position, and promote what Jackson calls 'differentiated citizenship' (see Chapter 1 above). Religious education can thus become a field of experience in the biography of pupils, showing them that it is possible to live their lives and hold positions without fear, self-discrimination or discrimination against others, while at the same time respecting the attitudes, positions and lifestyles of other people within their religions, ideologies and cultures. Religious education can be seen as a training ground for living in which differences do not alienate, but are part of everyday 'normal' life. In this sense, religious education deals directly with the question: can people from different cultural, political or religious backgrounds live together in peace?

Our empirical work in schools gives a tentative positive answer to this question. Especially in areas of social unrest, schools seem to be islands of relatively aggression-free communication. Our school-based research demonstrates that it is possible to perceive and talk about differences in religious education, without this leading to discrimination (Weisse, in Knauth *et al.* 2000: 141 f.).

I would like to conclude with another passage from the letter quoted at the beginning of this chapter. Despite some reservations about the social impact of religious education, I find the argument of this Muslim mother convincing. She writes:

I hope that my daughter will have the opportunity to learn that other religions are other possible ways to find God. In an open approach, she will discover things in common and different things, and learn to develop her own position and strengthen it. The alternative, religious education divided into religious groups, would draw unnecessary frontiers and miss a valuable opportunity. Ignorance of other 'foreign' religions provides a basis for assumptions, falsification, manipulation and hatred. I think inter-religious education is very important at a time when it is again possible in Germany to defame and burn people of other traditions and cultures. A school that refrains from inter-religious education is evading its social responsibility. I do not want my child to be 'foreignized'; I want her to live in calm and in a diversity of colour.

(Weisse 1999: 293)

References

Arkoun, M. (1992) *L'Islam: approche Critique*, Paris: Grancher.

Berger, P. L. (ed.) (1997) *The Limits of Social Cohesion*, Boulder CO: Westview Press.

Bourdieu, P. (1998) 'Der Neoliberalismus. Eine Utopie der grenzenlosen Ausbeutung wird Realität', in P. Bourdieu Gegenfeuer, *Wortmeldungen im Dienste des Widerstandes Gegen die Neoliberale Invasion*, Konstanz: Universitätsverlag Konstanz, 109–18.

Buber, M. (1962) *Das Dialogische Prinzip*, Gerlingen: Lambert Schneider.

—— (1986) *Reden über Erziehung*, Heidelberg: Lambert Schneider.

Doedens, F. and Weisse, W. (eds) (1997) *Religionsunterricht für alle. Hamburger Perspektiven zur Religionsdidaktik*, Münster and New York: Waxmann.

Falaturi, A. (1996) *Der Islam im Dialog. Aufsätze*, Hamburg: Islamwissenschaftliche Akademie.

Giddens, A. (1994) *Beyond Left and Right: The Future of Radical Politics*, Cambridge: Polity Press.

Grünberg, W., Slabaugh, D. and Meister-Karanakis, R. (1994) *Lexikon der Hamburger Religionsgemeinschaften. Religionsvielfalt in der Stadt von A-Z*, Hamburg: Dölling & Galitz.

Habermas, J. (2001) *Glauben und Wissen. Friedenspreis des Deutschen Buchhandels 2001*, Frankfurt am Main: Suhrkamp.

Huntington, S. P. (1996) *The Clash of Civilisations and the Remaking of the World Order*, New York: Simon & Schuster.

Jepsen, M. (2000) 'Dialog – Religion – Bildung. Religiöses Lernen in einer pluralen Welt', in W. Weisse and F. Doedens (eds) *Religiöses Lernen in einer pluralen Welt. Religionspädagogische Ansätze in Hamburg*, Münster and New York: Waxmann, 11–18.

Knauth, T. (1996) *Religionsunterricht und Dialog. Empirische Untersuchungen, systematische Überlegungen und didaktische Perspektiven eines Religionsunterrichts im Horizont religiöser und kultureller Pluralisierung*, Münster and New York: Waxmann.

Knauth, T. and Weisse, W. (eds) (2002) Akademic der Weltreligionen. Konz-eptionelle und Praktische Ansätze, Hamburg: Universität Hambürg (Faculty of Education).

Knauth, T., Leutner-Ramme, S., Weisse, W. (2000) *Religionsunterricht aus Schüler-perspektive*, Münster and New York: Waxmann.

Knitter, P. F. (1991) 'Religion und Befreiung. Soteriozentrismus als Antwort auf die Kritiker', in R. Bernhardt (ed.) *Horizontüberschreitung*, Gütersloh: Mohn, 203–19.

—— (1997) *Horizonte der Befreiung. Auf dem Weg zu einer pluralistischen Theologie der Religionen*, Frankfurt am Main and Paderborn: Lembeck & Bonifatius.

Küng, H. (1990) *Projekt Weltethos*, Munich: Piper.

Lange, H. (2000) 'Religionsunterricht und öffentlicher Bildungsauftrag', in W. Weisse and F. Doedens (eds) *Religiöses Lernen in einer pluralen Welt. Religionspädagogische Ansätze in Hamburg*, Münster and New York: Waxmann, 19–32.

Lehberger, R. (1999) 'Religionsunterricht in Hamburg. Eine stellungnahme des Landesschulbeirates', in W. Weisse (ed.) *Vom Monolog zum Dialog. Ansätze einer dialogischen Religionspädagogik*, 2nd edn, Münster and New York: Waxmann, 303–9.

Levinas, Emmanuel (1993) 'Penser Dieu à partir de l'èthic', in E. Levinas, *Dieu, la mort et le temps*, Paris: Grasset, 155–8.

Margull, H. J. (1992) *Zeugnis und Dialog. Ausgewählte Schriften*, Ammersbek bei Hamburg: Verlag an der Lottbek.

Neumann, U. (2000) 'Religionsunterricht im Gespräch', in W. Weisse and F. Doedens (eds) *Religiöses Lernen in einer pluralen Welt. Religionspädagogische Ansätze in Hamburg*, Münster and New York: Waxmann, 111–26.

—— (2001) Die Rolle des Islam in Deutschland, unpublished paper, Istanbul, 11 April.

Nipkow, K. E. (1991) 'Ökumenisches Lernen-interreligiöses Lernen-Glaubensdialog zwischen den Weltreligionen. Zum Wandel von Herausforderungen und Voraus-setzungen', in G. Orth (ed.) *Dem bewohnten Erdkreis Shalom. Beiträge zu einer Zwischenbilanz ökumenischen Lernens*, Münster: Comenius Institute, 301–20.

Peukert, H. (1984) 'Was ist eine praktische Wissenschaft? Handlungstheorie als Basistheorie der Humanwissenschaften. Anfragen an die praktische Theologie', in O. Fuchs (ed.) *Theologie und Handeln*, Düsseldorf: Patmos, 64–79.

—— (1992) 'Die Erziehungswissenschaft der Moderne und die Herausforderungen der Gegenwart', in D. Benner, D. Lenzen and H-U. Otto (eds) *Erziehungs-wissenschaft zwischen Modernisierung und Modernitätskrise*, Weinheim and Basle: Beltz, 113–27.

—— (1994) 'Bildung als Wahrnehmung des anderen. Der Dialog im Bildungsdenken der Moderne', in I. Lohmann and W. Weisse (eds) *Dialog der Kulturen*, Münster and New York: Waxmann, 1–14.

Sandt, F-O. (1996) *Religiosität von Jugendlichen in der Multikulturellen Gesellschaft. Eine qualitativ-empirische Untersuchung über christliche, atheistische, spiritualistische und muslimische Orientierungen*, Münster and New York: Waxmann.

Weisse, W. (1989) 'Ökumenisches Lernen. Möglichkeiten und Grenzen einer neueren pädagogischen Dimension', *Ökumenische Rundschau*, 38, 181–99.

—— (1995) 'Christianity and its neighbour religions: a question of tolerance? Impulses for the education of religion from the experience of ecumenical dialogue',

Scriptura: International Journal of Bible, Religion and Theology in Southern Africa, 55, 263–76.

—— (ed.) (1996) *Interreligious and Intercultural Education: Methodologies, Conceptions and Pilot Projects in South Africa, Namibia, Great Britain, the Netherlands, and Germany*, Münster: Comenius Institute.

—— (ed.) (1999) *Vom Monolog zum Dialog. Ansätze einer dialogischen Religionspädagogik*, 2nd edn, Münster and New York: Waxmann.

—— (ed.) (2002) *Wahrheit und Dialog. Theologische Grundlagen und Impulse gegenwärtiger Religionspädagogik*, Münster and New York: Waxmann.

Chapter II

Religious education and citizenship

Some reflections

Lat Blaylock

Synopsis   This concluding chapter draws together some of the insights and experience of both academic and practical settings in a number of countries, and applies the themes of democratic citizenship, global citizenship and diverse citizenships. The current and emerging context of citizenship education in the United Kingdom, where it has a clear frontier with the well established and flourishing practice of a plural model of religious education, has much to learn from the global field. For example, the idea of distinct communities based upon religion inside the United Kingdom, whose members participate on an equal basis in the nation-state as citizens, has been undermined by the experience of exclusion found among many Muslims or members of other religious minorities. Moreover, the idea that a shared citizenship may require some sort of shared story, or narrative of history, functions in ways that contrast religious shared stories with any attempt at a national shared story. The overview of the book draws out some key questions for educational practitioners about the ways religious and national identities relate to each other, the need for a pedagogy of diversity, and the positive consequences for teachers of a deepening engagement with both religious and national culture. Far from drawing shared answers from the studies presented in the book, the discussion identifies some questions and propositions which suggest ways forward for teachers of religious education or citizenship in the light of the key chapters. This makes it appropriate that answers remain tentative and exploratory in the face of the continuously changing contours of the debate about citizenship and religion in education.

Some meanings of citizenship

The concept of citizen is clarified in many ways through the contributions presented in this book, but readers may still ask for a definitive account: what does the word mean? Concepts which relate to ultimate questions are essentially contested: it is of the essence of ideas such as 'humanity', 'spirituality' or 'reality' that different individuals, schools of thought and societies will clash over their meanings. From such clashes new insights and convictions drive societies in new, sometimes visionary, directions. Thus, in this concluding chapter, I do not draw a definition of citizenship from the views presented, though I do suggest that the educational applications of the concept are powerful in driving new thinking about religion in school.

In the UK government's citizenship education curriculum for England, the issue of the meaning of citizenship is never clearly and definitively prescribed: pragmatism prevails, perhaps wisely, and being a thoughtful, informed, active citizen of the diverse nation-state is seen as a self-evident good, requiring no further justification or definition of terms (DfEE 1999).

But Thomas Paine, over 200 years ago, proclaimed himself beyond national citizenship, and beyond the specifics of religious identity: 'My country is the world and my religion is to do good' (Paine 1792). His sense of self, so pithily expressed, challenges all tribalisms with a breadth of vision that commends itself to many educators.

However, Tom Paine's clarity does not diminish the complexity of our field. Within this collection of theory and reflection readers may have identified meanings of citizenship which are national, post-national or global. Chapter 2 examines questions of cultural or transcultural citizenship. Consideration has been given to the idea that older concepts of citizenship, largely national, have given place to newer meanings that are both local and international, plural and flexible, diverse and plastic. (Jackson considers these issues in Chapter 1.) You may also have noted, with me, the particular challenges that come from considering citizenship issues in a feminist context, with reference to ecological issues, or for sexual minorities (see Chapters 7 and 10, for example). Moreover, each religion offers its followers some reasons for engagement in responsible citizenship, and sets some limits on their loyalty to an object so small as a nation-state (when compared with a transcendent object, as God may be conceived). Any – or all – of these particular ways of constructing the concept of citizenship can also be deconstructed. This only leads to a situation in which, as Tobler demonstrates in making a powerful case for drawing attention to feminist readings of the debate, you can choose which 'citizenship' you construct (Chapter 7). The responsibility of the teacher is weighty.

Those who teach young citizens owe the learners access to these debates, information about the potentialities and possibilities of being a citizen today and tomorrow. In our situation, the functions of religion in citizenship education include questioning, challenging orthodoxies with alternatives from beyond dominant traditions of discourse and reframing questions about national citizenship in moral or spiritual terms. Who is excluded? How can that exclusion be challenged? How can the meanings of humanity be compassionately enlarged?

In the popular movie *Independence Day* invaders from Mars are defeated by a globally united military and human force. The plot line of the film invents an imaginary Martian 'other' or 'them' to unite diverse human communities. This is a common device, and serves here to illustrate the simple point that 'we' often define ourselves negatively over against 'them'.

But citizenship programmes in education may seek to define 'us' broadly, without a 'them'. RE and citizenship education share leading roles in the construction of an inclusive sense of 'us', whether in the rainbow nation of South Africa or in the increasingly religiously and culturally diverse settings of Europe from which the studies in this book are drawn. Hollywood does not offer us any help here: the model for a shared humanity in *Independence Day* is that everyone else should fall into line behind the US President, with global peace achieved by killing your enemies, enabled by technological ingenuity. If only the respectful building of community cohesion were so simple!

When it comes to the description of what should be taught to children in school, we might take examples of the aims of religious and citizenship education programmes in isolation from their subjects and find it very hard to distinguish the subject context that bred them. If it is only the professional initiates who can identify the difference between the specialist languages of the aims of RE and citizenship, then perhaps the identity of concern between the two areas is so close that only method will distinguish them. Religious education has, for many years, aimed to prepare young people for life in a diverse community by promoting attitudes of tolerance and respect towards those who believe and live differently from themselves. If religious educators in Britain had made a better publicized success of this aim, perhaps citizenship education could be more reliant on that success.

In the light of these summary considerations, teachers may find it helpful to ask these questions. Given the contested nature of the terminology of citizenship, what accounts of the citizen's rights and responsibilities can be found within religious communities? How do they inform national debates about citizenship? Can education in citizenship or religion make a significant contribution to identity formation, or are such intentions essentially over-ambitious? What contribution to the meaning of citizenship can be made from religion?

Community, story and religious traditions in education: what possibilities are there of the well-being of all?

A thread that runs through many of the chapters in this book is to do with how we identify ourselves religiously. Can human identity in relationships be created through cultural communities, or built by participation in a shared story, or in a stream of meaning-making tradition? Can secure identity, seemingly important in accepting difference positively, be established without shared story or tradition? In South Africa, Norway, Germany and other settings the spread of non-religious, secular ways of identifying oneself may be less pronounced than in England, where measures such as church attendance and community membership are comparatively very low. But religious identity is perhaps more deeply embedded in many lives than political or national identity; being Christian or Muslim may often matter more to individuals or communities than being English or British. Both religious and national identities are plastic and can be remoulded: one common religious identity in England can be described as 'emigrant from Christianity'. Those who emigrate leave their place of belonging for another uncertain place. The metaphor applies to ethnic and national identities too: British Muslims may see themselves as 'Pakistani British' in national terms. If, as Østberg's review of the evidence (Chapter 5) suggests, national identity is often more fluid and less bounded than religious identity, perhaps educationists need a clearer deepening awareness of what it is to be Muslim today to inform their citizenship curriculum. And where national identities are fragmentary or fluid, how should educational systems respond to the interconnectedness of religious identities, which seem to harden and fix, sometimes into particularly conservative or inflexible forms?

This question is illuminated by Steyn's analysis of the example of Christian education in South Africa: manipulative or liberating (Chapter 6)? The South African debates about citizenship acknowledge that religion served as an agent of oppression under apartheid but simultaneously was an agent of liberation in the anti-apartheid struggle. There is, of course, much for pupils to learn from the study of how faith has inspired citizenships of various kinds in this context: the worst response would be to edit religion out of the political context of citizenship. Shared story, strong community, deeply rooted identities with layers of national, tribal and religious meaning can be found on all sides of conflict around injustice or oppression. What can the educator make of such contradictions? How can a school clarify its role in contributing to the creation of meanings, including religious or spiritual meanings, for citizens of the next century?

Religious education, as the writers of this volume see it, draws from many religions, and must do so selectively. One principle of this selectivity could be that RE promotes as a dominant discourse the examination of harmony-related questions. Recognizing that religious traditions have their own integrity, RE ought not to assume that equality means sameness. Østberg's evidence (Chapter 5) is that assimilationist political discourses of nationality or citizenship may engender an increasingly firm marking of religious boundaries by members of minority faith communities. I think this makes some sense of the negative response of some Muslims and Christians to citizenship orders written by Professor Bernard Crick, and adopted by the UK government. Is it also true that some young Muslims, for example, use their clearly bounded religious identity to assert themselves in a national culture that marginalizes them?

Is the study of world religions in education always instrumental to some other purpose? Need it be free of such instrumentalism? If you are a purist, and hold that the study of religion is an end in itself, a good without the need of instrumental justification, that does not preclude the idea that, in particular times and circumstances, instrumentalist accounts of the place of RE can be adjunctive to purist purposes. So RE has been publicly justified as 'for' the multicultural, the anti-racist, the spiritual, the nurturing and (long ago) the creation and support of belief in the 'national religion', or the buttressing of colonialism. In the present moment, should RE accept the purposes of citizenship? Our writers may cautiously favour such a course, but also draw attention to the inherent difficulties. Out of the tension comes a possibility, that religion and religious education may have a special role in educating young citizens with regard to the profound engagement with story, tradition, identity and questions of value and aspiration which in RE are handled with careful skill.

Temporary and functional justifications for the place of religious education in the curriculum are always subordinate to more purist understandings, for example that religion is a distinct form of human activity, connecting vast human communities with traditions and philosophical ideas in distinctive manners that concern the pursuit of truth, meaning and value. The public acceptance of the value of a religious element in secular education is, however, often dependent on the second-order merits of temporary and functional justifications of religion in education. At present, in English education, RE may make common cause with citizenship education in drawing attention to the importance of learning for life, not just for work or economic activity. In English schools, RE and citizenship education share concern for the examination of what it means to be human, and together may focus upon the idea that a school is a workshop of humanity, a place where the pursuit of truth in community is the primary justification for its existence. This idea will be contested, but the learning may be in the love of the questions rather than in the dissection of the answers.

One established function for inter-religious dialogue is to explore whether and how far the different theologies and traditions of participants establish a shared idea of human well-being. Those who participate in inter-faith dialogues often take the enterprise far more seriously than those politicians who seek electoral advantage from communitarian rhetoric, and education must follow the lead of inter-faith dialogue if it is to make much difference to young people's attitudes to the questions thrown up by plural societies. The writers in this book make significant arguments for deepening the dialogical functions of RE. Weisse raises the theological question: what does it mean to say that God is God, rather than the chief of one group? From this he develops the idea that dialogue may move beyond the sharing of diverse perspectives to focus on social and political issues in the light of the differing religious standpoints of learners. Ipgrave (Chapter 8) shows similarly how classroom dialogue, even among younger children, may produce fruitful, rich opportunities for learning not just about the phenomena of religion, but also about applied ethics, social questions and other aspects of the citizenship agenda. Leganger-Krogstad (Chapter 9) adds further weight to the evidence that such classroom dialogue is not only a possibility for the exceptional RE teacher but also a practical, interesting and valid approach to learning in RE in a variety of settings. I think RE and citizenship education must also ask the political question: what does it mean to say that humanity is one group, laying emphasis on a uniting 'us' rather than just a collection of fragmenting 'thems'?

One key aspect of the authenticity of religious education requires that work on religion in school should represent the characteristic passions of religion, not merely the aspects of faith which educators may find useful. Such passions vary over time, but may include sacrifice or forgiveness in Christianity, or the one-ness of the *Ummah* or the appropriation today of the transcendent teaching of the holy Qur'an in Islam. If RE genuinely makes space for some of these characteristic passions to be felt by learners from any background, then perhaps the learning from religion that it enables can function for some learners as a spur to challenge the ways the 'citizen' is constructed at present. Where in the school curriculum can we make room for issues of identity, meaning, purpose, value, origin or destiny? If Tobler is right that 'justice can be created' then the RE curriculum, itself a small space, may be the focus of aspirations to make space for some things too easily excluded: religious diversity, the non-vocational human questions of purpose and ultimate meaning.

In the light of these considerations, teachers of religion in any national education system will continue to offer their answers to some key questions. Research evidence suggests that functioning in two cultural situations (or nationalities or identities) is not so problematic for young people. So what is to be learned from this evidence about the national 'us' of citizenship education? Is it the case that shared stories, national or religious, seem desirable or essential for the establishment of educational purpose? If so, what happens to educational purpose in a time when all such stories are fragmenting under pressure? Does the practice of dialogue between religious people provide a model for religious education? What are the strengths and weaknesses of such a model?

Embracing diversity: an essential condition of world citizenship?

It is not necessary to problematize diversity. Religious difference can be a source of controversy, challenge, learning, personal growth or spiritual insight, and religious educators are used to finding and developing these potentialities: Chapter 8 exemplifies this in an inspiring way. Religious difference is often seen as problematic by secular authorities, but those who present religion in the public sphere of citizenship can perhaps present it as potentially a virtuous circle of relationships between Muslims, Christians, Humanists or Sikhs.

For example, Christian Aid is the world development charity of the Council of Churches in Britain and Ireland. The charity used UK government money during 2001 to develop and provide freely to all schools a package of curriculum materials, including video resources, which posed questions about responsibility, care and thoughtful living to the 5–14 age group. The resource, under the general title 'An RE Curriculum for Global Citizenship', presented insights from six different religions into the problems and issues of global justice which are at the heart of Christian Aid's development agenda. The example simply shows how national government, globally alert, can enable learning through funding a challenging educational input from faith (plural) to school. Its general positive reception and very wide use are evidence that the idea of global citizenship commends itself to teachers and pupils for exploration.

Chidester's contention (Chapter 2), that citizenship of a nation is challenged increasingly by new forms of belonging or of citizenship that may be globally or culturally focused, is an insight that sparks some useful considerations for those concerned about the interaction between religious and national ways of belonging. Religious educators are rightly concerned here. What is needed is a form of religious education that enables pupils to hear the clear challenges of any particular religion to the demands, visions, goals and purposes for education and national life which governments and national identities construct. The opportunity for education that draws upon religion here is particularly valuable to the many young people in education who are religiously anonymous, or dis-traditioned. The idea that all young people can learn from religions to which they may not adhere in a plural school community makes RE more significant in largely secular local cultures, precisely because many other local cultures in the global multiculture are intensely driven by religious traditions and perspectives.

The fast-moving and re-forming versions of socially constructed human rights, which have become a feature of national and transnational political debate and legislation in the West over the last half-century, are often rooted in values which originate within religious ways of life. The 'new rights' of citizens (who used to be described as subjects) may also be informed by the fast-moving and re-forming versions of spirituality that are increasingly observable in the ways postmodern young people appropriate religious traditions for themselves.

One aspect of the debate prominent in the United Kingdom is the organization of schools by faith groups, for faith groups: how far should such segregated schooling receive the support of the state's common citizenry through taxation? Jackson's consideration of these issues (Chapters 1 and 4) allows for the complexities of the interaction between identity, culture, nation and faith, encouraging the presentation of that complexity to young people in the classroom through pedagogies informed about diversity by ethnographic sensitivities. But he also attends to the ways in which the construction of the idea of justice can clarify the rights of smaller faith communities to influence educational provision in pluralizing societies in ways that are beyond tokenism. In this, Skeie's modelling of the purposes of RE around the process of fluctuating debates about truth, goodness and community points a powerful way through the complexities of the territory that draws attention to the rights of the learner (Chapter 3). A challenge to current RE practice and pedagogy emerges: does RE yet manage to give pupils opportunities to debate these ultimate questions of community, identity, truth and goodness and access to the enrichment that comes to the debate from traditions of faith?

An example of such a question is this: what accountabilities should citizens in a democracy exercise over the schooling of the young? Racial segregation and separate development are discredited by the structural disadvantaging of minorities or disempowered majorities that has commonly resulted from such policies. From Gandhi through Dr Martin Luther King to Desmond Tutu and Jean Bertrand Aristide of Haiti, it has often been those whose religious vision of equality or freedom has been coupled with brave and inspired social coalition making between, for example, Jews, Muslims, Christians and Hindus who have led movements to remake the idea of citizenship in a more inclusive manner. In the less apocalyptic field of curriculum design, RE and citizenship education offer pupils in school the chance to study what makes for communities that cohere. Answering this question must include dimensions of spirituality, theology, dialogue and social relations. The alternatives to these kinds of RE owe a lot to the idea of religious segregation. The track record of segregation as a basis for equality and freedom in society is deeply flawed.

In Chapter 10 Wolfram Weisse draws powerful attention to the need for new thinking that the multi-religious situation in Hamburg has created. The emphasis on the perspectives of parents, the local community and its political representatives draws attention to the fact that local politicians in Hamburg see religious education as a new opportunity, while in the United Kingdom it often appears to politicians as an old problem. The same contrast emerges between the South African and English approaches to RE. One major challenge to British RE professionals from the studies presented in this book is to envisage how the subject can change its image in the public eye, so that in future years it can be seen as a democratic space in the school curriculum where diversity is prominent, handled with effective care and profound respect, and in ways that yield some community cohesion. If this is our reality, then what must be done in order to present the potential of the RE curriculum to promote citizenship outcomes that are for the well-being of all? There is a continuing need to develop clearer and more effective educational programmes that enable young people to engage with some of the complexities of identity issues, for example connecting gender, ethnicity and religious identities. As these areas involve models of attitude formation, democratic educational contexts all share a need to articulate appropriate and legitimate ways of forming attitudes in diverse educational settings. Particular attention must be paid to the sharply contested nature of educational values, and it must be noted that the contest is not fair: the balance of power and privilege is normally stacked against minorities.

The contours of suitable pedagogy for RE and citizenship: theory into the classroom

The varieties of citizenship encountered in this volume have implications for the ways in which learners develop. The subtle diversity of needs of young citizens demands a subtle and diverse range of teaching and learning styles. The citizenship orders in England pay close attention to this: how you learn matters in citizenship, and participative, active, discursive models are promoted. Given the particular need of learners to form identity as citizens for themselves, what would be the characteristics of excellent pedagogy for citizenship in a diverse society? Recognizing that young people's learning is embodied, so that one might learn as a Christian, or as a Muslim, or as an agnostic, must publicly funded schooling deny or neutralize the influence of these key constructs of personal identity? Or can diverse ways to affirm and enrich religious aspects of identity find a place in state schooling? From the studies in this book I want to draw attention to four observations.

Sometimes young people need a pedagogy of liberation. Ideas of citizenship are inextricably linked with concepts of equal treatment. Second-class citizenship is an affront to all citizens; this can be seen clearly wherever refugees or asylum seekers are denied the rights of citizens. It is also exemplified by Jackson, who points out how poor economic conditions marginalize minorities within the wider society in his consideration of plural education in Bradford. In education, equal protection for all and equal opportunities to flourish may be available to all citizens. But if this formal or legal equality of opportunity is not matched in the experience of minorities, whether ethnic, religious or grouped around some other aspect of identity, then discontent based on a sense of injustice will ferment. Chapters 6, by Steyn, 8 by Ipgrave and 9 by Leganger-Krogstad discuss this set of concerns, and raise for me the question of the place of pedagodies of liberation. If, for example, for many Muslim minorities, the feeling of marginalization and discrimination is common, can religious educators play a part in drawing out the learning from the experience of marginality? In such situations, whether in RE, citizenship education or in education generally, a pedagogy of liberation for the oppressed is needed to create some equality of flourishing. What may its characteristics be? At the least, citizenship education aims to free young people from ignorance, but may also target uncritical assumptions, single models, stereotypical roles or discrimination in opportunity. The idea that citizenship programmes intend to set learners free to flourish can take many forms, but should never be absent from the aims of such programmes. So citizenship, like RE, needs pedagogical tools which raise awareness, inform consciousness, enable young citizens to take power for themselves and make a change to their community. The community of the school could be the first focus of democratic action by young citizens, but many schools are structured to prevent this. If, as Tobler insists (Chapter 7), the relationship of citizens is first and foremost a moral one, then more school space for ethical inquiry, modelled into the life of the school institution, must follow.

Sometimes young people need a pedagogy that will root them deeply and profoundly in a tradition of meaning making, such as a religious tradition. The call for faith-based schools for Muslims, Christians or others is often related to a community's desire to deepen through education the sense of tradition, meaning, shared story and identity which it offers the next generation. Much of the fear which arises when plural models of RE are developed, in South Africa, Hamburg or England, comes from religious communities where the identity and membership of the young are seen as fragile. An urgent question lies behind many of the studies in this book. Is it possible for the young to learn to put roots down, and to pull walls down? Can there be an education which strongly roots the young but doesn't encourage them to build walls against the 'other' in a demonizing fashion? The research reviewed in this book offers grounds for a tentatively affirmative answer.

Sometimes pedagogy needs to offer values clarification, and opportunities to test and explore attitudes and values for oneself. This pedagogic need is even more urgent for teachers than for learners. The problems of identifying and building on democratic values are easy to describe. What are the limits of tolerance? What is the place of the distinctive traditions of particular communities that participate in national life? Can curricular ownership and control be shared? Unless some such enterprise is attempted, the ethical base for shared education cannot be established at all. The South African experience is parallel to related endeavours in other national settings in drawing attention to three issues. How can teachers move from positions of false neutrality or objectivity to positions of affirmation towards diversity in harmony? What will equip teachers most effectively to handle religious diversity in the plural school? How can teachers resolve the personal and professional issues of fear, conscience and pedagogy that religious diversity raises? The South African case identifies such values as integrity and trust as the basis of a focus on outcomes and on the full use of classroom strategies that make the exploration of values central.

Young people as citizens themselves may need a pedagogy of action, a learning model which includes some political involvement. This may include exploration of the establishment of shared story and community. Such action is likely to be more effective if it starts where young people are at, that is, within the school community itself. What learning activity will teach young citizens to embrace diversity? Julia Ipgrave's study offers one answer, based upon the combination of challenging teaching with individual dialogue. The aims of RE and citizenship education, as seen by contributors to this book, often include some version of the transformation of intercultural and inter-religious relations. Such aims will not be achieved unless learning activity enables reflection on the need to engage with the profound questions of common humanity, set in life (including religious life). Mere factual learning will not suffice. This pedagogy of action relates to democratic values: it seems a legitimate and positive intention that citizenship education should widen and deepen participation in democracy.

Clearly, religious values which are particularly significant within one faith community may be a challenge to, and be challenged by, citizens' values in the national community. This kind of mutual challenge and interpenetration could occur only where a pedagogy of faith is at work to enable learners to identify themselves in relation to their tradition. Such nurturing pedagogy may be largely the result of activity within the faith itself, but subtle relationships between the learning in church and school, or *madrasah* and classroom, can strengthen the ways in which young people function in and between the different communities with which they identify. Because religious educators are poised on frontiers between religion and school, they can use their alertness to these relationships to open some profound questions for pupils themselves, affirming but not replacing the role of faith communities in young people's learning.

A final concern about pedagogy arises from the idea of 'second class' citizenship. Tobler draws attention to large populations excluded from the front-rank 'citizen class', referring primarily to the feminist critique of traditional constructions of the citizen. RE and religions in Western democracies often perceive themselves to share marginal status. The citizens who are most alert to this status learn from it and have something to contribute, because it is more than just a quip that societies can judge the quality of their civilization by the way they deal with those at the margin. So does 'second class' status in citizenship actually provoke the kinds of personal learning and engagement which subvert any fixed model of the citizen for today, and give birth to the potentially new model of the citizen of tomorrow? Or, to put the point another way, does exclusion carry its own lesson, the experience of exclusion its own pedagogy, so that only slaves can learn how to end slavery, only the oppressed can learn to challenge oppression?

As religious education's curricular relations with citizenship become clearer and more embedded in England, diversity will be identifiable. Some schools will dig a trench between the two subjects and some will merge them in partnerships of mutual esteem. Some, where anti-religious prejudice guides curriculum planning (and these schools are shockingly common), will make RE a dully tokenistic and colonialized annexe of the citizenship territory. But I think that where RE teachers are brave, visionary and professionally expert, RE will open the frontier with citizenship and ask a lot of awkward questions about the ways in which national citizenship is postulated on privilege and advantage. Some kinds of national citizenship, in their description and inclusion of 'us', produce implications of exclusion, creating 'them' – second-class citizenships experienced by racial minorities, women and those who march out of step with the uniform drum struggling for their rights. In schools where religious education practice is alert to this, the subject may make a bigger contribution to citizenship education than citizenship education does.

The meaning of citizenship is, to some extent at least, open to new construction. RE teachers – bearing with them the insights of faith into oppression and liberation, equality and injustice, freedom and constraint, which religious teachings offer – may seek to construct the meaning of 'citizen' today in ways that are global in reach, transcultural in awareness, fluid enough to accommodate the religious diversity of our societies and welcoming plurality as challenge and inspiration rather than problem. They will not be alone in doing this, but may have a special pedagogical contribution to make from the theological and religious fields that are their home territory.

Conclusion

If civil society is to claim to hold the ground shared between members of different religious and secular traditions, it needs to be suitably modest in offering something useful. The state does not offer objectivity between different life stances, or a secular ideology to compete with religious or spiritual views of life. Perhaps all that can be offered is a limited space made open to all. Education, of course, is where the tussle about who owns the space, and how it will be shared, comes sharply into focus. Examples from South Africa, Scandinavia, Germany and the United Kingdom all draw attention to the need for those who establish national citizenship structures to listen carefully and deeply to the aspirations of citizens from diverse religious traditions. Religious communities continue to draw from their transnational traditions visions and insights which inform their participation in the national political culture. People who are Sikh, Muslim or Jewish in Britain today may also find their traditions lead to a creative and dynamic critique of the national culture. Surely a good programme of citizenship education would make this diversity a strength.

Even if it is argued that national citizenship remains a primary shared form of belonging as citizens in the twenty-first-century world, the education offered by the nation must respond to globalization's challenges. These include, for example, the challenge to identities and nationalisms, the challenges of cultural plurality and the ethical challenges associated with high mobility, poverty and community cohesion. Teachers of religious education are particularly well placed to engage with these challenges, because their curriculum and their pedagogical expertise are linked in practice with the diverse response of religions to the profound questions of identity, community and values which religious meaning making has always addressed.

What may be the role and significance of the RE teacher in the preparation of the young citizen for all the opportunities of adult life in globalizing, pluralizing, post-national and, in some ways, post-Christian societies? Perhaps it is to make space for classrooms in which ideals of liberation drawn from many spiritual traditions are polished up as treasure, and held up to the attention of young citizens. In secular debates about citizenship, religion is often perceived as a negative force: conservative, legalistic, repressive or aggressive. While the authentic study of religion in practice in individual lives, communities and global traditions may confirm that any or all of these strands can be found within a faith, it also often exposes the strands of liberation from these negatives. So, for example, Muslim feminists may find in their tradition the sources of their liberation from sexist institutions. Hindu egalitarians draw inspiration from their ancient Dharma. Christian visions of gay rights are fed from biblical sources, and Buddhist environmentalists learn more from ancient and traditional practice of non-harming than from modern environmentalism.

Religious education can offer young people the space, the stimulus and the tools of reflection that enable them to examine liberations and empowerments in local communities, in nation-states and in the global context, and to learn from the diversity of religious life and practice. Where religious education focuses upon the ways religions enable individuals to make meaning out of experience in the light of a community's traditions, learners can find opportunities to reflect on their own sense of the meaning of identity, community or tradition. If religious education does this, its contribution to citizenship education may be out of all proportion to the time and attention the subject often attracts.

References

DfEE (1999) *The National Curriculum for England: Citizenship*, London: Department for Education and Employment and Qualifications and Curriculum Authority.

Paine, Thomas (1792) *The Rights of Man* II, 5, quoted in G. Parrinder (ed.) *Dictionary of Religious and Spiritual Quotations*, London: HarperCollins (1990), 1.

Index